Darkness and Hope

Sam Halpern

Introduction by
Elie Wiesel

SHENGOLD PUBLISHERS, INC.
New York

Acknowledgments

Heartfelt thanks to Miriam Sivan. My appreciation cannot be adequately expressed to her for her dedication and devotion which made a true labor of love of this work. Her tireless efforts created order from chaos and enabled me to achieve my goal of "telling the story."

To Moshe Sheinbaum, the publisher of this volume, for his wise counsel and guidance. He made invaluable comments. My cordial thanks.

My heart overflows with gratitude to my beloved sons, Fred, David, Jack and Murray, for their comments and excellent advice during the time when I retold and resurrected the days of destruction and renewal, of darkness and hope.

Library of Congress Catalog Card Number: 95-067139
ISBN 0-88400-181-4
Copyright © 1996 by Sam Halpern
All rights reserved

Published by Shengold Publishers, Inc.
18 West 45th Street
New York, NY 10036

Printed in the United States of America

Darkness and Hope

Dedicated
to my parents

Mordechai Dov and Bella Halpern
my brothers
Naftoli and Avrum Chaim
and the rest of my family

And to my wife Gladys' parents

Ephraim and Sara Landau
and their family

Table of Contents

A Moving Testimony

by Elie Wiesel

"I was liberated by the Red Army on March 22, 1944. . ."

That is how Sam Halpern opens his poignant and moving narrative about his wartime and postwar experiences. I read and reread this deceptively simple sentence, I stop at the date, and I am shocked by its implied significance: when his nightmare was over, mine hadn't yet begun. In fact, we knew nothing about its horror-laden dimensions.

Whenever I meet Sam Halpern, we come back to the fact that Hungarian Jews were kept uninformed about the fate of their brethren in Poland. How was it possible? Why weren't we warned? I wish I knew the answer.

Sam speaks often of his native town of Chorostkov. He speaks about it with tenderness and nostalgia. He remembers everything about its social structure and religious environment. The *Hasidim* and their *Rebbes*, the *heder* and its children, the merchants and their problems, he recalls them all with amazing precision. Naturally he evokes his family. His parents, his brothers, his relatives: he brings them back to life.

Many of them have shared the tragic destiny of Eastern European Jewry. His parents perished in Belzec, one of the six extermination camps for Jews established by Hitler's hate-filled armies on Polish soil.

Sam himself, with his older brother Ari (Sam calls his Zunio), were spared. Why they and not others? Sam says: "Among our people, there were many Jews who were smarter, richer, stronger and more educated than I. . ." And yet. Call it a miracle, divine providence, or chance. What is clear is the awareness for Sam that "we find purpose and create meaning for our survival through what we do—what we take from the world and, more importantly, what we give back."

He has given back, and is still giving, quite a lot. He gives to Israel and all other Jewish causes. But his generosity is not limited to financial contributions; it includes his personal recollections. In sharing them with readers, he helps them to acquire an essential measure of knowledge about what will be remembered as one of the greatest events in Jewish history. Sam considers it his duty to tell his story of how he vanquished death.

At first he describes for us the "before," when Chorostkov was a typical Jewish "shtetl" with its characteristic customs and traditions. It could be called by any other name. They were so alike, all those small towns and picturesque villages, where our grandfathers and grandmothers dreamed about the coming of the Messiah who was forever late in coming. They were all swept away in the tempest of fear and fire.

"I was nineteen when the Russian tanks arrived in Chorostkov. . ." Thus Sam relates the end of Poland. Its army, though gallant and valiant in its resistance to the German onslaught, was forced to surrender. As a result of the infamous Hitler–Stalin pact, Poland was divided. Chorostkov became Russian. Life quickly changed and was marked by a series of hardships. Zionist activities were forbidden. Large businesses were nationalized. Sam Halpern went to Lvov to involve himself in business to be able to support the family in Chorostkov. Eventually he returned home. How did Sam cope with the upheavals? Rather well. Initiative, courage, luck: he combined them all. When Germany invaded Russia, Sam could have followed the Red Army but his father was against it. "Remembering the German occupation in 1917, he argued that they had not been so bad." Says Sam: "I sometimes wonder what would have happened to me and my family had I gone to the Soviet Union. . . Would we have spared ourselves years of horror under the Nazis? Could we have saved my mother and my father?. . ."

They were not saved. The atrocities began as soon as German SS soldiers made their appearance in Chorostkov, murdering thirty-four Jews and terrorizing all others. Local anti-Semites collaborated with them. At one point, the Halperns went into hiding. A Christian friend of the family gave them shelter. Sam's description of all these episodes is evocative and poignant.

As is the day he tells of his new life in America. He made good in business and found a place of distinction in the Jewish communities in New Jersey, and in Israel. These post-war episodes are uplifting in more than one way.

Many immigrants, Jewish and Gentile, have written autographical success stories about the opportunities they had found or invented in this new world's greatest democracy.

Halpern's is special.

That Jewish men and women from many lands and cultures could find enough energy and ingenuity in themselves to overcome bitterness and rancor is an inspiring tale in itself; it does honor to themselves and to their adopted countries.

Instead of wallowing in anger and hatred, they became community leaders and friends of humankind, they chose social involvement instead of selfish pursuits, they are now determined to remember the past and fight for its sacredness, all of which represents a victory for Jewish memory.

Therefore I congratulate Sam Halpern for sharing with us his tragic wartime experiences and his subsequent achievements. They prove that, indeed, it is possible to build on ruins. They constitute an unusual testimony. I hope it will be read by those Jews and Gentiles who, in spite of everything, still believe in man's right to hope and to have faith in humanity.

Chorostkow Childhood

I was liberated by the Red Army on March 22, 1944. Although the war would go on for another fourteen months, on this day, when the Nazis retreated from our town, my brother, Arie, and I were finally able to leave the hayloft in which we had been hiding since we escaped from Kamionka, the forced-labor camp where we had been imprisoned. We walked into the light of day feeling hopeful, lucky, thankful to have survived the worst. We were also stunned to learn how many of our people—parents, family, friends, neighbors—had not been so fortunate. We counted our losses and mourned them. While the murders were occurring, the horror was too great for us to comprehend fully. When the bestialities were finally over, we could feel the terrible weight of what had happened to our people. Spring had come, and the air was sweet with blossoms. But for us there was just bitterness. Only twenty-six of over two thousand Jews from our shtetl, Chorostkow, had survived the Nazi slaughter.

Cut off from the past, I thought about my future. I reasoned that there must be some purpose to my survival. Through all the darkness of the Nazi years, I held onto the hope that in the end, no matter how unlikely it seemed to us during the years of horror, out of the evil some good would come.

Among our people, there were many Jews who were smarter, richer, stronger, and more educated than I. But Arie, whom I call Zunio, and I lived through the war when many others did not, and I realized the importance of *mazel* (luck). In the face of the arbitrary nature of life and death, we find purpose and create meaning for our survival through what we do—what we take from the world and, more importantly, what we give back.

In the concentration camp—even as people were selected for death—they would say to me: "If you get out, tell the story." I know that one of the main reasons I survived was to relate what happened to the Jewish people in Europe during the Second World War. By describing what I and my loved ones endured—by recalling the ghettos, *Aktionen*, labor and concentration camps—I am fulfilling the promise I made to those who cannot speak for themselves.

My father was a Chortkover Hasid, a branch of Hasidim that traced its lineage to the Rizhiner rebbe. One of the stories attributed to the Rizhiner expresses both the strength and inadequacy of words to capture the events of decades, the complex web of prayers, dreams, and horrors my people and I experienced.

One day the Baal Shem Tov, the founder of Hasidism, recognized that the Jewish people's prayers were not reaching heaven. Understanding the danger in this situation, the Baal Shem Tov asked Dov Baer, the future Maggid of Mezhirech, to accompany him into the forest. Under a full moon, the Baal Shem Tov hurried to a secret place and lit a fire merely by touching together branches of a tree. The branches were not consumed, and Dov Baer could not help but notice that they resembled the biblical burning bush. With closed eyes, the Baal Shem Tov sat in deep meditation and then stood to pray with intensity. When at last the Baal Shem Tov finished praying, he smiled broadly and said that Israel's prayers would be received in the heavens.

Years later, when the Maggid became the leader of the Hasidim, the Jews were confronted with the grave danger of blood libel. The Maggid took his future successor, Reb Moshe Leib of Sassov, into the forest to the secret place of the Baal Shem Tov. The Maggid could not light the fire, for he knew that a soul like the Baal Shem Tov burned only once in a hundred generations. He told the story to Reb Moshe Leib and said, "Perhaps we can no longer light the fire, but let us pray, for I still remember the prayer of the Besht." The Maggid repeated the words aloud for the first time since he had originally heard them. Although Reb Moshe Leib listened with concentration, he could not remember a single word. When the two men returned to the city, they were told the danger had passed.

A generation later, Reb Moshe Leib—leader of the Sassov Hasidim—was again faced with a catastrophe. Since there was no longer a clear successor to accompany him, Reb Leib went alone into the forest. He could not light the fire or say the prayer, but at least he knew the place. And that proved to be enough.

But when the time came in the next generation for Reb Israel of Rizhin to perform the task, he said to his Hasidim, "We cannot light the fire, we cannot speak the words of the prayer, we do not even know the place. But we can tell the story of what happened." And he did. And that was enough.

*

My generation has seen the darkest and brightest of times for Jews. We have confronted the unfathomable destruction of an entire people: young, old, Hasidim, Zionists, *Mitnagdim*, merchants, artists, and intellectuals. A complete way of life, with a unique culture, was obliterated. The shtetls, the Yiddish language, hundreds of yeshivas—

from the most prestigious Yeshivat Chachmay Lublin, founded by Rabbi Meir Shapiro, to the small *heders* in every hamlet— were all obliterated by the Nazis.

And then my generation witnessed the miraculous establishment of the state of Israel. Given Jewish losses in this century, the best insurance against another Holocaust is a strong Israel. In addition to the story of what happened in Europe, I must also tell of the state of Israel, for this saga includes me, my family, my friends, and my people. At this point, *all I can do is tell my story and pray that the tale will be enough.*

My brother, Avrum Chaim, seven years my senior.

*Meeting with Prime Minister Itzchak Rabin, at one of the Israel Bond drives.
Left to right, myself, Prime Minister Rabin, my brother Arie Halpern.*

My eldest brother, Avrum Chaim, *z"l*, seven years my senior, was an ardent Zionist. He always spoke of wanting to live in the land of Israel. Because of Hitler, my brother's dream never came true. I remember Avrum Chaim teaching the family Zionist songs when I was a little boy. He recounted stories about pioneers from Europe farming the land and living as Jews in their ancient home. Right after the Second World War, I wanted nothing more than to go to Israel, to help fulfill the commandment of building the land. I did not go because of the rigorous British embargo. After Israel's independence when Jews could resettle in Israel, I was already married with one son and another on the way. Still, I wanted to go and always expected I would be part of Israel's unfolding drama. Instead of following this dream, however, I listened to another voice inside me that longed for a family, longed to reconnect. I came to the United States to live near my only living relative (aside from Arie and my cousin Mina, who now lives with her family in Canada). My mother's brother, Paul Wolfson, wanted me and my family to come and be close to him.

But I never forgot my responsibility to the redemption of my people in their own land. On the shores of a generous America, I built a new life for myself and my family, and remained dedicated to helping Israel develop into the wonderful country it is today. From the first donation I made shortly after arriving in New York to a recently completed office building in Tel Aviv, I have observed the commandment to build and beautify Israel. Among all the charities and organizations I support, I give the most time and resources to United Jewish Appeal and Israel Bonds. This commitment to Israel lends meaning to my survival.

A number of years ago in the early 1980s, I met with the mayor of Jerusalem, Teddy Kollek, when he came to New Jersey. He told me about a vacant piece of land in Jerusalem, located outside the Dung Gate, that was being used as a parking lot. Archaeological exploration at the site had uncovered an amphitheater built during the time of the Roman occupation of ancient Israel some 2,000 years ago. Following this discovery, a world-renowned Jewish industrialist contacted Mayor Kollek and said he wanted to build a modern, outdoor theater to reinstate the tradition of open-air theater.

Mayor Kolleck inagurates the Gan HaTekumah, the Garden of Redemption. My wife and myself in foreground, Mayor Kolleck at the podium.

*Standing beside the dedication
tablet at Gan HaTekumah.*

The mayor was not happy with this idea. The site, he felt, was too close to the Western Wall, and performing all sorts of music there might not fit the sacred character of the environment. For Judaism, the Wall, the Temple Mount, is the holiest place in the world, and the last thing Mayor Kollek wanted was to make any Jew uncomfortable while praying at the *Kotel.* Kollek had another idea. He wished to create a park where people of all ages could enjoy trees, flowers, and shade. Kollek came to the United States to gather support for this park, but the project was not doing well. Someone suggested that the mayor contact me.

I was enthusiastic about the project and embarked on raising the necessary funds. I contacted Arie, Harry Wilf, *z"l,* Joe Wilf, Isaac Levinstein, Morry Pantirer, and Avraham Zuckerman, my partners in a number of American projects and the Jerusalem Renaissance Hotel in Israel. The men were easily persuaded that the park would be an important addition to the city of Jerusalem. Today, *Gan HaTekumah,* the Garden of Redemption, is a restful place of natural beauty by the Western Wall in the independent state of Israel.

Not long ago, I led a UJA group to Jerusalem. On the way to the

Kotel, we stopped to see the park. When someone pointed out the names on a dedication plaque by the entrance, I was proud to be a part of the rebuilding of Jerusalem, but I was also uncomfortable with the attention. Then another person in the group turned to some schoolgirls who were strolling past and said to them, "I'd like you to meet Mr. Halpern. He played a major part in building this park."

The girls' faces lit up and they smiled broadly. Now I was really embarrassed. I am rather shy and didn't know what to say. I just stood there and nodded my head. But when one little girl came over and gave me a hug, I thought I would burst with joy. With great warmth, I returned the affectionate embrace.

To understand why this moment meant so much to me, I must start from the beginning and tell the story of my childhood in the shtetl of Chorostkow. Located in what was then southeastern Poland and is today the Ukraine, Chorostkow was a farming hamlet south of the city of Tarnopol. It was one of many Jewish communities in the region of Galicia. None exists today. Until the Nazi invasion, about 500 Jewish families lived in this shtetl.

Jewish life in Chorostkow dates back some 500 years. In the fifteenth century when the Jews were expelled from Spain, the center of Jewish life at the time, they began a trek across Europe. Even earlier in the century, Jews had begun to move east, responding to the invitation of the Polish king, Casimir the Great, who wanted Jews to settle in his country in order to develop trade and commerce. Some Jews remained in Germany, but most continued on and settled in Eastern Europe.

In Hebrew, Poland is called *Polin*. According to legend, when the Jews first arrived in Poland, they were told, *"Po lin,"* which in Hebrew means "here you will rest." In spite of pogroms, persecution, and discriminatory taxation, by the time I was born in 1920, Poland had become the center of Jewish culture in Europe.

Two major events in the eighteenth and nineteenth centuries shaped Jewish life in Poland and, for that matter, in the rest of the world. The first was the birth of a religious movement, known as Hasidism, in the late eighteenth century in Galicia. The second was the start of a political movement, Zionism, in the late nineteenth century. On the surface, these two movements appear to be contradictory. Hasidism sought to save the soul of the Jew from despair by creating a highly personal, even mystical, relationship between the individual and his creator whereas Zionism aimed at finding a political solution to centuries of European persecution by establishing an independent Jewish state in the historical homeland of Israel. While Hasidim waited for God to send the Messiah who would, as part of a new world order, restore them and their ancestors to the homeland, Zionists sought ways to achieve Jewish sovereignty on their ancient land in the here and now. Rarely were both beliefs supported simultaneously. I was privileged to be raised in a household where that ideological gulf was bridged. My parents sustained a deep faith in God and the Jewish people, and thus both movements had a profound influence on my childhood and the man I was to become.

Until about 1750, Chorostkow had been just a quiet shtetl surrounded by many other towns. Then Count Sieminski, who owned the land of the village, gave Chorostkow the rights of a town and invited more Jews from the surrounding area to come live there. For the most part, the Jews lived in the center of town and the Gentiles on farms that fanned out around Chorostkow. For nearly 500 years, from the time Columbus began his Atlantic voyages until Hitler invaded Poland, there was a Jewish presence in Chorostkow.

The first leader of the Jewish community, Yaakov Feffer, persuaded Count Sieminski to allow Jews to build a synagogue, which became the center of Jewish worship and learning in town. For nearly two centuries it served the local Jewish community and became the spiritual home for several illustrious rabbis.

The economic profile of the newly organized Jewish community remained the same during this period of time. Most Jews were retailers, innkeepers, artisans, and peddlers who sold their wares in neighboring villages and in return bought produce from local farmers. There were some doctors, of course, and a lawyer or two. The artisans included tailors, carpenters, shoemakers, furriers, and blacksmiths, who worked for both Jewish and Gentile clients in town and on the surrounding farms. Farmers would pay with produce and poultry, which could then be sold in town. In Chorostkow, Jews sold their services, like all other exchanges, for zlotys.

Chorostkow itself, as noted by some of its survivors in a memorial published in Israel in 1968, *Chorostkow Book*, did not stand out among other shtetls. It did not have art treasures or cultural institutions to make it famous, yet from its inception, the town held its own among older, more established neighbors. Among Chorostkow's prominent rabbis were Meshulam Rath, author of *Kol Mevaser*, and Yeshaye Rappaport, a son-in-law of the famous Babad family. When the winds of national renewal began to blow, Chorostkow produced a number of personalities who contributed to building the state of Israel. Fishel Werber, Shmuel Epstein, and former Housing Minister Avraham Ofer came from my hometown. The Jews of Chorostkow were neither rich nor influential, but they did distinguish themselves in two areas: piety and good deeds. The town was spiritually fortunate to have many rabbis who served with distinction and were devoted to their congregants. In addition, some of Chorostkow's Jews belonged to

Rabbi Meshulam Rath,
with his son-in-law,
Rabbi Israel Haitner.

illustrious Hasidic groups: Chortkov, Husiatin, Sadegura, and Kopychince, which were descendants of the Rizhin Hasidim, a prestigious dynasty whose impact continues to be felt in the Hasidic world.

My father was a Chortkover Hasid. He had a long, beautiful beard and *peyes* (earlocks). On *Shabbat* and holidays he wore a *shtreimal* (a fur trimmed cap) and on weekdays an elegant black hat. The Chortkov dynasty was founded by the son of Rabbi Israel of Rizhin, who himself was the great-grandson of Rabbi Dov Baer of Mezhirech (the successor of the great Rabbi Israel, the Baal Shem Tov). The Chortkov Hasidim considered themselves spiritual children of all these luminary leaders. When my father visited the Chortkover rebbe, my brothers and I were always fascinated by the stories he recounted about this great man whose teachings were inspired by the Hasidic figures who preceded him.

My father taught us that Hasidism focused on three essential factors: the God of Israel, the people of Israel and the land of Israel. The key to the relationship of Hasidism to all three was love: boundless love for the God of Israel, whose will is manifested in the Torah; love for His people, who carry God's divine spark; and love for the Holy Land, where the Temple once stood and to which the Jews would return again some day to form a sovereign nation in their own country.

The disciples of Dov Baer, the great Maggid of Mezhirech, were among the first European settlers of the land of Israel. A group of them settled in the Holy Land over two hundred years ago and laid the foundation for the Jewish resettlement that was to come. The great Maggid used to say, "The entire world is nourished by Zion, which is the essence of the world and its vitality."

This attention to redemption, to the reestablishment of a Jewish state on the land promised to Abraham, is seen in the philosophy of the Rizhiner rebbe. Rabbi Israel of Rizhin wanted to renew a Jewish monarchy capable of ruling Israel once the Jewish people returned to the land, a concern that differed from the teachings of all other Hasidic leaders. While most other rabbis wore simple caftans, the Rizhiner dressed in dark, elegant clothing befitting an esteemed leader. Somehow, the rank and file of the Hasidic movement, and even non-Hasidic leaders, found this rabbi's bearing acceptable, as though he had a special dispensation to behave as he did. Even when the Rizhiner publicly denounced Czarist authority over Jewish subjects, he got away with a short prison term and banishment from Russia. Thousands of this man's followers and those of other rebbes came to Rizhin, and later to Sadigor, a town in Austria to which the Rizhiner moved his court after being exiled, to see the "prince of Israel" and spend time in his presence. To the downtrodden masses of Eastern Europe, the Rizhiner represented the hope of restoration and Jewish independence. *Hadesh yamenu kekedem*, "renew our days as before," recited every time the Torah is replaced in the synagogue ark, seemed one step closer to reality for a long-suffering people.

The Chortkover Rebbe, Rabbi Israel Friedman.

The Rizhiner is quoted as saying, "There will come a time, when the nations will expel us from their lands to the land of Israel. It will be a great disgrace, and it is a pity that after such a long exile, redemption should come in this way. But come what may, at least we will have escaped them at long last, and the rest will follow."

Although many scholars argue that Hasidism and Zionism are in conflict, the stories of the Rizhiner, as told to me by my father, paint an entirely different picture. One major Hasidic sect was clearly not anti-Zionist but was devoted to ending Jewish exile and restoring national sovereignty.

*

The Chortkover Rebbe, grandson of the great Rabbi Israel of Rizhin, was one of the most admired rabbis in Poland when I was a little boy. The head of the yeshiva in Hebron once remarked that someone in his family, upon seeing the Chortkover, said: "When redemption comes, there will be no need to look for a king, for we already have a king, the Chortkover rabbi!" And the person who made this observation was a Lithuanian Mitnagid (an opponent of Hasidism).

Besides being a leader who attracted tens of thousands of followers, the Chortkover was also a great scholar. He wrote several commentaries providing new insight into complex questions in the Torah and Talmud. Among the Chortkover's admirers was the famous Rabbi Meir Shapira of Lublin, who often visited him. Rabbi Shapira of Lublin founded the Yeshivat Chochmay Lublin and *"Daf Yomi,"* the system by which the same page of Talmud is studied daily by thousands of Jews the world over in a seven-year learning cycle.

The Chortkover was deeply concerned about Jewish affairs all over the world. Once the rebbe gave a speech at a general assembly attended by prominent Jewish leaders. His address dealt with the hardships facing Jewish pioneers filtering into the land of Israel from Russia and Poland. The Chortkover, who ordinarily spoke in measured tones, suddenly burst into tears and recited Psalm 137: "If I forget you, O Jerusalem, let my right hand wither. Let my tongue cleave to the roof of my mouth, if I do not remember you, if I do not set Jerusalem above my highest joys." He cried out, "One's heart aches at the thought of all the holy things we used to have in the land of Israel. All the fibers of one's being tremble. What is left to a father who has exiled his own children? Oh, Holy Father, when will you bring us back to Jerusalem?"

He continued, "All that is left to us of the Holy Temple is a piece of the Western Wall where, we believe, the *Shechina*, the Holy Presence, has remained to this day. King Solomon has pleaded that all the prayers pouring out of Jewish hearts rise directly to Heaven from there."

The Chortkover rebbe taught that the Holy Presence of God has always been safely harbored at the *Kotel.* When Theodor Herzl, the founder of Zionism, began to seek support for his movement among Hasidic rabbis, he wrote to the Chortkover rebbe. In this letter, which he sent through the chief rabbi of Botoshan, Romania, Leibishe Mendel Landau (one of the organizers of the Mizrachi movement), Herzl outlined the principles of Zionism.

A secular journalist from Vienna, Herzl made most Hasidic leaders suspicious. They could not understand why a nonobservant Jew would be the man to lead the people back to Israel. But the Chortkover rebbe had a different attitude. His own father, the first rabbi of Chortkov, said, when asked about Herzl's efforts to purchase land in Palestine from the Turkish sultan, "What do we care if those who appeal to the sultan are nonobservant Jews? When we need a lawyer, we may also turn to someone who is nonobservant, but who knows how to be a faithful representative before the law. Similarly, we the Hasidim will establish yeshivas that will spread Torah in Israel, while they will be busy with external matters." The Chortkover rebbe responded to Herzl's letter by saying he would endorse its contents if two other Hasidic rabbis endorsed it as well. Although Herzl tried, he could not secure these two additional signatures. Had two other supporters been found, tens of thousands of Hasidim would have made their way to Israel before the war and consequently escaped the Holocaust.

The Chortkover and his son also participated in the Palestine Agricultural Bank, which later became Bank Leumi. The Chortkover rebbe continued to speak of the Holy Land and influenced many Hasidim to settle there before the Second World War.

After the First World War, the Chortkover rebbe moved his official residence from Chortkov to Vienna. Once or twice a year he would come to Chortkov (about twenty miles from Chorostkow) to meet with his followers. On these visits, my father would go and see the rebbe.

I was about eight years old the first time my father took me and Arie to see the Chortkover rebbe. A constant flow of visitors came to the rabbi's house, and most people waited in line for a long time. But my father, who was a busy merchant with no time to waste, whispered something to one of the rabbi's assistants. The man nodded in agreement and led us to a back door. We were soon admitted into the rabbi's presence. The rebbe asked me what I was learning and then gave me a blessing for a long and prosperous life.

The Chortkover rebbe was a charismatic, learned, and faithful man who inspired all who came before him to do good deeds. This man taught me that the Jewish people need both the Torah and a strong, independent state.

*

The youngest of four sons, I was born on July 2, 1920 (Tammuz 17) to Mordechai Dov and Bella Halpern. The oldest was Naftali followed by Avrum Chaim, Arie, and myself. My parents named me Shmaryahu (meaning "Guarded by God") but also called me Shmerele. My father, who was called Motio by the Gentiles, was a native of Chorostkow. He owned an all-purpose store where he sold groceries, textiles, and leather goods. He also dealt in large quantities of grain, which he would buy from local farmers and then resell to wholesalers. The people in town would say, "If you cannot get it at Motio's, then you can't get it." My mother, who came from the neighboring shtetl of Tarno-Ruda, was a loving, conscientious *balabosta* (Jewish homemaker). My parents were strong and faithful people, devoted to Hasidut—the principles espoused by the Baal Shem Tov and his followers.

When I was little, I went to the local public school in the morning. At one o'clock I came home to eat lunch and then went to heder to learn Torah until eight o'clock at night. As a teenager, I also attended Hanoar Hatzioni, a Zionist youth organization where I was taught Palestinographia, the history and geography of the land of Israel, and modern Hebrew. Sometimes the boys and girls would be brought together to sing pioneer songs and do Israeli folk dances. Most of the boys in town followed a similar schedule. When I wasn't in school, I was in my father's store.

Like all Jewish boys, when I reached thirteen years of age, I celebrated my Bar Mitzvah. On the Thursday morning after my birthday, I went with my father to the Chortkover synagogue where I bound my head and arm with *t'fillin* (phylacteries). Now I was eligible to be a member of a *minyan* (quorum), and was required to perform all the *mitzvot* commanded to adult Jewish men. On the following Sabbath, I was called to the podium to read the *haftorah*, the prophetical section recited after the reading of the Torah on Sabbaths and festivals. My mother baked a special cake, and my father brought bottles of vodka and herring for a simple but festive *kiddush* after the prayers.

By the time I celebrated my Bar Mitzvah, I had mastered the art of buying and selling by watching my father and jumping in when help was needed. I also learned compassion for the needy.

On Friday mornings my father gave charity to poor people who came to the store. Other storekeepers might dismiss them with a coin and a nod, but my father greeted these people like any valued customers, inquiring about the health of their loved ones and making them feel comfortable.

This dedication to charity was not limited to Friday mornings. During the week people came to our home, and my mother would give them food and clothing. Even though we had a small house, my mother would often take in visitors from other towns. (My parents had the one bedroom, all the boys slept in a large area that was a living room, dining room and kitchen combined—Arie and I sharing a bed— and the front room was occupied by the store.) My parents practiced *hachnasat orchim* (hospitality toward guests). At our Friday evening Sabbath meals, there were always a number of other people at the table. Some of them were local residents who could not afford to celebrate the Sabbath properly. Some were travelers who needed a place to stay. My father would bring them home from synagogue after prayers, and my mother was always prepared. My mother used to cook for the Sabbath all day Thursday and Friday so that the Sabbath meal would be a feast.

My mother spent hours preparing gefilte fish, baking the challah, making noodle pudding, roasting meat and chicken, and baking my favorite pastries. As a child, I dreamed all week of the Sabbath. I loved the smells from my mother's cooking and baking.

On the Sabbath, the long, wooden table was covered with a white tablecloth upon which sat Sabbath candles and freshly baked bread. My father, who worked hard all week and could not afford the luxury of intensive Talmud study on weekdays, made up for it on the Sabbath. He and my mother grasped the teachings of the Torah and Hasidic masters, bringing the sources into harmony during these special meals. The feeling of love for God and the Jewish people and the longing for the Holy Land have inspired me throughout life.

Before dinner, my father would rise and chant the *kiddush* over wine. As was customary, each male at the table would then make his own separate *kiddush*. This tradition is still observed in our home and in those of our children. After washing his hands, my father removed the linen cover from the two braided loaves and said the *motzi* (blessing over bread). Every male at the table took two smaller challahs and make his own *motzi.* Then we would eat the delicious, rich bread that captured all the love my mother poured into it. During the meal, my brothers and I would tell what we had learned in heder that week. My father would tell some Hasidic stories, and then he would start singing songs. I always had a good singing voice and would join my father in Sabbath *zmirot.*

My father often asked Avrum Chaim to update the rest of us on the latest news from the land of Israel. I did not know at the time that this was not typical in Hasidic homes, but we were deeply concerned with the building of a future state of Israel. Avrum Chaim described the struggle against Arab and British opposition to a Jewish presence in the Land. He told stories about residents of Chorostkow who had gone to settle there. Avrum Chaim was determined to join them as soon as he turned eighteen. He had already joined an *Achvah*, a general Zionist youth movement.

The part of the Sabbath I remember most vividly was the singing during *seudat shlishit* (the "third meal") eaten between *mincha* and *maariv* on Saturday afternoons in the synagogue. All the men would raise their voices in praise of God for creating the world and its mysteries. The harmonies expressed hope and joy that transcended the material world.

Soon afterward, I would slip out of synagogue to see my friends at Beth Am where Hanoar Hatzioni (the Zionist Youth Movement) was housed. As I approached the ornate, old building. I could hear my comrades inside singing, "David, King of Israel, is still alive!" We would also sing songs written by poets and pioneers in Israel. Singing these songs made us feel as though we were ourselves helping to build the land, digging into the earth and watering our roots.

> *Anu banu artza*
> *L'vnot ool'hibanot.*
>
> We came to the land to build
> And to be rebuilt by it.

Everyone joined in the singing. Tears would fill our eyes, and for a moment, everyone was transported to the Holy Land; we had become a part of the dream.

In the evenings, Beth Am was filled with young people. In the library I listened to Marcus Tannenbaum, the well-known heretic who drew many listeners to his lectures. On the other side of the meeting hall, rooms were occupied by other Zionist organizations like B'nei Akiba, Hashomer Hatzair, Betar, and Poale Zion Achva. Even though Chorostkow was a small shtetl with only five hundred Jewish families, many of which were Hasidic and not affiliated with Zionist organizations, the entire political spectrum of movements was represented, as was also true for adult groups. We raised money for Keren Kayemet and Karen Hayesod, among other funds.

My friends and I in Hanoar Hatzioni would sing, dance and talk. During the week everyone came to the meetings wearing green scout shirts. Pictures of Dr. Herzl and the Hebrew poet Chaim Nachman Bialik hung on the wall along with a banner that read "The Scout Speaks the Truth."

In 1926, Dov Ofer, of the famous Israeli Ofer family (then known as Hirsh), organized a dozen young pioneers. They met in Godziecki's apple orchard, for want of another place, where they sang and danced and decided they would realize their dream of living in the land of Israel, even if they had to walk there! My brother Naftali wanted to join them, but he was too young.

A big send-off party was held for the idealistic young men. Many townsfolk attended, singing Hebrew and Yiddish songs. Then everyone walked with the young people to the city limits. I was only seven at the time, but I was filled with awe as I watched these young people walk out of sight, carrying with them only small sacks of clothing and some books. They had little money, so they hitchhiked or caught short train and boat rides, and did a lot of walking. A year or two after leaving Chorostkow, they joined 125,000 Jews already in the land of Israel.

Dov's younger brother, Avraham, was a year younger than me. We belonged to the same Hanoar Hatzioni group, and our fathers prayed in the same Chortkow synagogue. Every Friday night before *Kabbalat Shabbat*, Keren Kayemet wanted a few boys to post slips on the synagogue wall showing who had and had not given money to the

Jewish National Fund. Some Hasidim did not like this practice and would rip the paper off the wall when they came to pray *mincha*. Not to be outdone, we youngsters decided to outsmart the men and began to post the slips immediately before the Sabbath. Once *Shabbat* came, nothing could be done since ripping down papers was considered a form of work that was prohibited on the day of rest. Avraham Ofer, Berche Somerstein, and I—all devoted Zionists even at the ages of eight, nine, and ten—enjoyed performing this service in the name of the Zionist cause.

There were about eight synagogues in Chorostkow. Although just a shtetl, Chorostkow had Mizrachi synagogues, Hasidic *shteeblach* (small houses of worship), and Mitnagdim *shuls*, just like in the big cities. The largest synagogue was known as Zionist. A number of smaller synagogues were affiliated with the Chortkow Hasidim, and my father prayed there. All other *shuls* and *shteebels* in town were connected with various Hasidic groups, except one synagogue called Yad Charutzim, which was organized exclusively for working men, drivers, package carriers, smiths, and carpenters who wanted to pray separately during the week because they were always hurrying to work. On *Shabbat*, everyone, regardless of trade or profession, rested, basking in the peace and beauty of the day.

The large synagogue in Chorostkow.

The *Shabbat* atmosphere began on Friday afternoon. Stores would close early, and everyone went home to change into better clothing. The houses were clean, and everyone waited in anticipation for the Sabbath Bride. Shalom, the *shammash* (synagogue sexton), stood on a hill by the synagogue and loudly called out over and over, "Time to go to *shul*."

Everyone was happy. Poverty did not diminish the Sabbath joy, and Yiddishkeit filled every heart.

On Rosh Hashanah and Yom Kippur, the entire community woke earlier than usual and stayed in synagogue late into the evening. The atmosphere of piety had actually begun at the start of the month of Elul, four weeks before. At midnight, Shalom, the *shamash*, would walk through town knocking on doors and windows. In a sweet, melodious voice he would sing, "Get up and pray to God." On *Selichot* night, the community would begin to recite prayers of forgiveness. The sense of repentance and contemplation would build during the month, gaining momentum during the Ten Days of Awe and climaxing on Yom Kippur. People asked *selicha* (forgiveness from God and one another) throughout this period. Even though we lived among Gentiles and were a small minority in Chorostkow, indeed in Poland generally, Jews followed the cycle of the religious calendar. Time was measured from one *yom tov* to another, from one *mitzvah* to the next.

When I was nine years old, like all other youngsters in town I wore a costume and mask on Purim—a time during which students put on skits poking fun at teachers, turning the world topsy-turvy in good-natured jest. One Purim Arie, Avraham Ofer, Wolwa Nagler, and I went to Rabbi Yeshiya Rappoport's house. As is the custom on the holiday, the rabbi wanted to give us some *shalach manos* (a gift of two kinds of food), but in the trickster spirit of the holiday, we refused. Avraham said we didn't want food, only money. The rebbetzin (rabbi's wife), who caught on to our antics right away, said she wouldn't give money but was willing to negotiate. Would we like some wine? We declined the offer. Some cake? Again, we shook our heads. The spoof worked because we were in costume and anonymous. No one spoke aloud. As long as we wore our masks, we could continue the *spiel*, the fun-loving pranks allowed on Purim. For another fifteen minutes we tried to negotiate with the rebbetzin, Avraham in the lead, until tired and hungry, we took off our masks and sat down to eat and drink with the rabbi.

That year on Chanukah, Arie and I came down with measles. As usual, we were sleeping together in one bed, and when the holiday arrived, relatives came to our home bearing Chanukah *gelt* (gifts of money). In total, we received thirteen zlotys, which was a lot of money at the time. We lay in bed and thought about the toys we wanted to buy. Then we remembered that our father needed to purchase salt for the store. Unlike other commodities, which were bought on credit, salt had to be paid for in advance, in cash. At that time there was a monopoly on salt imports and distribution in Poland; whoever wanted this "luxury" had to pay dearly for it. We called our father into the room and handed him our Chanukah *gelt*. *"Tate,"* we said. "Father, take this so you can buy salt." We knew that toys meant little compared to helping our father provide for the family.

In 1929, my family suffered a tremendous loss. My eldest brother, Naftali, died on the fourth day of *chol hamoed* (the half-festive days between the first and last days of Passover). Naftali had been sick with tuberculosis for many months, and my father and mother ran from city to city looking for a doctor who could offer a cure. But in the days before penicillin, little could be done for TB. Naftali was sixteen years old, a brilliant student and an ardent Zionist. That he left us during a festival, a time of rejoicing and congregation, was doubly hard to bear. Jewish law prohibits eulogies and outward gestures of mourning during festivals, and although we observed the commandments, we were crushed with grief.

At the time, I didn't look well myself. I was pale and thin. My parents were concerned and started taking me to one doctor after another. A well-known professor finally concluded that my tonsils were inflamed. I was thin, he said, because I could not eat enough.

My mother then took me to an ear, nose, and throat hospital in Lvov, the largest city in Galicia, where the professor's opinion was confirmed. An appointment to remove my tonsils was scheduled two days later. But first mother took me to see the Husiatiner rebbe in Lvov. He knew our family, and I sat on his lap. "Please, don't worry. It's an easy operation," he said, telling me about people who had gone through it without any problems. Then he put his hands on my head and blessed me. The rebbe predicted the operation would go well, and it did. I was reassured by the blessings, which quelled my fears. In those days in Poland, only local anesthesia was administered for this operation. Two doctors held me down and a third cut out my tonsils. It was very painful, but for days afterwards I ate only ice cream.

Although my tonsils were out, I still didn't gain weight. My mother tried to make me to drink lots of milk, but I did not like milk. So she bribed me: a piece of chocolate and then the glass of milk. The milk feeding proved as unsuccessful as the operation, so my mother took me to see Doctor Klar in Chorostkow. He told her I would have to go to Micolichin, a resort in the Carpathian mountains known for clean, fresh air. Since neither of my parents could take me—my father had his business, my mother had her other children—Aunt Chayke, my father's younger sister, was recruited. We stayed in the mountains for four weeks. (Chayke was later killed during the war along with her husband, Moshe Morgenstern, and their three children.) When Chayke and I returned to Chorostkow, my mother and father were waiting at the station, waving enthusiastically as the train pulled in. I leaned out the railcar window, holding up two fingers as in the "V for victory" sign, yelling: "Two kilo, two kilo!" I had gained two kilograms and felt like a hero.

Of course, life in Chorostkow was not all joy and singing. While the young Zionists dreamed of going to live in the land of Israel and while the Hasidim waited for the Messiah who would come and usher in a better world, one still had to make a living. From the turn of the century, through the teens, the difficult twenties, and eventually through the horrific thirties and forties, the Messiah did not come to help the Jews of Europe. And the reality of making ends meet only became grimmer with each passing decade.

In 1918, Poland became an independent country for the first time in 130 years. Two years later, Chorostkow, so close to the Russian border, became part of Poland (having originally been held by the Ukrainians and later the Bolsheviks). During the 1920s, Poland sought to become economically stable, but in 1929 the stock market in New York crashed and with it much of the world economy.

In Chorostkow, as in many other Polish towns and cities, many businesses went bankrupt. The value of goods dropped some 80 percent, and merchants, who had always signed promissory notes to obtain merchandise, suddenly found themselves owing large sums of money and having nothing with which to pay them back. For many, life became quite hopeless. A sense of despair settled over the town.

My father had been dealing in leather and had a large inventory that had been produced in local factories using a simple tanning and curing process. At the same time as the crash, the Margosches factory in nearby Stanislavov began producing high-quality leather using modern techniques at a much lower cost. The value of my father's leather fell not only because of the general devaluation of goods but also because of the introduction of Margosches leather into the market, and my father was almost pushed out of the market entirely. A pair of boots that he had previously been able to sell for a hundred zlotys was now worth only twenty.

One evening my father called his three sons over to him and said, "Times are very difficult. We owe a great deal of money. But we must

*Above: Shmuel Itzhak Halpern,
my paternal grandfather.*

*Right: Naftali Hertz, my maternal grandfather.
Unfortunately, no pictures of my parents
remain extant.*

not despair. We must find a way to repay our debts and continue to uphold our reputation as reliable merchants. I will go and talk to the wholesalers and see if I can get an extension on our debts. I am sure that if we put our minds to it, we will succeed."

That night I lay awake and thought about my father's words. I was proud that my father had so much faith in Avrum Chaim, Arie, and me, even though we were only sixteen, eleven, and nine years old! I was proud of my father for not letting despair overtake him. I thought painfully of all the poor Jews in Chorostkow who had such a hard time making a living. I knew my father would find a way out of his dilemma, and taking his sons into his confidence would only give him strength.

The next evening my father called us to him again. This time he was smiling. He told us how he had gone to see two of his leather and textile wholesalers that day. They agreed to extend his six-month promissory notes to two years. Relieved and hopeful, my father figured that with Avrum Chaim, Arie, and me helping, we would be able to repay the notes.

Having weathered this crisis, much of the town's economic life stabilized, and the routine of market day resumed its usual pace. For many Chorostkow residents, including the town's two thousand Jews, two thousand Ukrainians, and two thousand Poles, Monday was the day of the week when one earned one's living. Monday was market day, and it seemed to take over, sparking anticipation and eclipsing other activities. On market day, the number of people in Chorostkow swelled from a manageable six thousand to an almost riotous but wonderful twenty thousand. People came from the surrounding villages and even from nearby cities to the large market where a wide range of merchandise was bought and sold. Everyone had a hand in it.

God forbid it should rain or snow on a Monday! Then everyone's source of income for the week would be lost. When it rained, the market grounds were reduced to mud. The horses would struggle to pull the heavy wagons through, and buyers and sellers would hurry to transact business. It was hard enough for most to earn a living, and being at the mercy of the weather did not help matters. Too often families did not have enough to eat, and the local Jewish family service would have to help out. Most people did not live in large, com-

fortable homes but in simple, houses that were too hot in the summer
and too cold in the winter.

This is why everyone was vigilant on Mondays. Those Jews who
normally settled comfortably into their morning services during the
rest of the week, prayed early and quickly on Monday mornings. Even
the Husiatyn and Chortkov Hasidim, who during the week studied
Mishna or a page of Talmud, did not always do so on Monday mornings. Their minds were primarily on the market. Surely the One on
High was aware of market day and the need to earn a living, and He
would forgive them this morning of haste.

Like most Jewish children, on Monday afternoons I would leave
heder early. Often, I helped my paternal grandparents, Shmuel Itzhak
and Chana Halpern, in the market. They sold lace, which was sewn
onto the collars of women's dresses and blouses as a decorative acces-
sory. Lace had been a very good commodity before the First World
War, but afterward it was out of fashion, and customers were scarce.
My grandparents also sold red coral beads, but this too became harder
to sell after the War since the local population could no longer afford
them. Fortunately, though, there was a strong demand for this semi-
precious item in both the United States and Canada, and salesmen
came all the way from North America to search out my grandfather,
who had a large stock of coral beads, on market day. He was able to
make good money selling to these exporters.

On Mondays, many of our heder teachers also left their classrooms
to work in the market. A common product for sale was fabric remnants bought in Tarnopol. One of my teachers, Hirsh Leib, had a stand
where he sold small items like soap and matches. And some, like my
Hebrew teachers Eli and Gavriel helped their wives. Eli's wife sold
cotton at her stall, and Gavriel, helped his wife sell glass beads. The
husbands often stood guard near the stands to make sure nothing was
stolen. Even Gittel, who sold only lollipops, insisted that her husband
help her on Mondays, arguing that she would go broke if he did not
keep on eye on her merchandise. On Mondays, they were merchants,
not just Hebrew school teachers. And in order to eke out a small
living, they had to be both and began preparing for market on Sundays.

The Market in Chorostkow.

What really helped make the Chorostkow market thrive, though, was the livestock fair where farmers bought and sold horses, pigs, and cattle. The farmers would arrive on Sunday with their livestock and stay at the inn where they drank and argued in loud voices. The livestock merchants would arrive the next day, make deals, and load the animals onto cattle cars that waited at the nearby train station.

In addition, there was a grain market on Mondays. The grain would be delivered in sacks and piled high, and the grain merchants would

Sam Halpern, Izthak Goldfleiss, and Arie Halpern.

come and look them over. My father bought grain from the local farmers and sold it to the wholesalers on market day. I would often join my father on market day, learning the basic skills of buying and selling.

I also remember well, and fondly, some of the other merchants of Chorostkow, like Itzhak Goldfliess, who owned a tavern and restaurant in the center of town. And Asher Baruch Klar, the wealthiest Jew, a large landowner who every year donated enough wheat so that those less fortunate could make *matzot* for Passover. Then there was Shmuel Kimel, a prosperous businessman; Pinchas Elenberg, who owned a big textile business; and Shmerele Stein, a wholesale grocer.

When I was not in school and not helping out on market day or in my father's store, I was involved with Zionist youth activities and with sports, neither of which held my heder rebbes' attention. I belonged to Hanoar Hatzioni's sports club, and for many years, until the Russian tanks rolled into town, I played soccer. I was quite good, and the hours I spent playing a defensive position in front of the goalie, kept me in good physical shape.

One day, a soccer team of older boys from a neighboring town came to play a more advanced team from our town. I asked my heder rebbe for permission to go watch the match. He objected, saying that nobody would be going to the game, that we had to stay put and learn. He could not appreciate the sport or the importance of athletics in my life. I asked him again, and this time my question was met with a chilly silence. After some time passed, I asked him if I could go to the bathroom, and when I was out of the classroom, I left the heder. I walked to the field outside of the town where the match was taking place. The young men ran with grace and discipline, and I waited in tense anticipation as attempt after attempt to score a goal was thwarted. I studied every move of the defensive players, looking to learn from them, to adapt their plays into my own game. For an afternoon I was transported into another world, that of athletics and physical skill.

*

Managing to survive the blight of the twenties hardly prepared us for the events of the following decade. The thirties, the era in which I grew from a little boy to a young man, was a grim time. In 1933, when I was 13 years old, Hitler came to power in neighboring Germany. He soon informed his citizens and the world that he intended to rid his country of Jews. With Hitler's public pronouncements, the ghost of anti-Semitism, which hovered over European history, was given permission to show itself, and in small towns and shtetls it became harder and harder for Jews both economically and socially.

In the late 1930s, when Skladkowski was the Polish prime minister, there were sporadic incidents of Jews being caught in the streets or on the trains and having their beards cut off by local Gentiles—both Poles and Ukrainians. Although Skladkowski denounced these incidents, telling the nation that the Polish people were too sophisticated to engage in this sort of shameful activity, he also echoed some of Hitler's themes, claiming the Jews had too much economic power. Indeed, he went so far as to repeat the lie that the Jews controlled the banks and the world economy and threatened the livelihood of the native population. To redress this supposed imbalance, Skladkowski encouraged Poles to take over businesses from Jews by creating their own. Poles were offered low rents in prime commercial locations and large, low-interest bank loans. In spite of these incentives, in 1939 when the Second World War began, many of the businesses in Chorostkow were still in Jewish hands.

This situation was not without its problems, however. It was increasingly hard for Jews to secure loans and merchandise on credit. As anyone in business knows, this hardship can have a terrible effect on an enterprise's ability to weather difficult periods or grow profitably. It was not uncommon in those days for people in Chorostkow to go to bed hungry. In response, many young men went to the larger cities to look for jobs.

Meanwhile, the German monster was continuing to prepare one of the worst wars ever inflicted on the human race. In Russia, Stalin, a ruthless despot, was destroying millions of human beings in the name of justice and brotherhood. He also launched an anti-Semitic campaign that made it all but impossible for Jews to practice their religion. The Western powers, which should have been preparing for the coming catastrophe, chose instead to hide their heads in the sand and maintain isolationist positions. Poland, in a deep economic crisis, vented its frustrations and fears on its Jewish citizens.

I had left both public and religious school and had begun to work full time in my father's business. Since he was not rich, my father could not afford to send me to school after my Bar Mitzvah. My eldest brother, Avrum Chaim, had studied for a few years in a yeshiva after his Bar-Mitzvah, and Arie, too, studied with one of the local rabbis until he was seventeen years old, but times had changed and money was tighter than ever. Venues of commerce were being denied to Jews, and jobs were become more and more scarce.

A year later, in 1934, like many other young men, my brother, Avrum Chaim, left Chorostkow in search of work. He spent a number of years in Lvov, the largest city in Galicia, working as a bookkeeper in a quilt factory owned by my father's cousins, Mechyl and Gittel Halpern. Lvov had a rich cultural life, six-story apartment buildings, and the hustle and bustle of a large city. When Avrum Chaim returned to Chorostkow, he saw the town with big city eyes. He still loved it, though, as we all did, even if he continued to dream of leaving permanently for the land of Israel.

In 1935, a man in Trembowla by the name of Freund had a large dairy business. Every day he would deliver approximately one ton of butter to Lvov. He always had a large surplus of buttermilk and finally came to the conclusion that with it he could make Swiss cheese. No one made domestic cheese in Poland, and all the imported ones were very expensive.

Freund invited a specialist from Switzerland to examine his product and he too concluded that a domestic cheese could be produced. Freund enthusiastically approached the authorities with his idea. He needed a special license to produce the cheese.

Freund told them about the Swiss specialist. He told them he was willing to bring in the necessary machines. He told them his cheese factory would employ many local people.

The committee assigned to review his proposal was impressed. A Mr. Sommerstein, a Jew who had converted to Christianity, said to Freund that this was an excellent idea. Good for the local economy, good for Poland. But, he continued, it was not legal for a Jew to possess the necessary licenses and, therefore, Sommerstein suggested that

Freund take on a Gentile partner. Freund could remain involved but only as a silent partner.

Freund was naturally infuriated and told Mr. Sommerstein that from Nuremberg to Trembowla was not so very far and that Sommerstein should not be so high and mighty. He was a Jew as far as the Germans were concerned and might one day be subject to the same discrimination he was now delivering. Mr. Freund is no longer alive, but his son lives in Israel.

Not much time passed before my family once again faced an economic crisis. It was 1936, and my father's notes were coming due. For the second time in the span of a few years, our income plummeted. Again my father called his sons to him. After outlining the situation, he said: "I am now relying on you three to find ways to increase our trade. Find some new sources of grain. Also, we don't have to sit here and wait for customers to come to us to sell our merchandise. Every day is market day in a neighboring town. You will take fabric from the store and set up a stall in a good location in the rotating markets and sell it."

The next day I got out of bed early and made a list of all the people I was going to visit to try and add to my father's clientele. The first person I approached was the Ukrainian Orthodox priest, Lubovich, whose son, Piotr, had gone to school with me. It was late July, and the sun stood high in the sky. After a short walk through the narrow streets of the town, I found myself in the fields outside Chorostkow. They were filled with thousands of wildflowers. The reds, pinks, lavenders and yellows were dazzling. They lifted my spirits, and a surge of optimism ran through me. In the distance, I could see Father Lubovich's ripe, golden wheat fields. He owned 120 acres, and I was going to offer him a deal. I would buy all his grain at the going rate, and on top of this I would make us both a handsome profit. I knew it was a daring proposition. Why would Father Lubovich be willing to sell his grain to me, a young man who had recently turned sixteen, and not to one of the established grain dealers?

As I walked along the small lake to the priest's farm, I thought of the simple but loving birthday party my family recently had for me. I was given a bar of chocolate and a couple of pencils, and everyone

wished me a long and healthy life. This low-key celebration was typical of birthday celebrations in the shtetl. I considered how lucky I was
to have such a close and devoted family and shut my eyes, as I walked
along, and took a deep breath of the sweet, fresh air. "How great are
your deeds, O Lord, " I said quietly to myself. "In wisdom have you
done them all!"

When I reached the farmhouse, I pulled the rope hanging from the
large, metal bell over the gate. I pulled it three times, and then I saw
my friend, Piotr, running down the lane.

"Piotr," I called out. "Good to see you again."

"Shmercio! What a surprise!"

Piotr opened the gate and put his arm around my shoulder. I was
pleasantly surprised and uplifted by this warm reception. "Come inside," he said in a cheerful voice. "Say hello to my father."

Father Lubovich was sitting in the parlor, smoking his pipe. He too
was happy to see me. After some small talk, I told him why I had
come. He listened intently, drawing on his pipe, and kept nodding in
agreement.

"Well," he said finally, "it sounds like a good idea. Your father,
Motio, is a very responsible man. I trust him. Besides, he is known to
be very good to the poor, which I can appreciate. If you really think
you can do well with the grain, I am willing to give it a try."

I was elated. I had just landed a major source. Things were beginning to look better already.

In addition to finding new grain suppliers, over the next few
months Arie and I traveled to the neighboring towns selling textiles.
Each time we made enough money to enable my father to pay off a
promissory note, we were ecstatic because we could see how much
joy it brought him. As a Torah-loving man, my father took seriously
the responsibility to repay debts. To him it was not just a matter of
good business and honor but an ethical issue, an expression of God's
will.

As for the plan with the priest, at first it did not yield as much
profit as I had hoped, but the priest was satisfied and continued to sell
me his grain on a regular basis. This was wonderful, for it provided
me and my family with a steady, predictable income.

I continued to find new sources of grain, and each month I turned over more and more money to my father. By the end of the year, our steadfast reputation for reliability was further established, and more wholesalers began to extend us credit. My father's policy was a simple one: never to get into more debt than he could see his way clear to repay. This was one lesson whose logic and prudence I never forgot. To this very day I employ this policy in my business. It has always held me and my associates in good stead. My father continued to expand his business, but he did it carefully, one step at a time, without falling into the trap of making deals on which he could not deliver.

In the early spring of 1936 as I was on my way to the synagogue one day, a carriage drawn by two large, white horses stopped next to me. From the window, a man's head in a tall, dark hat appeared. He motioned that I should come close. When I did, I recognized the man as Count Michael Shatarsky, the richest landowner from the neighboring village of Ivanovfka. In addition to his land, he owned a large flour mill and a distillery.

He was not unfamiliar to me. He would sometimes come to our house before the harvest, in need of a few hundred zlotys. He would always repay the loan with grain. Often my father would lend him money in April or May, and although we would have to wait until July or August for repayment in grain, we knew his credit was good and his reputation as the Ivanovfka's wealthiest man certainly preceded him. Sometimes he would come to our store for groceries he couldn't find elsewhere. And every Christmas, my mother would make honey cake and gefilte fish, which my father would then bring to Shatarsky and a few local Polish and Ukrainian priests who were good customers. Shatarsky claimed that not one of his fancy Paris chefs could make gefilte fish as delicious as my mother's. I am convinced that these annual gifts of food helped my family gain entrance into these Gentiles' lives and that later, during the darkest days of the war, these same people helped me.

One day he came to us on the Sabbath asking for a loan. My father had just returned from synagogue and when he saw Shatarsky, he knew immediately why he had come. My father greeted him politely. Shatarsky looked around the room and saw the table set for the Sabbath meal. Shatarsky knew that my father did not handle money on the Sabbath, and he left our home without asking for a loan. I ran out after

him, asking if there was anything I could do to be of service. He then
told me he was in need of a few hundred zlotys. I told him that if he
could wait, I would be able to get him the money in the evening. In a
small town, this was the way you could get friendly with everyone,
even the most influential people. Possibly, Shatarsky still remembered
this incident.

"Are you young Halpern?" he asked me, leaning out of the carriage
window.

"Yes, sir, at your service," I quickly answered.

"Come with me to your father's store."

The store was around the corner, and I walked alongside the carriage. The driver put down the reins, stepped down from the bench,
and came around to the side to open the carriage door. Shatarsky
emerged slowly, putting on a monocle and taking off his gloves. My
father, meantime, had come out of the store to greet him.

"Mr. Halpern," Shatarsky said, "I would like to talk business."

They went into the store, and my father motioned to me to leave
the room.

"No, no," Shatarsky protested. "Let him stay. I would like him to
hear what I'm going to say."

He then explained that he had a great deal of grain to sell and had
heard that I was a very reliable grain dealer. He wanted to try me out.
Proud yet still humble, my father said: "I am sure you will be very
pleased with his dealings."

Shatarsky turned out to be my best supplier. He sold me grain
without asking for any payment up front. He trusted me since my
family had always trusted him. After working with Shatarsky for one
season, I brought home what was a substantial amount of money for a
sixteen-year-old. My father was overjoyed. "Well Shmerele," he com-
mented. "You have fulfilled the words *hamotzi lechem min haporitz*."
This was a play on words. Instead of the blessing for bread "which is
brought forth from the earth," he had punned the word *haaretz* with
poritz, Yiddish for landowner.

Selling was never a problem. Grain was a commodity that was always marketable. We would hire men to bring the grain to the mills
and to the railroad stations by horse drawn wagon. We sold to
wholesalers as close as Lvov and far away as Warsaw and even Vien-

na. The market often went up, and the clients would take as much grain as we could deliver. The crux of making money in the grain market was buying at the right price.

Since my father maintained excellent credit, he always tried to use it to help other people. If they had smaller stores without much credit, they often could not purchase merchandise. Without merchandise, they would have nothing to sell. When buying merchandise, my father would ask some of the smaller storekeepers for a list of what they needed. He would buy everything, give them what they had asked for at cost, and would be paid back after they sold the products.

My father also helped small storekeepers who did not have the licenses necessary to buy and sell certain merchandise, such as leather, grain, or textiles. We, of course, had a license to deal in grain since we bought and sold large quantities during the season. But these licenses were expensive, and many could not afford them. Therefore, if one of the smaller merchants was questioned by the local police about selling grain or something else without a license, he could avoid a penalty by claiming to work for the Halperns. All he had to say was, "This isn't mine. It belongs to Motio Halpern," and the police would leave him alone.

All of our permits and licenses were in perfect legal order. And when the police would come to the store, we would be polite and treat them nicely. We wanted no trouble and got along with everyone.

Through our combined efforts, my father managed to pay back all the promissory notes he had taken out. We were all so proud of being able to do so in such difficult economic times; it was an achievement.

After returning from Lvov, Avrum Chaim worked for twelve months in a *hachshara*, a training farm that prepared youth for the agrarian lifestyle in Israel. This work would enable him to enter Israel, then British controlled Palestine. A Jew either had to have a certificate proving that he could be a "productive" citizen, in many cases from a *hachshara*, or had to have a thousand pounds Sterling. This substantial amount of money assured the British government that a person could take care of himself financially and not, once there, be a drain on the Empire. In Chorostkow, there were many who wanted to emigrate who could not prove to have this much money. And then there were some who had the means but either were not Zionists or could not leave Poland at the time because of other family considerations. Even though the Jewish newspapers carried articles about Hitler and the Nazis, and even though we heard Hitler's hate-filled speeches on the radio in the town cafe, much of what we read and heard was met with a kind of numb disbelief. Then too, hadn't we heard this sort of hate speech for hundreds of years? After a period of persecution, things always seemed to have returned to a workable calm. We reacted to Hitler's propaganda, therefore, with a strange mix of concern and indifference. He seemed to us a deranged man in the neighboring country who would not last long. If only the Jews in Chorostkow had known what was to befall us within the next few years, I am sure we would have worked much harder at getting out of Poland and into Israel.

Since we were all working hard just to keep the family business afloat, we could not afford to bankroll Avrum Chaim's entrance into Palestine, and so he had to wait and work and train at the *hachshara*.

Avrum Chaim, preparing to be a pioneer.

Finally, his turn came to receive the cherished certificate. Everyone was thrilled. His friends threw a party for him where they sang and danced all night. Many cried with joy for him, and some cried with sorrow being unable to join him.

Our joy was short-lived. The very next day a telegram arrived from Lvov informing Avrum Chaim that he would have to give up his precious certificate. It was 1938, and the Nazis had just expelled all Polish Jews living in Germany. These Jews were sitting right over the German-Polish border in a small town called Zbonszyn; they had no place to sleep and nothing to eat. The Zionist authorities in charge of the British certificates decided to give all existing ones to these Germany Jews who had, overnight, become refugees. The Zionist authorities concluded that those Jews still living in the relative security of eastern Poland would have to wait a while longer to enter the land of their dreams.

Avrum Chaim was heart-broken. None of us knew if he would ever get another chance to go to Israel. The clouds gathering over Chorostkow were getting darker, and I cannot help but wonder how different things would have turned out for my brother, for my entire family, for my shtetl, for all the Jews of Europe, if the State of Israel had been born in 1938 and not, as it was, a decade later in 1948.

Overall, even though there was a long history of anti-Semitism in the Ukraine, and occasionally we could feel its undercurrent, for the most part the residents of Chorostkow, Jew and Gentile, merchant and farmer, lived and worked together on good terms. There may not have been intensive socializing, and certainly inter-faith marriages were almost unheard of, but the communities were friendly. My parents' gifts of cake and fish to Shatarsky and the local priests were but one example. For the sake of business and in the name of human decency, everyone made sure to go out of their way not to hurt one another.

On one occasion, the cardinal from Lvov visited Chorostkow. Thousands of people came to welcome him, including representatives of neighboring parishes and synagogues. A member of my family's synagogue came carrying a Sefer Torah. When the cardinal approached the crowd of people, the first thing he did was walk over to the Jewish delegation. He took the large cross that was hanging on his chest and moved it to his back. Then he bent over and kissed the Torah. I was deeply impressed.

Of course, all this changed. Judging by our lives before the war, I could never have predicted the hatred and sadism that was directed toward the Jewish community by some Gentile neighbors. A very small number did risk their lives to save Jewish friends. But were it not for such Poles—unfortunately, a very tiny percentage of the population—I, my brother, my wife, and countless others would not be alive today to tell the story of what happened. Very few righteous Gentiles risked their lives and the lives of their children to hide Jews, and unlike Oskar Schindler, most of them have not become famous for their good deeds. They remain unknown except to those Jews who owe them their lives.

Living with the Russians

I was nineteen when Russian tanks arrived in Chorostkow. That day, September 17, 1939, marked the end of an era and the radical beginning of another. It would be the watershed moment that closed the chapter on centuries of Jewish life in Poland; it marked the day that everything familiar to me, and to all the hundreds of Jewish shtetls in Galicia, would be forever transformed.

The invasion and division of Poland by the German army in the west and the Soviet army in the east had begun two weeks earlier, on September 1, 1939. Everyone in Chorostkow remained within earshot of the radio throughout the day. Many people gathered at the cafe in town to hear the frenzied news reports of the bombing of Polish cities by the German *Luftwaffe*. We wondered how far east their vicious tentacles would reach. Shocked at this blatant aggression and hopeful that the Western nations would not tolerate it and that the war would be short-lived, we nevertheless trembled in anticipation of what might happen.

From the moment that Hitler had been elected chancellor of Germany in 1933, we had heard about the hateful anti-Semitism contained in his book, *Mein Kampf*. We had also listened to venomous speeches on the radio and knew he wanted to rid Europe of Jews. After all, he said so straight out. But how far could he carry this hatred? How much of this threatening diatribe was rhetoric? And how much could he actually accomplish? In retrospect, had we taken his book and speeches literally, we might have acted differently. Still, the obsessive anti-Semitism seemed so extreme that many of us dismissed it as irrational, unbelievable. Even after the invasion of Poland had begun, few suspected the disaster it would bring for the entire country or the consequences it could have for Jews.

Facing little military opposition from the Polish army, the German Wehrmacht took over western Poland. The country was divided between the Soviet Union and the German Third Reich, in fulfillment of the infamous Molotov-Ribbentropp pact that had spelled out this conquest and sharing of spoils. The socialists in town were shocked that the Russians had entered into such a deal with the fascist Reich. They had made a deal with the devil. If only the shock and dismay could have ended there, but the atrocities that were to follow made this initial betrayal seem tame.

By mid-September, Nazi troops had overrun their allotted portion of western Poland, including the capital city of Warsaw, and the Red Army had taken over their portion with frightening ease.

Until the Russian tanks arrived, I had thought of myself as a young man living in a traditional society, the way my father had before me and his father before him, in a lineage stretching back for centuries. We were concerned with making a living in a family-owned business, with hoping for good weather on market day, with praying three times a day, with creating a Jewish, God-conscious home where *mitzvot* were more important than anything else and where wives and children could prosper.

With the start of the Russian occupation, everything had changed. Overnight, I became an adult facing the challenge of a frightening reality. No one could guess at that point what the outcome of a large-scale European war might be. Neither did we know what kind of life Jews would have under the Soviet secular, antireligious regime.

The air-raid sirens, which began to shriek throughout the town, ended, in one instant, hundreds of years of peaceable Jewish existence and relative security in Chorostkow. Since there were no bomb shelters, people merely left their homes and sought safety in the fields or down by the pond. When the high-pitched wailing of the sirens suddenly stopped, an eerie silence descended over Chorostkow. Today I count that time as the moment when I grew up.

A few days later, the railroad station near town was bombed. No one was killed and the area suffered little damage, but the incident caused widespread panic. On the day following the bombing, refugees fleeing from the Germans in the west began to show up. Among the refugees were known journalists and writers. I was in Trembowla selling grain at the time when a group of nine German planes appeared out of nowhere and swept over the city and its train station. They dropped bombs indiscriminately, killing eight civilians and wounding many. The people of Chorostkow started to wonder whether they, too, should take to the road and look for refuge across the border in Hungary or Romania.

On Friday night, two weeks after the war started, our family gathered around the Sabbath table, and everyone did his and her best to fulfill the *mitzvah* of greeting the Sabbath Queen with joy and song. Underneath, though, we were wondering how long it would take for the Germans to show up. We hadn't then considered that it might be the Russians. We were forbidden to discuss such grim matters on the Sabbath lest they spoil the sanctity of the day, and so we refrained from mentioning the war, despite the fact that each of us could think of nothing else. Finally, my father turned to his family and guests, and said in a halting voice, "My dear ones, we all know that there are difficult times ahead of us. But we must trust in the Rock of Israel, who has never allowed his people to suffer destruction. With His help, this too shall pass." Some around the table murmured, "Amen," and others nodded in agreement.

On Saturday evening, after the Third Meal of *Shabbat*, as my family was preparing for *Havdala*, the ritual at Sabbath's close, we heard airplanes in the distance. Silence fell over us as we waited for the bombs to fall. But there were no explosions. We waited some more, and when the airplanes seemed to recede, my father filled the cup with wine, opened the box with incense, and lit the special braided candle used only for *Havdala*. Over the blessings marking the difference between the sacred and the profane, between the Sabbath and the regular weekday, we prayed to the Almighty to protect our family and our nation, to usher in an era of peace and to help us find our way.

This was to be the last Sabbath we would celebrate freely as Jews. The next day I rose early to prepare for Monday's market. I heard an unfamiliar rumble and ran to the window to see what was happening. Strange vehicles with red stars painted on the sides filled the streets.

They had tracks instead of wheels, and each was fitted with what looked like a cannon. They were Russian tanks. I knew then that there would be no market that Monday.

The Red Army had crossed the Polish border during the night, and since Chorostkow was so close to it, they reached us early that morning. Russian soldiers in khaki uniforms began distributing leaflets to the frightened population. They read:

> "We have come to liberate the population
> from the Polish yoke."

Jews who had been hiding in cellars and attics started to appear on the streets, happy to see Russians instead of the murderous German soldiers. Some went over to the Russian tanks and kissed them with gratitude, not only for saving them from the German onslaught but also from the Ukrainian neighbors who were waiting for the first opportunity to attack Jews. There was good reason to fear the Ukrainian peasants. They had appeared from the countryside, armed with axes, pitchforks, and knives, waiting for the moment when they could begin assaulting the Jewish population and plundering homes. Their very presence struck fear in the hearts of Chorostkow's Jews.

It soon became clear, however, that Jewish life in Chorostkow and, for that matter, in the rest of Poland was not going to remain the same under Soviet occupation. Zionist organizations were declared illegal and forced to disband. With them went many people's hopes of emigrating to Israel. In addition, the Soviets were antireligious and did not look favorably on Jewish life, its practices and education. Finally, as Communists, the Soviets were against any private enterprise, no matter how small.

Needless to say, everything my family stood for—religion, Zionism, and family trade—made us suspect in the eyes of the new occupiers. The Russians appointed a common wagon driver, Hureh Singer, the town mayor. We braced ourselves for the worst. As it turned out, though, things were not so bad after all. The ones who fared the worst with the new authorities were Chorostkow's wealthy landowners and merchants, whether Ukrainian, Polish, or Jewish.

Large businesses and estates were nationalized immediately. The rich either had the presence of mind to flee or were sent to Siberia. Small merchants, like my father, were given some time to sell their merchandise and ease their way out of private enterprise.

We all worked in the store, helping out, but there was no problem selling goods. There was already a shortage of many commodities, and anticipating worse conditions, householders were beginning to stockpile. In addition, everyone wanted to get rid of Polish zlotys before the Russian ruble officially replaced them, and the townsfolk were spending and spending and spending. Russian soldiers, already almost twenty-two years into their post-Revolution economy, were overwhelmed by the variety and quantity of goods available, and they, too, kept buying.

In the meantime, shortages, particularly of food, were acute in the cities. We who lived near the farms had plenty of everything, and my mother, who was concerned for her relatives in Lvov, decided we had to send them some of the "plenty" we had. So Arie and I traveled two hundred kilometers to Lvov by train with sacks of food. After a few trips to the city, we decided to stay awhile.

We had already fully liquidated my father's store, and there was no way for us to make a living in Chorostkow. After some consultations with my father, it was agreed that we would return to Lvov. We took backpacks full of food—butter, honey, coffee—and went to stay with relatives.

They were happy to see us again and accepted the food as though it were a gift from heaven. They were quite poor, and with supplies already running low in the country, it was even harder for them to get food because of rapidly rising prices. After a few days, we realized that they could barely support themselves, let alone two young cousins from the country. We knew other family members in Lvov were big textile wholesalers. They were rich. I didn't want charity but an opportunity, so we looked them up and met with my father's cousin, Bezalel Nesate.

I told Nesate that I had extensive experience as a salesman and that I was prepared to do anything asked of me. I explained what had happened to my father's business in Chorostkow after the Russians arrived and that there was nothing for me or Arie to do back home.

He listened attentively, scratched his beard, and was silent. Then he told me to come to his store first thing in the morning to observe how he ran his business.

When Arie and I went, we saw two long lines of clients waiting to enter. We had never seen so many people lined up to buy goods from a store. There must have been hundreds of them. They were all buying two, three, or four yards of textiles. They feared that under Communist rule there would be little material available for clothing.

Uncle Bezalel said, "I'll give you boys some material. On credit. Go and sell it in the market. But remember, in the market you sell it for twice as much as you are paying for it."

I looked at him in surprise, not quite understanding what he meant. I had never heard of charging more than say, 10 or 15 percent above cost. But double?

"It's war time," he smiled at my puzzlement. "You'll see. They'll pay."

Arie and I took as much fabric as we could manage to carry in large suitcases and went out into the market. We were astounded by the great demand for material. Before the end of the day we had sold everything. We paid our uncle for the material and pocketed the profit. The next day, our uncle gave us more material and this time raised the cost of the material from the previous day. We continued to do business with Uncle Bezalel, selling textiles in Lvov and then returning home with material to sell out of our house in Chorostkow. Like some strange joke, every time I returned to Lvov, Uncle Bezalel charged me more for the merchandise. Fabrics that cost a dollar a yard in the store; he would sell to me for four dollars a yard.

Finally, one day, I asked, "Uncle, why do you charge me so much more?"

He answered, "When a customer buys in the store, he often waits two or three hours to do so and then can only purchase two or three yards. But a person who buys from you in the market or in Chorostkow doesn't wait at all, and for this privilege he has to pay more. Besides, the money is being devalued everyday, so the cost must go up."

Whatever our cost was, we were always able to double our investment, and in this way we continued to make a lot of money. However, though the sums grew, the value did not. Inflation was running wild at this time, and whatever profit we made one day, was substantially reduced the next. For the first time in our lives, Arie and I had pockets full of money, but it was like "funny money," colorful and fun to play with but of very little value.

Even with rabid inflation, the fact that we could steadily sell merchandise enabled us to ensure that there was food on the table and sometimes money for a little something extra. We could simply not believe that under Communism we were doing more business than ever. It was really a funny paradox.

Still, we did not have much time to sit around wondering about ironies. We learned quickly that life was a constant challenge, and, as the American expression goes, one must learn to make lemonade out of lemons. So Arie and I started looking around for other ways to expand our trade. We saw that Uncle Bezalel's stock was running out, and we wanted to find something else to sell. One day when we were on the train on our way to Lvov, I noticed people carrying knapsacks of flour. Stopping one man, I asked him what he was doing. He said that in Drohobycz, a town near the Carpathian mountains, there was a flour shortage and the bakeries were unable to function at full capacity. He said they were desperate to buy flour.

I knew that this problem represented our next opportunity. But I did not want to travel to Drohobycz with a knapsack of flour on my back. I knew I could get my hands on large quantities of flour and that I could move a great deal of it if the right customers were found. So Arie and I traveled to Drohobycz and walked into a large bakery. The baker came out from the back of his store.

"Do you need flour?" I asked him directly.

"Of course," he said. "I have a bakery, and I cannot get flour."

"How much will you pay for flour?" I asked him.

"I'll pay any price you name," he answered.

I then told him we could supply him with flour, but we were concerned. One needed a permit to sell flour. If caught without it, a person ran the risk of fines and imprisonment. This baker told us that not only was he willing to pay any price for the flour, but that his son was the chief of police in town. He would make sure nothing happened to us.

Excited by this verbal transaction, we traveled back to Chorostkow and made arrangements with a local flour mill to provide us with a ton of flour, not a knapsack's worth. Some mill owners had known us since childhood. They knew our father, his steadfast reputation, and were more than willing to do business with the Halperns. And we had the money from our textile sales for the down payment.

We made arrangements with a carriage driver in town to take the flour to the train. There we were stopped by a train inspector, a Pole, who questioned us about the merchandise. We explained to him that we were trying to help the people of Drohobycz who were suffering from hunger. We added, that he would be doing his part to save them if he made sure the flour arrived safely in that town, smoothing over any potential problems with the Russian authorities. He showed us a safe place on the train to store the sacks of flour, and we traveled to Drohobycz to see our man.

The baker could not have been happier. He took the flour sacks into the back of his bakery and came into the front with a sack full of rubles. We had never seen so much money in our lives. This delivery was merely the first major flour shipment we were to make to him. In the end, we supplied him and other bakers in Drohobycz with tons of flour from Chorostkow.

And so, at nineteen, living under Communist occupation, the most anti-bourgeois, anti free-trade regime that ever existed, I became a prosperous businessman. But I had no illusions about this success, and I knew that Arie and I were pushing our luck. Private enterprise had been officially banned, and we recognized that it was increasingly risky to continue making such transactions. Politically, economically, and socially, everything around us continued to be unstable.

The turning point in our thinking about living with the Soviets came on Yom Kippur of 1940, a year after the Russians had arrived in Chorostkow. I went to synagogue on this holiest of Holy Days, as I had ever since I was bar-mitzvahed, to spend the day praying, fasting, and in meditation. Gedalia Fink, a former classmate of mine from public school, came to the yard of the synagogue wearing his Communist Youth uniform and smoking a cigarette in front of the other young people. He turned to a group of children and said they had better go to school instead of wasting time praying to an old bourgeois

God. He threatened that if they did not leave and go to school, their parents would run into problems.

The Bolsheviks were trying to uproot all non-communist political views and religious traditions in the communities now under their control. One popular method was to turn children against their parents by teaching youngsters the virtue of weeding out anticommunist sentiment and the necessity of informing on anyone, including parents, who expressed them. One morning, soon after the Yom Kippur incident, we sat down with our father at the breakfast table and discussed the new reality. We all agreed that our wheeling and dealing days were over. All three sons had to find jobs that were approved by the regime. We reassured our father that we would have little trouble finding these jobs since we knew the local officials and got along quite well with them.

"The Communists have big ideas," I told my father. "They want to change the world. But we have skills that they need very badly, and we will find a way to work."

I was right. The Communists had big ideas about reorganizing the local economy. They intended to do away with all small merchants and businesses. All facets of commercial life were to be collectivized, and this approach would extend to the social spheres of life as well. But this was far easier said than done. The threat of war was in the air, and the Soviets were not fully prepared to take on the Nazi threat. They needed the cooperation of the local population to keep things running smoothly. I grasped this situation rather quickly and soon began befriending the town officials. Before long I won their trust.

One of the large factories around Chorostkow was the alcohol distillery. Following the Russian occupation, it had been "liberated" from the private ownership of Shatarsky, the wealthy landowner whose grain I once sold, and was now being managed by the state. The Russians were completely reorganizing the factory and needed help. I was offered a position as manager in charge of storage and distribution of grain and potatoes for the production of alcohol, which I gladly accepted. Arie was hired as a bookkeeper in a flour mill, and my eldest brother, Avrum Chaim, received a position as bookkeeper for the district management office of a distillery. He worked for Mr. Pekar, the director of nine distilleries in the area, at the main office in Trembowla.

For the time being we were set. We had legitimate jobs, we were receiving government salaries. We could not only ensure that we would not be jailed and sent to Siberia, but we knew that there would always be food on the table. No one in the family, especially not our parents, would be in want of anything.

I worked hard as manager and soon earned the trust of my superiors. Despite my youth, it was not very long before I was supervising over a hundred young men who delivered grain and potatoes to the distillery. I had to make sure that everything was accounted for and did so efficiently. Even though I received a modest salary, I had access to vodka, a valued commodity. Bottles of vodka could often buy what money could not. Merchandise was found and favors were delivered with a bottle or two of this coveted drink. I considered myself fortunate to have landed this position and decided to work hard and well to hang onto it as long as possible.

Meantime, at the distillery my responsibilities grew. I was put in charge of shipping large containers of alcohol, about fifty tons, every two weeks to a rubber factory about twenty kilometers away from Moscow. Ninety percent of the alcohol we produced was used to make rubber for defense purposes, the remaining ten percent being devoted to vodka production for local consumption.

One cold winter day in February 1940, we were told to load with alcohol a cistern that the Russians had sent to us from the rubber factory. It was enormous, and one of the employees told me that the container was partially filled with benzene. The people at the rubber factory outside of Moscow did not care what kind of alcohol came to their premises as long as they could use it for the production of rubber. But I cared. I did not want to mix our first-quality alcohol with benzene. In order not to be criticized by higher-ups for mixing the good stuff with the cheaper, I ordered that the benzene be pumped out of the container and into some open barrels that were kept at the railroad station.

As the operation was underway, one of the workers filling the barrels decided to smoke a cigarette. Suddenly, fifteen of these large barrels were on fire. I had been standing in the back of the railcar at the time, supervising, and had turned my back for a moment when this man lit the cigarette. I immediately felt the heat and turned around to face a wall of fire. There seemed to be no way out. The railcar door to the outside, the one leading to life, was on the other side of the fire. Covering my head and face with my jacket, I ran through the fire in the direction of the door, yelling the prayer, "*Shma Yisrael.*"

There were many people standing outside watching, wondering if I would emerge alive. I jumped through the wall of fire and came flying out through the open door. I landed in the snow on the ground, my clothing on fire. Everyone immediately started to cover me with snow. The flames were extinguished, and I was saved. This would not be the last time my life was threatened and thankfully spared.

After some time, I was taught how to run the factory with Dolek Bligreier, the chief's son. The work was not hard, but the hours were long. I had to be there at 4 A.M. when the distillery opened and supervise every step of production. But the money began rolling in. With vodka as king, I was able to live comfortably. My mother used to wonder how before the war we lived modestly, and afterward, under Russian occupation, we lived quite well. My father did not take our newfound "fortunes" for granted and gave a great deal of help and charity to families all around us who had little or nothing.

Until June 1941, I worked as a manager in the alcohol distillery and made a good living, enjoying prestige and responsibility. My family was cared for, and we had our home, we went to synagogue, and most importantly, we were together.

After two years of the Russian occupation, on June 22, 1941, Germany declared war on the Soviet Union. As German tanks began rolling toward the new Russian border, Stalin drafted all able bodied men into the army to fight the Nazi fascists. My two brothers and I were strong, young and healthy candidates for Stalin's army.

Actually, three months before the German invasion, Arie had already been drafted. He had been given extremely hard physical work to do, and we were all concerned about him. After about four weeks, I went to see him in Drohobycz where he was stationed. I asked one of his friends to show me where my brother was. I managed to find him and became even more concerned. He had evidently lost a great deal of weight. He looked pale and weak. I found out who his superior officers were and befriended them. Through this friendship, I was able to persuade them to have Arie transferred to an office where he would be employed in the physically easier job of bookkeeping.

My oldest brother, Avrum Chaim, was also drafted into the Soviet army on June 24, 1941, a Sunday—two days after Germany attacked. Officers came into town and told him and about a thousand other young men to come with them. The Germans were approaching Chorostkow, and there was little time to waste. The soldiers kept the young men congregated at the soccer field and remained there for the entire day. Not for a moment did I leave Avrum Chaim's side. When finally the young men were shepherded to the railroad station, I accompanied them. I said goodbye to Avrum Chaim with a heavy heart as though I had a premonition that I would never see him again. I held him close to me and cried openly when the train pulled out. His warm smile and waving hand are my last images of him. I loved and admired Avrum Chaim, not only as a brother but as a role model and the most ardent Zionist I ever knew. His entire life was devoted to the idea of building an independent Jewish state, and to this day whenever I land at Ben-Gurion airport, I think that it is he who most deserved to have seen his deepest dream come true. He is the one who inspired me to live, to make meaning from my survival, to channel so much of my time, effort, and resources into building the state of Israel.

Hoping against hope that when Hitler was defeated we would all be reunited, I left the station when the train was out of sight and walked slowly and sadly home. But Avrum Chaim and his platoon were captured by the German army, and despite his status as a prisoner of war, he was brutally murdered for the crime of being a Jew.

Prior to their retreat at the time of rhe German invasion, the Russians rounded up the Ukrainians in our town and its vicinity. Some were killed immediately, but some, especially the young people, were sent to Siberia.

One young fellow, Stefan Kuzak, realizing the great danger, ran into our home and asked me to save him. Although I knew that I was endangering both him and myself in case he was discovered, I felt a deep obligation to save the young man's life. I therefore hid him under my bed and enabled him to survive this period.

On Tuesday, June 24, 1941, all of Chorostkow's young men were ordered to enlist in the Soviet army. A marathon run through and around the town was held to determine fitness. As a future recruit, I too participated. As I ran, I saw all the sights so dear to me. The Great Synagogue, the smaller sanctuaries, the market grounds, my father's store. I ran as hard and fast as I could. All my years as a soccer player paid off, for out of a thousand participants, I came in second and received a medal! Because of my athletic ability, I was selected to join the air force and be trained as a pilot. I remember how proud I was of this distinction. Out of a thousand young men, only five were chosen for the air force.

While all my peers went that day into their regiments, I and the four other air force recruits were told to wait a week before we would be called up for service, but by that time the Germans conquered, and the Russian army was in full retreat.

The question, then, was what to do: stay in Chorostkow and await the arrival of the Germans or flee east with the retreating army into Russia? My supervisor at the distillery, Mr. Pekar, advised me to prepare three wagons, two for his family and one for mine, and together we would make the trip to Russia. I discussed this plan with my parents, but my father was against the idea. Remembering the German occupation in 1917, he argued that the Germans had not been so bad.

"They have certainly not gotten any better," he said, "but this, too, shall pass. The Communists are no friends of the Jews, particularly religious Jews like us. It is best to stay where we are and outlive the German occupation. We did business with them before; we can do it again."

I did not fully agree with my father and considered crossing the border into Russia to be with Arie. But within days, Arie was home. His army unit had totally disintegrated during a ferocious German panzer attack. He barely made his way out of the encirclement. After the battle, everyone dispersed. Since Arie was so close to Chorostkow and his unit no longer existed, he had no place to go but home.

I sometimes wonder what would have happened to me and my family had I gone to the Soviet Union. Would Arie have followed me? Would we have spared ourselves years of horror under the Nazis? Could we have saved my mother and my father? But I didn't go, and Arie, too, agreed we should stay home and not leave our parents alone at such a critical time. My father had not worked at all since the store was liquidated, and he and my mother were dependent on their sons to survive. If we left, who knew what might happen to them. So I gave up any notion of fleeing and stayed in Chorostkow, waiting for the Germans to arrive. Within a day, the Germans were in Chorostkow.

The German Occupation

The German demons of death and destruction entered Chorostkow in early July of 1941. For centuries, we Jews had lived under different rulers: Austrian, Polish, Russian, to name only the most recent. Time and again we had lost our livelihoods, had our rights curtailed, had suffered many forms of persecution, but somehow we always found a way to survive. Yes, we had heard by now about Nazi atrocities in Germany and the occupied part of western Poland, but what lay in store for us was something we could not imagine in our wildest dreams. By now the gang of murderers had reached the secret decision known as "The Final Solution of the Jewish Question," and all the Jews of Europe had been targeted for annihilation. Hitler played on the jealousy and base instincts of other nationalities and ethnic groups. Although he also considered these people inferior species, worthy only of enslavement, he recognized that their anti-Semitism could be used to help murder Jews.

We did not find out about the Final Solution and the collusion of many of our neighbors until much later, usually when it was too late. There were many among us, particularly young men, who considered escaping to Russia, but strong family ties prevented us. Somehow, we hoped, we would all weather the storm.

Looking back, I am certain that Jewish life in Chorostkow and the rest of Poland would have continued to this very day had it not been for the German invasion in the summer of 1941, not because we were so happy and prosperous and well accepted in Poland but because we had lived there for several centuries, and many of us knew no other life. That summer was the beginning of the end of Jewish life in Poland.

The atrocities began immediately after the Germans arrived in town, when thirty-four innocent Jewish residents were brutally murdered. Randomly, the German SS looked for excuses to kill Jews. The SS asked one Gentile to show them where Jews lived. He pointed to Itzhak Goldfliess' house. The SS walked into the home of my friend and killed his parents, wife, and two children, a little boy and girl. Itzhak happened to be away from home at the time and survived the slaughter. He managed to live through the entire war, surviving even Kamionka, and afterward made his way to America. He remarried, had a daughter and later on, grandchildren.

On the first Sabbath of the occupation, the Germans gathered all the Jews and ordered us to dig a wide, deep trench near the town hall. Next, they ordered us to bring bucket loads of excrement and sewage water from the public bathrooms to fill the trenches. We were then told to go home and dress in our Sabbath finery and ordered to show up again at noon to hear a speech by a local Gestapo officer who was going to outline what was expected of us and how we were to behave toward to the German authorities and among ourselves. The Germans were fond of laws and regulations for policing Jewish lives.

Unlike most of Chorostkow's Jews, my mother suggested that our family not respond as ordered. Instead, she told us to go into the attic, and there we watched everyone else return punctually at noon, trying to appease the new rulers. To everyone's amazement, the Jews were told to stand in the excrement-filled trenches. Many Ukrainian townsfolk gathered to watch this humiliating spectacle and rejoiced wholeheartedly. On the other hand, the deputy mayor of the town, Vasilenko, himself a Ukrainian, protested this barbarism and resigned his post. However, most of the Ukrainians and Poles willingly helped the Germans persecute and ultimately exterminate the Jewish community. The Jews were forced to remain in the sewage pits all day long. The Germans beat them with sticks and stepped back to allow the Ukrainians an opportunity to lash out with pitchforks, shovels, and clubs. Whenever someone tried to scramble out of the pit, he was immediately beaten back and knocked down by the assembly of German SS officers and Ukrainian civilians.

This was our introduction to the German reign of terror in Chorostkow. Each day brought new tortures, atrocities, and killings. Within a month or so, the Germans ordered us to organize a *Judenrat* (Jewish council) that would run our affairs according to German orders. The *Judenrat* would also create strife by pitting Jew against Jew and thus weaken the community. The head of the *Judenrat* was Shmuel Kimmel, and his deputy was Yekutiel Tannenbaum. The other members were Leib Bart, Feibish Morgenstern, Herman Tannenbaum, Shmeril Weisbrod, and Meir Gelman. Afterward, the Germans added Dr. Kotler and Doly Schutzman. Everyone thought the group was going to function as a prewar Jewish *kultusgemeinde* (community council).

At first, the Nazis ordered us to hand over all gold and jewels to the *Judenrat*. The head of every household gathered together the family jewelry, keeping aside as much as he dared, and delivered it to the *Judenrat*'s office. They then organized it, keeping a careful accounting, before delivering it to the German masters. Later on, the Jews of Chorostkow had to hand over silver, jewelry, and religious ritual objects, furs, and art. Every day the Germans came up with additional demands: linens, shirts, carpets. The *Judenrat* administered all commands. They had no choice but to fulfill German orders since the alternative would have been fatal.

Although fences and walls were never erected in Chorostkow, the town layout, with Jews in the center and the Gentile population living in the surrounding plots of land, created a kind of natural ghetto. Even though we did not look out on barbed wire, we could almost feel it was there. We knew that we were confined, oppressed by a curfew at sundown, and that we were at the mercy of German whim and policy.

About three weeks after the German arrival, all Jews over the age of ten were ordered to wear white arm bands with a blue star of David. We cut up sheets and white tablecloths for the arm bands and usually used blue writing ink to draw the stars. This shocking sign reinforced that we were going to be singled out at all times, never allowed to forget how much we were hated. Ukrainians, who detested Jews, suddenly began to act superior whenever they encountered a Jew with an arm band in the street. And when German soldiers were passed, anything from a tug of the beard to a kick in the kidneys was possible.

The contrast then was tremendous when Jan Gorniak, a Polish farmer with whom my family had done business over the years and whose mother, Tatyana, had gone to school with my mother, arrived at our doorstep at six o'clock one morning with a sack of a hundred kilos of flour.

"I don't know what will be," Jan said to us. "I don't know if the Germans will let me into the ghetto again. Take this flour. It will help you in the days to come."

We thanked Jan profusely since we too did not know what the future would bring and how much more restricted our access to food would become under German rule.

One day in late August, 1941, nearly five hundred Rumanian Jews were brought on foot from Kopychince to Chorostkow. Among them were about a hundred Jews from Hungary. This group of men, women, and children tried to follow the Russians when the army was retreating, but they were caught by the Germans. Driven on foot from town to town, they were hungry and thirsty, being beaten along the way until they reached Chorostkow.

When the Rumanian Jews arrived in our town, they were herded into a fenced-in, grassy field usually used for selling cattle on market day. Ukrainian police stood guard. The *Judenrat* of Chorostkow asked the Jewish women to prepare any food that could be spared for the refugees to eat.

I remember my mother, of blessed memory, baking bread and making soup. Arie and I helped carry large kettles of soup to them during the four days they were kept in Chorostkow. Many other Jews did the same.

Nights in August were often cool, and it was also raining then. The prisoners, who were kept in the open, were cold and wet and many, especially the children, were already sick.

Four young men from this group managed to run away. The Germans would not leave Chorostkow until the escaped prisoners were found. After four days, they were indeed found and the group left, supposedly to Tarnopol. We never heard another word about them.

It became clear to me in those early days that there would be no way of finding an accommodation with these new masters. I was only twenty-one years old, but I had already learned how to get along with

Polish and Ukrainian merchants, farmers, priests, and government officials, and later even with Communist officials. I could always get around hostile decrees, unfriendly attitudes, and deliberate obstacles. I knew how to cope, even under the most adverse circumstances. This time was different, however. These new rulers, with their Gestapo and SS and an assortment of other unpleasant names, had only one agenda: to make life impossible for us, to see us suffer and eventually die. The only hope left was for them to be defeated as soon as possible by the Allied forces.

Every day new decrees were issued against us. All Jewish men were ordered to shave off their beards. Everybody complied immediately, with the exception of Yeshiya Rappoport, the rabbi of Chorostkow, and my father, of blessed memory. My father tried to stay at home, but when he had to go out, he would wrap his jaw in a kerchief, which covered his beard, as if he had a toothache. With his beard still intact, he was taken to Belzec.

We were not allowed to work. We were not allowed to possess weapons. Desperate to warm the soldiers on the Russian front, the Germans ordered us to turn over all furs under pain of death. We were allowed to shop only in Jewish designated stores, and then only during certain hours of the day.

When the Germans formed a Jewish *ordunungdienst,* or auxiliary police, it was a dark day for us all. This police force, which operated as though it were an autonomous body, was in charge of enforcing German rule. Some members of the Jewish police did whatever they could to save their own skins by blindly obeying the Gestapo orders. Others tried to help their brethren whenever they could. Among the youth who joined the Jewish police force were David Edelman, Milo Rottenberg, Israel Wallach, Mayer Gelman, and Elisha Weber.

In addition to collecting valuables, the *Judenrat* had to fill quotas for workers at various hard labor tasks, such as snow removal, field work, and sanitation duty. The main objective of the Germans was to humiliate the people while they worked and to make them open targets for vicious beatings. A popular way to demean our young women was to force them to clean public toilets and animal stables.

I myself spent many days doing this kind of hard labor, mostly on the farm, but since I was young and strong, I was able to endure. Not everyone could. Every day, several people would fail to keep up with the pace, and they were beaten and often shot.

Soon the Germans ordered the *Judenrat* to compile a list of two hundred able bodied young men to undertake "special tasks," a euphemism for almost unbearable physical labor with little food under inhumane conditions. No one wanted to enlist for such work, and everyone tried to bribe his way out of it. Bribing often meant the difference between life and death.

My name was put on this list, and when we learned this fact, my father went to Leib Bart, a member of the *Judenrat*. He had been a prosperous businessman before the war who had had many dealings with my father: indeed, my father had considered him a friend.

"Please," my father said, "leave my sons alone. What is it that you need?"

My father understood the dictum that one hand washes the other, and his question was not only a bribe to keep us out of the special tasks work corps, but presented Bart with an opportunity to do a small favor for the German overlords, thereby improving his lot.

"Okay," Bart said. "I need tea for the German officers," he paused, "and I also need leather."

"Tomorrow at seven sharp the materials will be in your office. Thank you."

My father left quickly before Bart could change his mind and was grateful that over the years he had the foresight to hide such coveted items. In this way, my father was able to keep his children out of the work brigades for several months.

A while later, Mr. Kimmel, the head of the *Judenrat*, called my father in to his office and told him, "Reb Halpern, you have able bodied sons. Please let me have them work for the Germans. I will see to it that your family receives a larger ration of food. Some more bread."

"What kind of work do you have in mind?" my father asked.

"Nothing physical, don't worry. Your sons are good organizers," he said. "I'll put them in charge of recruiting other people. It's a good job. And it's safe."

My father hesitated. "I'll have to ask them," he said. "But I don't think they'll agree."

Kimmel shook his head sorrowfully. "Try to encourage them, Reb Halpern. These are different times. We have to do everything we can to survive. The Germans know no mercy."

When my father came home, he went over the discussion he had just had with Kimmel.

"What would I have to do?" I asked again.

"You would call people to work," he said.

"He wants me to make up lists of who will have to do forced labor? Am I going to call my friend to work? I would rather go and work myself. Am I going to call you, my father, to work? No, I don't think so. I will not accept this offer."

My father understood my position, agreeing with me ethically, but was still concerned for my welfare. He insisted that it was too dangerous for me simply to stay home. "With all young men working, you too have to work," he said. So I found work on a nearby farm of over a thousand acres that had once belonged to Count Sieminski. As a wealthy landowner, he had taken his cues from the Russians and had run away years before. This farm work not only kept me busy and out of sight, but I was still able to come home every night to sleep.

The farm was put under government control during the Russian occupation and was now being administered by the Germans. The day-to-day affairs, though, were run by local Ukrainians. The work day was hard and long, but the Ukrainians in charge were relatively fair. We were not beaten or harassed, and many times, since I was a good worker, they gave me extra bread and soup.

The men who were not so fortunate and worked in the special tasks division built and were eventually housed in a labor camp fifty kilometers outside of town. It was called Stupka and was only one of hundreds of labor camps the Germans set up in the early stages of the war. They were used to incarcerate and work to death Jews, Russians, and other political prisoners.

Compared to the horrible death factories like Auschwitz, Maidanek, Treblinka and Belzec, the smaller labor camps—like Kamionka and Stupke—may have caused more prolonged suffering; proportionally, more people died in the small labor camps. In a labor camp, life was a constant nightmare of grueling work and brutality. It was only a matter of time before one could no longer go on. Some sixteen thousand people lived and worked in Kamionka, the labor camp to which I was eventually sent, during the German occupation. Of these, only thirty-six survived the war.

From July 1941 to March 19, 1942 when I was taken by the Germans, I worked at that large farm every day and saw my family each night. I considered myself fortunate and, like everyone else, I kept waiting for Russia to start beating the Germans on the eastern front. I hoped beyond hope that the United States and the other Allied countries would mount an offensive against the German military monster.

My comparative safety ended abruptly on March 19, 1942 when an enormous snowstorm hit the region. All the streets and thoroughfares were blocked. The road from Chorostkow to the railroad station, a distance of about three kilometers, was completely snowed under. There were no snowplows or bulldozers to clear the streets. Even if there had been, the Germans enjoyed making Jews shovel snow. So on the morning of the 19th, the Germans told the *Judenrat* to assemble a large group of workers to clear the snow.

In all, eighty-four young men were rounded up. Many, like me, had worked on farms. Others worked cleaning the city streets and other facilities in the ghetto. (Only three of this original group of eighty-four would survive the war: Moshkele Fengold, Itzhak Goldfleiss, and me.) When I said goodbye to my parents upon leaving for work, I didn't know that this was the last time I would see them. We were given shovels and ordered to start clearing the road from town to the railroad station. It was very cold outside, and everyone was already weak from many months of hard labor and little food. For about a half hour we worked at clearing the snow when we were suddenly surrounded by the Ukrainian police.

"Leave the shovels," they said, "and come."

We did not know where they were going or why the important work of clearing the road to the station had been stopped. Some of the men panicked and tried to escape. They made a run for the trees. The police shot some and beat up the others.

The rest of us were frightened and decided to cooperate. The long trek began. At first they made us run, even though the snow was deep and it was freezing cold and we were clearly weak. Then they brought into our group another group of boys from Kopychince, and we were then about 160 young men. One of the policemen told me that we were headed to Chortkow, a town about twenty-five kilometers away, although he wouldn't say why. Nor would he tell us our exact destination.

All along the way, men tried to escape. Each one was caught and brutally beaten by the Ukrainian police. We had been rounded up at nine o'clock in the morning, and by the time we reached Chortkow it was evening. We had spent the entire day walking in the bitter snow without food or rest. Everyone was thoroughly exhausted.

We were taken to a jailhouse. There we had to pass through a receiving line of SS soldiers and Ukrainian police, each with a rifle or stick, each waiting for a turn to hit a Jew on the head. There were about eighty of them, and it took a long time for a Jew to make his way through the line, being clobbered by everyone. If you were by chance hit on the neck or chest and not on your head, you had to go back and give the soldier or policeman another chance to "get it right."

Like everyone else, I tried to shield my face and head and lessen the force of the blows by jerking my head away a little, but this had to be done carefully; otherwise, I would have had to return to the beginning of the line, and the second time I would surely have been hit even harder and more frequently. My technique seemed to make no difference, and by the time I got into the jail cell, I was bruised, cut, and bleeding. I wondered if the Germans intended to kill us or were just having fun.

After the ordeal, I was herded into a small jail cell packed with about sixty men. There was no room to sit down, let alone lie down. We had to stand, crushed one against the other, bleeding and in pain, frightened and hungry. All told, there were some five hundred men from the entire vicinity in the jailhouse, with every cell packed as tight as ours.

We stood packed together like that all night, and in the morning we were sure we would be let out a little and given some food, but we were wrong. Nothing changed. The entire second day and night we stood, jammed together, hungry beyond belief. On the third day, we began to talk about how the Germans meant to kill us. One way or another, from starvation or lack of oxygen, we thought we would die locked up like this.

Many of the men began to recite *Shma Yisrael*, a prayer Jews are commanded to say, when possible, before death. Just then the Germans opened the door to the cell and took us out. Everyone stretched their limbs and gulped the fresh air. Although we were still starving and parched with thirst, the freedom from being pressed up against other bodies on all sides felt wonderful. Then one German began to toss pieces of bread at us, like one would throw scraps to a dog from the dinner table. Men hurled themselves at the bread, like animals, and stuffed it into their mouths before anyone else could steal it. A tub was filled with water, and we all drank from it, like cattle at a trough. But no sooner than we began lapping the water, a German came over and started beating us, yelling: "Let's go, let's go." They permitted us just one sip of water after three days of extreme thirst, and then administered more beatings. I will never forget the sight of this tub and men bending over to drink.

We were made to run from the jailhouse to a railroad station about a kilometer away. All along the way the German soldiers were free with their clubs and boots. At any moment one could be felled by a blow to the neck or a kick in the side, so despite our weakened state, we ran as fast as we could. When we got to the train station, we saw cattle cars on the tracks. There were no steps or ramps leading to the doors, so the SS officers beat the people at the front yelling, "Crouch down, crouch down," to get them down on all fours and form human steps for the rest of the crowd behind them to climb on.

Once the human staircases were made, the Germans yelled and clubbed the rest of us to hurry into the cars. They were beating us so hard and their voices sounded so vicious that we had no choice but to obey. Painfully, we were forced to step on our brethren and climb into the train. The groans and cries from the men on the ground were nearly drowned out by the screaming of the SS and the cracking whips.

It took quite a while to fill the cattle cars. We were packed in tight, much as we had been in the jail cell, and all the while we were being beaten and clubbed by the Germans. About 120 men were squeezed into each car, the only improvement over the jail being that there was enough room for two men at a time to sit down and take a rest.

When the Germans were satisfied that enough of us had been packed into each car, they threw in some bread and swung the doors shut. I heard them lock us in from the outside. In my town at that time, we had not heard of the death camps of Auschwitz or Maidanek, nor did we know of the "final solution." We knew the Germans intended to use Jews as work horses, but we were unaware of plans for extermination.

The few who managed to get hold of a piece of bread ate it quickly; the rest of us turned away and tried not to think of the emptiness in our stomachs. We had already gone three full days without any food and only a small sip of water.

We sat idly in that sealed cattle car for hours. Despite the cold March winds outside, it quickly grew hot inside, and again the lack of oxygen threatened everyone. Whoever was lucky enough to be standing by the walls could try and draw fresh air from between the cracks of the cattle car. Then we took turns so that more of us would have a chance to breathe a little better.

Finally, the train started to roll. We traveled for three days in these terrible conditions until the doors opened again. We had been brought to the labor camp Kamionka located near the city of Tarnopol, about fifty kilometers away from Chorostkow. Normally, it would have taken only about three hours to travel from Chortkow to Kamionka, but the Germans had shuttled the train back and forth between many small stations and made long stops on the tracks to torture us further. They wanted to break our spirits with three awful days where there was no place other than the floor beneath our feet to heed the call of nature, no food, no information, no sense of destination. They wanted to make us believe we were really not part of the human race, as Hitler (and the hundreds of Amaleks in history before him) had been shouting for years. They hoped to convince us that we were truly a subspecies, that we were vermin.

A very wealthy family by the name of Marindorf lived in our town. They owned a great number of buildings as well as flour mills, exporting flour to several European countries. A year before the German invasion, their son, Willy, married the most beautiful girl in town, Ruchka Bergman.

When the Germans occupied our town, Ruchka's father was detained by the SS. Ruchka went to SS headquarters in the city of Tarnopol, where she pleaded for her father's freedom with the head of the SS. She said she was prepared to pay any amount of money for his release.

Rikita, the head of the SS said he would release her father, but she would have to remain with him as his lover. She pleaded for her freedom, explaining that she was a married woman, but nothing helped. He released her father and took her with him when he left Tarnopol.

Willy Marendorf, her husband, was so stricken by this tragedy that he died shortly afterward. My brother Arie attended his funeral.

What was behind this madness? Why were we suffering? Where was God? Where were the British and the Americans? But even as we stood in our own waste, we knew we were human beings, *b'nai adam*, and that we were Jews. When all the other vicious empires in the world had their fill of our blood, when they had disappeared from the earth, leaving behind only piles of stones and stories in history books, we, who had been around since the beginning and whose land at that time was a pile of stones—and whose books much of the world coveted and embraced as truth—we still had more than books and stones to show for ourselves. We were still living and procreating, generation after generation.

Although I did not yet comprehend the evil of the "final solution" or suspect that a full third of our people would ultimately be slaughtered, still I knew that the Jewish people, stiff-necked and faithful, were not easily pushed off the world stage. We were major players, despite our small numbers, and we would survive this latest onslaught, much as we had survived every previous exile and persecution.

Kamionka

After three wrenching days, the doors to the cattle cars were finally opened, and we were greeted with a flood of light, fresh air, and ear-piercing screams ordering us out.

"Los schnell! Los schnell!" the Germans screamed. "Do it fast, do it fast," all the while beating us with sticks and rifle butts. Again there were no ramps or stairs and we had to jump about four or five feet from the rail car to the ground. Then we struggled to get up as quickly as possible before being kicked by the German soldiers standing nearby. We were starving, dehydrated, and weak. Still, once the cars were cleared of their human cargo, we were made to run two kilometers to the labor camp. Some men were weeping from fright, others from relief. Surprisingly, we kept up the brisk pace forced upon us and had little time to notice the landscape. When we reached the camp, though, a hush settled over the group. We looked and carefully listened. The entire area was eerily silent. The cloud of death hung over the camp that stood before us, and the fields, which in the summer were filled with corn and wheat, were gray and brown and lifeless.

Before the war, this clearing in the woods had been the site of a large farm, of perhaps a thousand acres. The stables, formerly used for cattle and horses, had since been converted into barracks for inmates. The entire compound was surrounded by a high fence of barbed wire, and in each corner was a tall watchtower manned by Germans with machine guns. Two gates, one in front and one in back, were guarded by Ukrainian policemen.

The conversion of the farm into a labor camp, originally intended for Russian prisoners of war and then also used for Jews, was done by the special task work brigades months earlier. The men who built the camp never left it. By the time the group of five hundred men I was in arrived at Kamionka, there were already many people there—maybe three to four thousand in total.

When I walked through the gates of the camp, I saw terrible sights. German soldiers peered down at us from watchtowers, machine guns in hands. All the inmates—about fifty or so Russians, a hundred or so Poles, and thousands of Jews—were absolutely filthy. Everyone wore a two inch by two inch cloth square—the Russians and Poles a red one, the Jews a yellow one—and all were so thin they looked half-dead. The men moved around the yard of trampled dirt as if they were sleepwalking. For many, though the body lived on, the spirit was already gone.

Our group was stopped at the entrance and a German officer stood tall before us, scanning the group contemptuously. He cleared his throat dramatically before addressing us.

"You are to hand over your watches, rings, any other jewelry, and money that you have on you. If we find something that hasn't been turned in, you will be shot immediately."

I looked at his mean face and well-oiled gun, knowing there was no choice but to comply. As I took off my watch and went through my pockets for loose coins and bills, the Germans soldiers continued to lash out at us with a club to the stomach, a slap across the face. They never interrupted this sadistic amusement.

Once the confiscation of valuables was over, we were marched toward the central yard of the camp. In that we had not had anything to drink in days, the light snow that remained on the ground looked incredibly inviting. The problem was that directly underfoot there was no snow; the little that remained was close to the barbed wire fence about two or three feet away. We were steered in another direction. One man standing before me in line could not contain himself. Overcome with thirst, he took a couple of steps out of line towards the snow. No sooner had he stepped away from the formation and bent his back than he was shot to death!

The Germans and Ukrainian guards laughed at the look of horror on our faces; they were thoroughly amused by our fear. They seemed to take great pleasure in terrifying us and certainly wanted us all to see who was master in Kamionka and who was the slave. A man died for stepping out of line, for trying to scoop up a handful of snow, for attempting to quench his dry mouth and throat. This act posed no direct military or political threat. He was no spy sending signals or a soldier reaching for a weapon. He was a totally defenseless man, a creature in need of hydration. But it was precisely because he wanted to take care of a physical need on his own, and not when the "masters" dictated, that his innocent act was considered criminal. In this way, the monsters who controlled our fate informed us what our lives were worth to them: nothing.

Later the same day we were given tin cups, the only utensils we would ever receive. Each was thin and small with a narrow handle. Anytime there was something for us to eat or drink, we had to bring along the cups to receive our meager rations. Without the cup, a person received nothing. We were then told to stand in line for some nourishment; they called it soup, but it was really dirty water with some potato in it. I didn't care. It was something to drink, and I would consume as much as they allowed. There were between three hundred and four hundred people waiting on this line for food. I was somewhere in the middle and saw, closer to the front, a friend of mine, Dunio Winter from Chorostkow. He spotted me too and called to me. I went over to talk. Maybe he knew something no one in my jail cell and cattle car knew. Maybe he had seen someone in my family before being taken away from our shtetl at gunpoint. And maybe I just wanted to talk to a *landsman* for a few minutes, knowing there would be some comfort in exchanging words.

Just when I reached my friend, one of the kapos came up behind me and with a wide, flat stick hit me so hard across the back and shoulders that my eyes dimmed. It took a few seconds before I was able to see straight. "Go back to your place in the line!" he yelled. Just taking a few steps to talk to a friend brought swift, severe punishment.

This terrible, frightening blow, along with the man shot for wanting a lick of snow, were my introduction to the hell that passed for life in the slave labor camp of Kamionka.

Next we were lined up and ordered to call out our names in a loud, clear voice as we passed in front of the German officers. One of the men, whose father was a butcher in Trembowla, called out "Adolf Hitler" when asked his name. He was immediately hit in the face with great force. He fell to the ground and was again asked his name. He answered, "Adolf Hitler," for this, indeed, was his real name. The Germans pounced on him and began to beat him mercilessly. Realizing he would have to lie to save his life, he called out as strongly as he could his mother's maiden name. This worked. The Germans stopped the beating, and he was allowed to return to the line. This man survived Kamionka and today lives in New Jersey.

The same day I was taken away from clearing snow in Chorostkow, my mother had wanted to buy my freedom. Unlike in the large concentration camps, it was sometimes possible to be released from the smaller camps if the lucky inmates or family found an officer willing to accept a bribe for this favor.

My mother had a gold chain that my father had given her at their wedding. From Chorostkow, she walked all day to Chortkow. There she approached some SS men who turned a deaf ear to her pleas. She persisted, however, and then came to Podwolocsysko, which was about nine kilometers outside Kamionka. She thought for sure that having walked all this way she would be able to do something to get me out. She contacted a member of the *Judenrat* who put her in touch with a German who often released people. My mother offered him a lot of money. This German always took the money he received from desperate families but reserved the right to refuse release of the inmates. Old people, sick people he usually freed. But he often denied someone young and strong. The man listened to her pleas, looked at her money, but in the end refused the offer.

That first evening, after gulping down one tin cup of "soup," we were taken to the barracks. It is hard to describe the wretchedness of the place. Originally built for animals, the only modification the stables underwent to accommodate human beings was the installation of three or four levels of long, horizontal planks of unfinished wood for beds. The wind blew through the cracks in the old walls. The place was infested with lice, and within a matter of hours all of us were dirty with them too. Soon enough I learned to live with lice. Even though lice carried typhus, in comparison to other aspects of the camp, they were a small problem.

There were no mattresses on the wooden planks, no straw (as later I heard people had at Auschwitz and other camps), and certainly no blankets. For many of the sixteen months I was there, I used a short coat I had brought with me as my blanket. Hundreds of people were crammed into each of the barracks, and they slept on the planks, the floors, anywhere they could find space. We each had less than two feet to lie in, and if one person wanted to turn over, everyone on either side of him on the long plank had to turn over as well.

One of the main tasks assigned to inmates in this labor camp was to help fix the highway that stretched from Berlin to Kiev. Kamionka was located right beside this major artery (which also happened to run through Lvov), and our most important responsibility was to maintain the road. Day and night German trucks and tanks rolled along this route, taking supplies and soldiers to the eastern front and back again to Berlin. All this activity exacted a heavy toll on the road, whose surface demanded constant repair.

After being awakened at 5:30 in the morning, we were given two minutes to dress. If someone was not ready, he was badly beaten. Only after everyone in the barracks was ready were we allowed to stand in line for a cup of ersatz coffee, which was really dirty warm water. They also gave us a piece of bread (whose flour had been mixed with sawdust), often so hard and moldy that it could hardly be eaten. Since this was our entire food ration for the day, some people saved the bread for "lunch" while others, unable to abide the gnawing hunger in their stomachs, chewed on it immediately. I tried to save mine for later in the day, knowing that as hungry as I was upon waking, I would become much more so as the day wore on and the hours of physical labor took their toll on my body's limited resources.

After this meager meal, thousands of camp inmates were made to stand outside in the yard, in straight lines, from six until eight in the morning. It did not matter if the brilliant summer sun was shining, or the deathly winds of winter were blowing; we had to stand still for two hours. Rain, snow, withering heat. It was the second phase of torture routinely worked into every day.

A few minutes before eight, the *hauptsturmführer*, Paul Rebel, would come into the yard with his dog and watch Mr. Koltz, the *lagerführer* (who was also a Jew) delegate work details. In groups of 250 or 500, we were taken to work. Some men went to the *steinbrochen*, the stone chopping corps, others to the *strassenbau*, the road crew where the road was swept and cleared of snow and debris, and the rest went to the *eisenbahn*, the railroad corps. No matter which group I was in, there was always an eight, ten, or twelve kilometer walk to the work site. Often we had to carry heavy tools back and forth. No matter what the weather conditions, we had to walk, and always, *schnell!* *schnell!* (fast, fast). The Germans wanted us to do things quickly so we wouldn't have time to think, so we wouldn't have a moment's rest.

It took weeks before the *Judenrat* leaders of Chorostkow, Chortkow, Kopychince, Probyzna, Tluste, and Lvov were able to make arrangements with the officers at Kamionka to allow us to receive packages from outside. I was in a camp only fifty kilometers from home. Twice a month the *Judenrat* would come to Kamionka with food packages. What a difference it made to be able to receive something from home. There was bread, jam, and sometimes salami that my mother always sent, literally a life saver, and then a blanket, sweater, coat, and scarves. I would touch everything carefully as if the gifts were precious jewels. For these packages were not merely filled with items that would prove useful; they were my link to the outside world. They were evidence that I was not forgotten, left to die among barbarian rulers. But the wonderful connection was soon discontinued. Since this arrangement ceased to be sanctioned, someone from Chorostkow would come to Kamionka with smaller packages and bribe a German guard to let the supplies into the camp. Over time, this practice occurred less frequently but still sustained our ties with the rest of the world.

When I first arrived in camp, I was fortunate with my work assignment. Instead of having to chop stone into one cubic meter blocks by hand with a sledgehammer, the most grueling physical labor of all three work corps, I was taken to the road crew and assigned the task of clearing the snow. Aside from being less strenuous, the other major advantage of this job was my proximity to large quantities of snow.

Even though it was filthy from constant vehicular traffic, I would use the snow to wash myself. Keeping up some degree of personal hygiene contributed greatly to maintaining a strong psychological profile. It helped bolster my feeling of still being a human being. I would not allow myself to drift into the kind of bodily filth usually associated with certain animals or the mentally ill who no longer know how to care for themselves. In fact, it was a known symptom in the camps that when a person stopped picking the lice out of his head and clothing, he had given up hope of surviving. The other crucial benefit of the snow was that I was able to eat it. The Germans only gave us two small portions of dirty water a day to drink—early in the morning and in the evening. This was not enough to keep up proper hydration, and so throughout the day I would chew on snow to quench my thirst.

Once, en route to the road, there was a heavy downpour of rain—a real thunderstorm that only brought greater misery to us. The road became muddy where there was no snow and thick with slush where there was. It made the trek, carrying our heavy tools, that much more difficult. The dampness cut through our thin clothing and settled in our aching joints. Everyone's spirits were low.

About two hundred of us were walking, four men to a row, when one of the Ukrainian policeman ordered us to sing *Vitaher Libaynu* (a Jewish song *"Our Hearts Quicken"* to do God's work). Everyone complied. Only I didn't. I was hungry, thirsty, and tired and in no mood to sing. A Ukrainian policeman came over to me and hit me, shouting: "Sing *Libaynu*," and then he hit me so hard on my shoulder with his rifle butt that I blacked out momentarily. After that incident I of course had little choice but to join in song. Once again I learned how a man in uniform feels he has the power of life and death over inmates. This man told us to sing, he was wearing a uniform, so he concluded that I had broken his law and needed to be punished. We were their puppets and they the evil puppeteers relishing their sadism.

One officer, a German whose name was Klein, liked to see blood. He would hit a person over the head for no reason. If he saw blood right away, he would stop hitting. But if the injury did not bleed, he would continue to pummel the individual until blood flowed from the body. Then he would stop, satisfied. He would smile and walk away, daring anyone to stoop to help the bleeding man, and would scan the rows of laboring men in search of a new victim. Luckily, I was never hit by him.

After about two months, my job was switched and I was sent to the stone works. I was given a sledgehammer to chop stone for road repairs. Today in America, in Europe, in most countries, this kind of work is done by machine. But there, on the Berlin-Kiev road, just like our ancestors before us in Egypt, Jewish labor created the bricks for the empire.

At the end of the day spent breaking stone without stop, without anything to eat, we would walk the eight or nine kilometers back to camp. Then we would be given some so-called soup. Again, it was really dirty water with, if we were lucky, a piece of cabbage or slice of potato in it. Sometimes, if a horse were killed or an old one died, they would throw its flesh into the soup. Even though these were desperate times and I doubt many rabbis would rule against eating the horse's flesh, I could never bring myself to consume it. On the nights when it was in the soup, I drank only the liquid and gave others the meat.

On Friday nights, we tried to recreate the custom of *Lechem Moshne* (two loaves), to honor the Sabbath, by hoarding our bread so that we should have two pieces. Even on those nights when it was impossible to save enough bread, we welcomed the Sabbath Queen with *Shalom Aleichem* (Welcome to you) and other *z'mirot* which reminded us of better days at home.

We worked seven days a week, from eight in the morning, until seven in the evening, except for Sunday when we would stop work at one o'clock in the afternoon, after which most people collapsed into sleep.

Considering these conditions, it's a miracle any of us survived. Most did not. So many people died as a result of the beatings they were given while working on the road, while chopping stone, while standing around inside the camp, that in my barracks about fifteen or twenty men (out of the hundreds that lived there) would rise earlier than was necessary in order to gather together a *minyan* to recite the Kaddish for the dead. Later, after I learned of my father's death in Belzec, I joined the *minyan* and said *Kaddish* every morning.

Not only Jews worked on the road. Since all Jews had to wear a yellow, two-inch square sewn onto their clothing, it was easy to differentiate Jew from Gentile. The Poles and Ukrainians who were interned in the camp for some sort of criminal conduct in civilian life, from a bar fight to bad debts, wore a red patch. The local population could be sent to the labor camps as a punishment, like a prison sentence. They would be worked for a few months and then let go, but they were not treated any differently than the Jews. They were given the same barracks conditions, the same meager amount of food, and the same back-breaking work. Most of them, being farmers, were accustomed to difficult physical labor and managed to get through their quota of work more swiftly and efficiently than us. It was to the Jews' detriment that we had little experience working so hard with our bodies. What we lacked in experience, though, we made up in spirit.

After three months when everyone's endurance had been tested, the Jews proved they could learn to work quickly and survive while many Poles and Ukrainians were fading away, unable to maintain their physical stamina with little food. And, as with the Jews, the first show of weakness for the Polish or Ukrainian inmates would mean death at German hands.

For no reason at all, literally at random, any one of the SS or Ukrainian policemen who watched over us all day would single out a man and beat him practically to death. One Pole named Janek was especially vicious. Pleasure glowed in his face when he brutally beat a weak Jew. He was a sadist who had never had so much fun in his life.

I would watch out of the corner of my eye as I continued hammering the rock with a sledgehammer and wonder how a person was able to tuck away his soul to such an extent that he could treat another human being as if he were a rock in a quarry. The Germans and Ukrainians ruling our lives acted as if we, like the stone we worked on, felt no pain. They seemed to believe that we existed to fulfill their needs and desires, as if the meaning of our lives was to provide them with props for their evil drama. They treated their dogs and horses with greater compassion and gentleness.

Sometime later, I was sent to lay railroad track for the Berlin-Kiev line. By hand we had to drag enormously heavy railroad ties into place. The Germans permitted us a half-hour break during the day to rest. Here, too, there were guards who seemed to thrive on spilling Jewish blood. They enjoyed beating us with their own hands. The direct contact, flesh against flesh, was far more satisfying to them than a bullet from a gun, though there was no shortage of that either.

One day, my friend Zigale Freisinger from Kopychince, was working by the railroad when a Ukrainian police officer told him to lift one of the very heavy rail ties. Zigale was still a young boy and was weak and tired. Not thinking clearly about his future and how he might best survive the war, he simply answered the Ukrainian's order: "I can't do it."

The Ukrainian hit him with a shovel and repeated his order. "Lift it!" he thundered at Zigale. And then Zigale shouted back at him, "You shouldn't hit me. The Russians are coming, and then you'll be sorry." Everyone around him shuddered with fear. We had all heard news from the ghetto that the Russian front was advancing, but it certainly was not very wise to throw this information in the face of a Ukrainian police officer who had everything to lose and everything to hide from his enemy.

The Ukrainian grew red in the face with rage and started to pound Zigale with the shovel, time after time after time, only stopping when Zigale's body lay motionless on the ground, curled up in a fetal position, like a small boy sleeping. He was dead, killed for voicing the hope that all of us carried within us like a burning torch—the hope of liberation, of survival.

A few weeks into the work, in February of 1943, during our rest break one day, we saw many rail cars of soldiers pass by. Their uniforms were not familiar. They certainly were not German. When they stopped at the nearby Kamionka station for water, I strained to listen to them speak. I recognized only a few words, but that was enough to for me realize that these were Hungarians on their way to the Russian front.

All of a sudden, an elegant young officer, maybe in his mid-thirties, came over to us and saw our yellow patches. He spoke in German.

"Are you Jews?" he asked.

"Yes," many of us replied. "We are."

He then dug into the deep pockets of his army coat and threw chocolate and cigarettes to us. These were precious gifts. He then gave us the most meaningful gift. He said:

"You Jewish people should know that Hitler has lost this war." He paused and looked at the convoy of railroad cars halted temporarily on the tracks nearby. "Thousands of soldiers are headed toward the front. Every half hour more and more. Hungarians. Croatians. Ukrainians. But they will not make a difference. They are simply cannon fodder."

Of course, we hung on his every word, each one sweet like fruit, ripe with hope.

"The Germans were defeated at Stalingrad," he continued. "All these soldiers will be killed."

We wanted to jump up and start singing and dancing with joy, not because these soldiers, many of whom were not Nazis but ordinary conscripts, were going to die but at hearing that the war would soon be over. We might survive after all. In fact, though, we did not sing or dance, but sat huddled together as if nothing unusual had just been said and calmly thanked him for sharing this critical information.

"Stay strong," he said. "This war is going to end."

We then watched as he walked away to join the ranks of men doomed to die in Hitler's vainglorious war. When they pulled out, we saw that these Hungarians had left us packages of zwieback, a hard, biscuit-like bread. Of course, we greatly appreciated their kindness.

When we returned to camp that evening, we told the story to some of the Hungarian Jews there. One of them said to me:

"Listen, you are all Polish Jews. You know no Hungarian. I speak fluent Hungarian. Let me go to the railroad with you tomorrow to find out more about the war."

Everyone agreed that this would be a good idea since it was nearly impossible for us to gather information about current events. It was quickly arranged that the next day this Hungarian would come out with my group to the railroad tracks and someone from the rail crew would go out with the Hungarian's group to the stone works.

The next day, during our rest break, we again watched rail car after rail car of soldiers stop for water. The Hungarian from Kamionka, seeing how the day before the Hungarian soldiers had been so good to us, went over to talk to one man from the new group of soldiers. But when the soldier saw the yellow patch sewn onto his clothing, he started yelling *"Jude, Jude,* I'm going to kill you" and grabbed his rifle in order to shoot. The man from camp, understanding perfectly well that his life was being threatened, ran away as fast as he could. Luckily, the train whistle blew, and the vicious Hungarian soldier had to return to his rail car.

One day we encountered a fine, kind Hungarian, the next day an evil, small minded one. When I had asked the Hungarian from the first day why he was being so helpful, he told me that though he was born in Budapest, he had studied medicine in Vienna. Many of his friends and colleagues were Jews, and he felt bad about what was happening to them all over Nazi dominated Europe. The contrast between his behavior and that of the murderous Hungarian on the second day was painful, and the lesson I learned was important: every nation had good people and bad. In Poland, there were vicious anti-Semites, and there were those very rare individuals who saved some Jewish lives, including my own and that of my brother, my wife, and my mother-in-law.

I am reminded of a Ukrainian police commander in Chorostkow, Ivan Ratinsky, who before I was taken to Kamionka rode his bicycle to my house one day. He wanted to talk privately with me, so we went outside and stood in front, out of everyone's earshot.

"Look, Shmerko," he said to me. "You're my friend. I want to help you. Come with me, and I'll save you."

When he saw me hesitate, he said again: "I want to help you. You can trust me. I'm the commandant of the police and, I can save you."

But I didn't trust him. He was an ardent Ukrainian nationalist known for killing many Russians when they ran away from Hitler's advancing forces. Even without these murders, I would have been reluctant to place my life in the hands of a Ukrainian policeman. When I ran away from Kamionka, I knew I would have to find shelter with a Polish family. I just couldn't bring myself to believe in the Ukrainians. But I had been wrong to prejudge a nation of people. After liberation when I returned to Chorostkow, I learned that the very same Ivan Ratinsky had hidden three Jews, Yosele Steinig, Mrs. Keller and her daughter, throughout the war and saved their lives. He had been serious all along, and I was reminded of my experience with the two Hungarians and how it was an error to judge a nation exclusively by those among them who commit evil.

*

The local headquarters for the Firma Otto Heil was located in the town of Kamionka, which was the large German construction company, from Bad Kissingen, that was in charge of the road works. The firm was helping the war effort with its work on this critically important road link. And the SS were doing its part by supplying the Firma Otto Heil with slave labor, meaning Jews. The Firma Otto Heil was by no means the only large German company to move operations to Polish soil to reap greater war-time profits. I.G. Farben had a large chemical factory in Monowitz, part of the Auschwitz complex. Primo Levi, the Italian writer and chemist, wrote about his experience working as a concentration camp inmate at this factory. German and Ukrainian civilians were also employed at these factories as were local Poles. Whenever the claim is made that no one knew about the death camps and exploitation of Jewish labor, it should be remembered that these giant companies, many still in business, made use of this labor and that thousands of their employees sometimes worked right alongside the dying, skeletal Jews.

A year after I was in camp, my mother and Arie again tried to buy my release. This time my mother gave her money to Nierle, a member of the *Judenrat* in Skalat, a shtetl fifteen kilometers from Kamionka. He took her money, but when he was unable to secure my release, he later returned it.

Sometimes, efforts to get relatives out of the camps proved disastrous. One day, Mr. Kupfershmidt, a member of Sushastow's *Judenrat*, came to Kamionka with a wagon full of packages that the people of his town had sent along for their loved ones. His son was in the camp, and he was going to use this opportunity, as the bearer of packages, to try to obtain his son's release. He had the misfortune of meeting up with the Nazi *Scharführer* (Squad Leader) Miller.

"Look," Mr. Kupfershmidt said. "I have all this gold and money. I'll give it to you if you let my son out."

Miller took the gold and money and then thundered, "You're trying to bribe a German SS officer?" The lieutenant proceeded to rain blows on the father; we who were watching thought this tirade would surely end in his death. It did. In the end, Miller had the wagon unloaded, and he kept the gold and money.

It became quite clear after this incident that anyone coming to the camp with packages for relatives or with gifts for the Germans and Ukrainians ran a tremendous risk. At any point in any exchange, one could be killed.

When I first came to camp, I had to sleep on the bottom bunk. The longer someone stayed in the camp, the more people were killed, the more space opened up on upper bunks, and a person would eventually work his way up. The major drawback of the bottom bunk was that dust and dirt from other people sleeping on the upper planks always fell through the sizable cracks and onto my face while I slept. But the one advantage to sleeping on the bottom bunk, in fact the only advantage, was that it was close to the floor where a small board had been pried loose to create a cubby hole where small items could be hidden. During the days when I still received packages, my father had sent me a little wooden box, and I hid it in the cubby hole. Also, it was in there, in the box in the cubby hole, that I would put the contents of anything sent to me from home: some bread, shoes, a pair of pants. And I wasn't the only one. A few of us would use this secret space beneath the floorboards to hide prized possessions. Anything left lying around casually on the bunk or on a hook would inevitably be stolen. Ours was a desperate situation, and men who in normal times would never commit a crime, even a petty one, were driven to do things that they would have never considered previously. After all, another pair of pants might mean the difference between freezing to death and staying warm; a piece of bread could mean the difference between surviving another day and succumbing to death.

One late afternoon in October, right after the holidays, I returned to the barracks after work. I saw that the floorboard I had used as a locker had been nailed shut. Not only had our things been taken, but we could be identified since our names were in the box. The other men who also had placed things inside there for safekeeping were wondering, like me, what was going to happen next. We knew this sort of offense was often punished by death, and we supposed all we could do was to wait for the guards to point to us, march us outside into the yard, and then kill us in full view of the other inmates to teach them a lesson about maintaining personal possessions. Needless to say, I was tense with anticipation.

The next day when I returned to the barracks, one of the older men came up to me. He no longer worked outside because he was too weak and was basically waiting for the order to be killed. In the meantime, he had been given the task of cleaning toilets.

"You have to report to the main office," he said blandly.

This was it. I expected the worst; death had come to greet me.

When I reached the main office, I quickly found out that another one of the men, Abba, the ritual slaughterer's son from Chorostkow who had kept things under the floorboards with me, had asked for his possessions back. He had also tried to explain to the Germans why he had hidden them. But when he began to speak, they hit him. The more he spoke, the more terrible were the blows. They were not interested in explanations or reasons; rather, they hated him even more for his efforts. They did not want to be reminded of his humanity, so they silenced him. He would fall down from the blows, then get up, and would be hit some more. When he could no longer move, they made him lie on his stomach and gave him twenty-five lashes on his back. Among the men who did the whipping was a Jewish kapo named Zuckerman. Zuckerman, who always wore his World War I lieutenant's uniform, was alternately vicious and compassionate to fellow Jews.

I knew then, when it was my turn, that explanations would not help, that they would, in fact, only make matters worse. So I said nothing more than answer their questions.

"Are you Shmerko Halpern?" I was asked.

"Yes, I am Shmerko Halpern."

"Is this your box?" they asked.

"Yes, it is my box."

"Lie down," they said.

I lay down on my stomach, and they began to strike me with a heavy wooden stick. I did not cry out but absorbed the pain as quietly as possible. Each blow was so painful I thought I would faint. I did not expect to live through it. When the Germans were through with me, my backside was bruised as black as a leather shoe, a solid plane of ruptured blood vessels. The entire area was numb from shock, and I could barely walk and certainly could not sit. Then they gave me what amounted to a death sentence. The Germans said I was too sick and hurt to go to work. Everyone in camp knew that whoever didn't work was sure to be killed.

However, two friends from my barracks assured the authorities that I could still work. They helped me walk the eight kilometers to where the rail ties were being laid, discreetly holding me in the middle so the German guards on the road would not notice. I was in extreme pain, thinking all along that I wouldn't make it, that at any moment I would collapse on the road and a German bullet would put an end to my suffering. My friends, Itzhak Goldfliess among others, wouldn't let me drop off, though. They were determined to give me a chance to live and held onto me tightly. I was very lucky that they cared; otherwise, things would probably have ended for me right then.

I was also fortunate in that the German officer on duty that day knew me as a good worker. He appreciated that I was young and strong. The Germans, for all their evil, continued, even in these hellish circumstances, to respect hard work. People who demonstrated this quality sometimes received a little better treatment, and in the camps, a little better treatment could mean the difference between life and death, as it did that day.

This German came over to me when he saw I could barely walk, that I could hardly straighten up, and asked what had happened. I told him the entire story, about hiding small things under the floorboards, about being beaten with the heavy wooden stick. I stopped short of showing him my blackened skin. Miraculously, he was sympathetic. While everyone else worked laying ties on the railroad track, he permitted me to rest on the ground. "Rest," he said, "today you will not work."

A couple of days later, I went to one of the Jewish doctors who treated the inmates to show him how black my skin still was. I was worried, as was everyone else who got sick in the camp, about infection and gangrene.

"Look," the doctor said to me after examining the area. "Today it's black, later it will be blue, and after that it will be red. Thank God you're alive. In a few days, you'll be able to walk better."

And he was right. It took a while, but after the skin was black, it turned to blue, and then to red, and with each change, walking became a little easier, until finally, after two months, I was fully healed. I was fortunate, very fortunate.

Anyone who survived knew himself to be fortunate. One never knew when a random shot would end a life. One Sunday afternoon in June during our only afternoon off, I was bathing in the outdoor shower that, after months without any water for personal use, had been installed. This was our only opportunity to bathe ourselves, and whoever wasn't too tired, took advantage of it. On this particular Sunday afternoon, many of us were standing outside naked, waiting to feel the clean water on our bodies, when the SS *Scharführer* Miller came by with his girlfriend. They stood there watching us and laughed and laughed. We were very embarrassed to be standing naked in front of a woman, and even though we could tell they were both drunk, we were still humiliated and nervous. The affair did not end there, however. Suddenly Miller took out his gun and shot one of the men who was standing just a few feet away from me. For no reason at all, he just pointed the gun at one man's head and pulled the trigger.

It was like a man who goes out into the forest to hunt animals just because he has the power to do so. Miller was trying to impress his girlfriend with his power over Jewish life. I was paralyzed by this callousness. For the life of me, I could not understand how a man could take out his gun and kill another in cold blood, on a whim, and indifferently observe the thin, naked body collapse onto the dirt. Ashes to ashes, dust to dust. Dear God, how did these monsters permit themselves such cruelty? Miller and his girlfriend laughed some more when they saw our expressions. Then they got into his car and drove away to enjoy what remained of their Sunday afternoon. These Germans never forgot to remind us of how worthless our lives were to them.

*

Yom Kippur of 1942 was spent in Kamionka. Without the aid of a calendar, Jewish or Gregorian, we had managed to determine the date of this Holiest of Holy days by counting the weeks since we had been brought in and by keeping track of the lunar cycle. Everyone in the barracks fasted, even those Jews who before the German occupation had not observed religious laws. The previous day, right before *erev* Yom Kippur, we begged the Jews working in the kitchen to give us our evening ration before sunset. We carefully ate everything, and once the sun set, not a morsel of bread, not a drop of water, passed our lips.

We returned to the barracks and prayed *Kol Nidre*, the opening prayer of the Holy Day. Out of hundreds in our barracks, only a few did not join in prayer. We did not worry that the Germans would hear. They were so afraid of the lice and typhus in the barracks that they never entered. Knowing we were not likely to be disturbed, we prayed with great devotion.

In the morning after waking and dressing, no one lined up for the warm liquid and moldy bread. Of the three thousand Jews in the camp, only a few of the very sick ate that day. We did go to work as usual, however. Most people had a little money hidden here and there, and I had collected a considerable sum before the holiday. When we got to the road, I began to talk to one of the German soldiers who happened to speak Polish and with whom I had become friendly. I knew he wasn't a Nazi by ideology, so I asked him whether he had ever heard of Yom Kippur. He had. I told him it was the holiest day of the year for Jews, and if he let us pray, I would give him some money, enough to buy four yards of fabric for a good suit. He said he knew how important Yom Kippur was to the Jews and agreed to turn a blind eye on us as we prayed.

All day long as thousands of German soldiers passed on the road, headed to the Eastern front, we bent over and attacked the road with sledgehammers, shovels, and brooms. When there was a lull of five or ten minutes between convoys, the group of about 150 of us were led in the prayer service by Mr. Pick, whose son had been a friend of mine. He had had the insight to run away to Russia when there was still time. Fortunately for us, Mr. Pick, a fine and educated man, knew a great deal of the service by heart. He stood by the construction trailer, facing it as if it were an ark, and sang the *nigunim* (melodies) of the Yom Kippur prayers with all his heart and soul.

In this way, we observed the laws of Yom Kippur, fasting and praying, and while working on the road. As with the fasting, even those who once would not ordinarily have gone to synagogue did so on this day. Everyone, under these horrendous circumstances, felt a deep need to pray for redemption. The lines "Who shall live, who shall die" were not abstract phrases for those of us who had witnessed scores of deaths every day. We lived with the sight, feel, and smell of death minute by minute. We knew death so well that we were utterly committed to life.

We prayed to live, we prayed for deliverance. Among us, there were men who did not believe in God or did not think God was paying attention to our suffering, but even they prayed on that Yom Kippur. We prayed and cried, prayed and hoped. There was little room for philosophical speculation. We were in desperate circumstances, and everyone knew that a miracle was needed to survive. Even though we were being treated as subhuman, we retained our sense of humanity. By asserting ourselves through prayer, we affirmed our dignity.

I had always maintained a deep belief in *Hakodesh Baruch-hoo (The Holy One, blessed be He)*, and when I prayed in the morning in the barracks *minyan*, and especially when I prayed that day on the Berlin-Kiev road, I did so with all my heart and soul. I pleaded with God that He hear the cries of His people as He did when He parted the Red Sea for the Jews on their way out of Egypt, that He show the evil masters on earth the true ruler of the universe, that He demonstrate His ability to intervene in the events of this world in order to protect His beloved people, Israel, the innocent victims of the Nazis.

Although there was no sign of redemption that day, over the next few weeks, amid all the despair, I beheld a vision of such devotion to God that I was moved to renew my beliefs. In my barracks, there lived a father and his twelve-year-old son. They usually worked together and were very nice. (We also had old men in the barracks who were not taken out to work and who, as a result, were hardly given anything to eat.) We knew that in only a matter of days men who could not work—whether because of age or ill health—would be taken out and shot. This father approached one of the old men in the barracks and said:

"I'd like you to teach my son Torah. For each day that you tutor him, I'll give you my portion of bread." The father continued. "I can't give up my bread every day because I'll grow too weak, but every other day I can manage."

So a deal was struck. Every other evening, after we returned from work, the old man and the young boy sat together, and from memory the words of Torah came forth from the old man's mouth. They filled the air, uplifting not only the soul of the twelve-year-old but of everyone within earshot.

I was deeply moved by this father's willingness to sacrifice his own lifeline so that his son, whose chances of surviving the camp were also small, could celebrate life through study. A people that chooses to give away bread, more valuable than diamonds in the face of starvation, out of love for Jewish knowledge, is truly unique. Like a pearl for which you have to pry and dig out of a hard shell, this story remains as a gem in my memory.

A few weeks later I came down with typhus and was taken to the infirmary, which was only a small room with six to eight beds lined up one beside the another. In fact, the beds were no more than slats of wood, each with a small blanket. There were no medicines in the camp, no thermometers or stethoscopes. The infirmary only provided an opportunity to rest, drink some water, and eat a little extra food. Like almost everyone else who went there, I was not expected to survive. For eight days I ran an extremely high fever, but I did not succumb. I got to know the doctors quite well; they too were Jews and inmates, but they worked at their professions, at least for the time being. One of them, after he saw that my fever had subsided, said to me: "I have no medicine for you, but your mother built you well. She probably gave you lots of good food. Maybe this care and God's love will help you survive." For almost twelve days I stayed in the infirmary, and then the doctors told me that if I wanted to live, I would have to return to work, sick or not. Everyone else who remained in the infirmary this long had been shot.

My temperature had gone down, so I got out of bed and stood up. I told the doctor that I saw flecks moving in front of my eyes, like little flies. He explained, "These 'flies' you are seeing come from your body's weakness. If you go to work now, you won't make it, I'm afraid." Then he paused. "But if you got enough food, you would get better, and your eyesight would clear up." He paused and then spoke the words that probably saved my life. "With so many people getting sick, I'll need help. Stay here as my assistant. That way you'll get stronger before returning to the road and working with the sledgehammer in the bitter cold."

*Sam's uncle, Dudio Wolfson, who was with Sam in Kamionka, with his wife
Yente and his mother, who was Sam's grandmother.*

With the doctor's help and that of other friends, I arranged to stay
in the infirmary, caring for others who were sick with typhus. For
about two and a half months I worked with this doctor and received
extra food, a privilege reserved for the sick and the doctors. God
helped me, and I became healthy once again. Many were not so lucky.

My mother's brother, Dudio from Trembowla, was also in the
camp for a while. He was later bought out and reunited with his family. They were all killed in the *Aktion* in Trembowla on June 3, 1943.
Dudio had first started coming to visit me in the infirmary when I was
sick, but even after I recovered, he continued coming to comfort other
sick people. He sat by their bedsides and made small talk, trying to lift
their spirits. Even in this place of death, he observed the *mitzvah* of *bikur
cholim*, visiting the sick. Afterward he would come sit and talk to me.

Often there was a little leftover food in the infirmary since patients
were too sick to eat; also, the doctors and other infirmary workers did

not always finish their portions. I would get up around two o'clock in the morning and cook whatever food was available. Then I would sneak over to the barracks where my friend Itzhak Goldfliess from Chorostkow and Uncle Dudio were sleeping. Normally, Itzhak and I slept next to each other. Although he was older than me, we always went out of our way to help each other.

I would nudge them gently so as not to scare them. When they were awake, I would say: "Here, I've got some food for you." Of course, they were very happy to have something extra to eat, and I was pleased to do my share to help others survive.

However, most of the people in the infirmary died from typhus; others were shot when the gangrene in their legs and feet was discovered. One day seventeen people with gangrene were taken out and executed. Quite a few were my friends, like Freyke Gurtman. We had spent months together, nursing each other back to health. They knew where they were going and what would happen to them.

"If you survive, remember all this, and tell the story," one man said to me as he hobbled toward the door. Another said, "Tell the world what these devils did to our people."

In truth, there were times when I did not know whether *anyone* would survive. Hitler and his henchmen killed right and left, young and old, women and children. Nonetheless, I promised these men that I would not betray their lives, that I would recount the *kiddush Hashem* (sanctification of God's name) that these deaths represented. I begged God for the opportunity to tell the world what the German people did to us.

Among the seventeen men with gangrene who were killed were Freyke Gurtman from Chorostkow and Dr. Bloch. I had become fond of the doctor, and I watched with great pain as he was taken outside to be shot. The Germans boasted that it was more efficient to kill a Jew with gangrene than amputate the infected limb. As Dr. Bloch was being led to his death, he decided to tell the Germans his story, and in an elegant, educated German he said:

"I am a professor of philosophy from Vienna. I was an officer in Kaiser Franz Josef's army during the First World War. I was a loyal supporter of the Hapsburgs. I helped many people in Vienna, Christian and Jew, rich and poor."

Then he paused, even though they were about to kill him, and he had nothing to lose.

"You really think you are going to win this war? You think by shooting me, one little Jew, it will help you win this war? Well, I will tell you, with this act you will not win the war. In fact, not only are you going to lose this war, you are already losing it."

We all stopped working momentarily, and those of us who understood German listened to his brave words. We knew his speech would anger the SS, that the truth would make them nervous. I am convinced that many Germans volunteered for the SS because they considered themselves good, loyal Germans and thoroughly believed Hitler's doctrines. But others saw the SS as a way to avoid serving on the Eastern front and thereby increasing their chances of surviving the war. The last thing they wanted was to be reminded of the collapse of the German war effort. Nonetheless, Dr. Bloch persisted, speaking aloud what we had already heard from the Hungarian officer and in hurried gossip and whispered rumors.

"You have been repelled at Stalingrad. Hitler knows, as well as anyone, that the war is over, that he has lost. Like Napoleon, you lost because you took on too much. Russians in the Russian heartland— you cannot beat them there. They wounded your depleted forces, and now it is only a matter of time. The Russians are advancing, and it will not be long before Germany is forced to surrender, with Russia bearing down on the Eastern front and the Americans and British on the west. You can shoot as many of us as you want, but it will not help you win the war. It is over."

Then the soldiers dragged him forward and put a gun to his head. I looked away as one of them pulled the trigger.

After most of the sick people were killed, there was nothing more I could do to help the doctor, and since I had recovered from my illness, I returned to laying railroad ties. I was still weak, however, and the work proved hard for me. I don't know how long I would have lasted with the rail gang. Still, I was determined to outlast the Nazi beasts, and I worked as hard as I could to avoid drawing attention to myself. However, I rested whenever possible to conserve energy.

Then I had a lucky break. The Jew who had been working for

Hauptsturmführer Paul Rebel, the SS captain, had run away, and for some reason I was chosen to replace him. By camp standards, this job was wonderful, and everyone coveted the position. People who were stronger and smarter and had the means to bribe their way into a better situation, all wanted to be the *hauptsturmführer*'s servant. Perhaps my friendship with the doctors had helped. Or perhaps Zuckerman, the kapo who had given me the horrible beating that left my backside black with bruises, had felt the need to make amends. God only knows, but I was glad to have landed the position.

Every day I had to wake up a little earlier than the rest of the inmates to walk two kilometers from camp to the *hauptsturmführer*'s house. Once I arrived, I would carry about fifteen pails of water from the well, which was a kilometer away. I chopped a great deal of wood for the fireplaces and stoves, and throughout the day I shined the *hauptsturmführer*'s boots. He had several pairs of high, black boots and was constantly changing from one to another. Each had to be polished to perfection.

This job had many good aspects. First, since the kitchen of the household was staffed by Jews, enough food was available for everyone who worked there. Each evening before I returned to camp, I stuffed my pockets with leftovers to take back for my hungry friends. I often say that the act of giving a piece of bread to a starving Jew in those days meant more to me than all the *tzedaka* (the charity) I am, thank God, now able to give to numerous American and Israeli causes. To smuggle a piece of bread or cheese out of the *hauptsturmführer*'s house and put it into the hands of a fellow Jew meant that I was literally helping him live a little longer, which could prove long enough for him to survive the war.

A piece of bread meant life then, and I cherished the act of *chesed* (loving-kindness) that giving it provided for me. Helping others made getting through each day a little easier for me.

I was also allowed to wear regular clothing, not an inmate's uniform with a mandatory yellow patch sewn onto the breast, and I could keep my hair at a normal length rather than closely cropped like everyone else. These two privileges would increase my chances of blending in with the civilian population were I to decide to run away. I spoke Polish and Ukrainian. Of course, I didn't forget for a second that the Germans, the SS, and the Ukrainians could kill me at any moment.

*

Some time after the event, we in the camp learned that during Sukkot of 1942 the SS had again raided Chorostkow. They had planned an *Aktion* and immediately killed a hundred Jews on the streets. Then they took over a thousand Jews, which represented fifty percent of the entire Jewish population of the town, and placed them in cattle cars as they had done with me and my group. The intention of the SS was to make Chorostkow *Judenrein* (Jew-free). Whoever was not transported managed to survive by hiding in underground bunkers or attics, which everyone had built by then in anticipation of another, more thorough *aktion*. The survivors, my mother and brother Arie among them, were later ordered to leave Chorostkow for other ghettos. Almost all of them went to the ghetto in Trembowla.

My father, uncles, aunts and cousins were not so fortunate. My father was hiding in an underground bunker in Yosele Shwartz's house along with forty-one other Jews. To ensure safety, the bunker needed to be camouflaged from the outside, and Melach Foden, Yosele Schwartz's father-in-law, volunteered for the job, which amounted to sacrificing himself. He hid behind the door and waited. When the SS eventually came into the cellar, they shot him and despite the camouflage, discovered the underground bunker as well. All the Jews were herded onto this transport.

At the last minute, Arie decided not to join our father, but instead went with his friend, Vova Nagler, into another bunker, a small one with room enough for only two people. Dudio Edelman, a Jewish policeman, covered the hiding place and checked periodically to see that they were all right. My mother, unable to tolerate the idea of hiding in an underground bunker, managed to remain undetected in an attic.

Upon learning that his wife and children had been taken from their hiding place into the transport, one member of the *Judenrat*, Shmuel Weissbrod, decided to join his family. He could not know then that, instead of transporting these thousand Jews to Kamionka, the SS planned to take them to Belzec, a death camp about fifty miles outside Lvov.

There they were not to be put to work. Before the Germans packed every cattle car with about 120 Jews, squeezing them one against the other like herring, they lined the floors in the train with three inches of caustic quicklime. Normally used in construction, this lime burns the flesh on contact. Therefore, most of the Jews died before the transport ever arrived in Belzec. Those who managed to survive this horrible ordeal were shot once the doors of the cattle cars were opened. All the bodies were then burned in the crematoria, and the ashes were buried in the surrounding forest.

At this point, we did not know that Avrum Chaim, who was in a P.O.W. camp in Chelm, would be killed. My father's death was the first tragic loss for our family. When I found out the terrible way in which my father lost his life, I could not eat nor sleep. I cried constantly. Even though death was all around me, I still could not accept this loss. My father, such a gentle and giving man, was only fifty-four years old. He had written to me in camp to keep up my morale. I would work all day on the road, thinking of him and crying.

I have visited Belzec many times since the 1970s. The death camp is right next to the small city of Belzec and is completely surrounded by dense forests. A block of granite near the entrance to the fenced-off site reads, in Polish: "Here in Belzec, from the beginning of 1942 until the end of 1942, 600,000 Jews, and 1,500 Gentiles who helped Jews, were killed." My father was one of these 600,000. My uncles, aunts, and cousins were also among the murdered. Our entire section of eastern Galicia, with many towns and cities like Chortkow, Chorostkow, Tarnopol, Lvov, and Zolkiew, was made *Judenrein*, with Belzec serving as the Jews' final destination. Since there is no actual grave over which to pray at Belzec, when I visit, I say *Kaddish* near another memorial on the site, the statue of a skeletal figure supporting another, which bears the Polish inscription: "In memory of the victims of Hitler's terror murdered from 1942 to 1943."

The story of how Jews were murdered and burned at Belzec is known primarily because of Jan Karski, currently a professor at Georgetown University. In 1942 he wrote a book, *The Story of the Secret State*, in which he recounted what he had personally witnessed both in

Entrance to the Belzec deathcamp.

the Warsaw Ghetto and the Belzec death camp. Karski was a recent graduate of the Lvov law school and was also a member of the Polish underground. A Catholic, he responded to a request by the Warsaw *Judenrat* by volunteering to risk his life to tell the world what the Nazis were doing to Polish Jewry. He was smuggled into Belzec dressed in an Estonian guard's uniform, and for two weeks he made a mental record of all that he saw. In his book he writes:

"Alternately swinging and firing with their rifles, the policemen forced still more people into the two cars, which were already over-full. The shots continued to ring out in the rear,

Plan of the Belzec deathcamp.

The author with his wife, his son David, daughter-in-law Sharon, and grandson Jeremy, in Chorostkow at the monument which was erected in 1995.

the driven mob surged forward, exerting an irresistible pressure against those nearest the train. . . .

"These were helpless since they had the weight of the entire advancing throng against them and responded with howls of anguish to those who, clutching their hair and clothes for support, trampling on necks, faces and shoulders, breaking bones and shouting with insensate fury, attempted to clamber over them. After the cars had already been filled beyond normal capacity, more than another score of human beings, men, women and children, gained admittance in this fashion. Then the policeman slammed the doors across the hastily withdrawn limbs that still protruded and pushed the iron bars in place. . . .

"The floors of the cars had been covered with a thick, white powder. It was quicklime.

"The moist flesh coming into contact with the lime is rapidly dehydrated and burned. The occupants of the cars would be literally burned to death before long, the flesh eaten from the bones. Secondly, the lime would prevent decomposing bodies from spreading disease.

"It was twilight when the forty-six (I counted them) cars were packed. From one end to the other, the train, its quivering cargo of flesh, seemed to throb, vibrate, rock, and jump as if bewitched. Inside the camp a few score dead bodies remained and a few in the final throes of death. German policemen walked around at leisure with smoking guns, pumping bullets into anything, that by a moan or motion betrayed an excess of vitality. Soon, not a single one was left alive."

A few years ago when I visited Belzec, I was told by a Pole who lived in the neighborhood that there was still one more witness to the horrors that had taken place there. The witness was the only Jewish inmate to survive this notorious concentration camp. He had been a mechanic who worked on the crematorium where the dead bodies were burned. One day, a certain oven part was needed, and he said he knew where to find it in Lvov. He was taken to the city by two SS officers, and after he went into the store to purchase the part, he ran out the back door and escaped, saving himself. After liberation, he had returned to Belzec and helped organize not only the erection of a fence marking the site of the camp (the Germans had dismantled everything before retreating to destroy all evidence of their crimes) but also six concrete monuments, one for each group of 100,000 Jews butchered there. The mechanic emigrated to Israel where he lived until he passed away.

Sam Halpern, Jan Karski, and Abe Zuckerman.

Jan Karski published his book in London so that the English-speakers, most importantly in the United States—the only country with the power to stop the German slaughter of innocents—could learn what was taking place in Europe. When American Jews say they had no idea about the killings, I always think of Karski's book and wonder how intelligent people could have ignored the atrocities. Why didn't they read everything they could about Europe's Jews once there was a hint of persecution? Not only did American Jewry fail to learn what was happening to their brothers and sisters in Europe, Americans did not press their government to act even when news of the atrocities was confirmed.

Karski did not solely rely on his book to inform leaders in London and the United States about the mass murders being committed by the Nazis. In November, Karski met with the British undersecretary for foreign affairs, Lord Selborne, and personally recounted what he had witnessed. In the United States, Karski briefed President Roosevelt, Herbert Hoover and Stephen Wise, among other leaders. Tragically, nothing came out of these meetings.

Karski himself told me about his meeting in 1943 with Felix Frankfurter, a Supreme Court justice, one of President Roosevelt's most trusted friends and advisers, and a Jew. Karski spent forty-five minutes telling Justice Frankfurter everything he had seen in the Warsaw Ghetto and at Belzec. Karski wanted to convince Frankfurter that the reports of Jewish genocide that were crossing the Atlantic from Europe were absolutely true. Karski wanted Frankfurter to persuade Roosevelt to save the Jews who were still alive. When Karski finished speaking, Frankfurter said: "I cannot believe you."

The Polish ambassador of the government-in-exile, who had arranged this visit, protested. He explained that Karski's story had been checked and rechecked. The information was confirmed. Frankfurter said, "I did not say he was lying. I said that I cannot believe him. There is a difference. My mind, my heart, they are made in such a way that I cannot conceive it."

Karski said he did not understand Frankfurter's distinction. He claims that Frankfurter deliberately suppressed the information within himself so that he would not feel personally compelled to act. As Alan Dershowitz wrote in his book *Chutzpah,* "Frankfurter did not want to be regarded as one of those soft-hearted Jews who put Jewish lives before the American war effort. He did not want to endanger his valuable credibility with the president over an issue of Jewish sentimentality. And so he said and did nothing as millions of his brothers and sisters and their children were slaughtered."

How, I often wonder, could American and British Jewry have been galvanized to action after Samuel Zygelbaum's suicide? This highly publicized event had been Zygelbaum's reaction to world apathy. In the spring of 1942, Zygelbaum was living in London as the Bund representative to the national council of the Polish government-in-exile. During this period of time, Hitler's "final solution" was at its height. As a member of the council, Zygelbaum was receiving information about the on-going Holocaust and immediately alerted Polish, American, and British authorities. He wanted them to intervene to stop the mass killing. When all his efforts fell upon deaf ears, he felt utterly deserted and depressed. When the Warsaw Ghetto uprising was brutally repressed and nearly everyone inside the ghetto slaughtered, Zygelbaum could no longer endure the indifference. In his suicide letter, he wrote that he was taking his life because of the world's indifference to the deaths of millions of innocent Jews. It was a world he could no longer inhabit. After news of the protest suicide spread throughout the Jewish world, many said that Zygelbaum was trying to accomplish through death what he was unable to achieve in life.

But Zygelbaum's efforts were to no avail. Although his tragic act and letter stirred public opinion, the actions he hoped for were never undertaken. No government or private group initiated any substantative protest. American Jews did little, and their leaders—men in positions of knowledge and power—abandoned their European brethren.

When my son David was still a small boy, he came into my room one *Shabbat* afternoon and found me reading Karski's book. I was crying. I had just finished the section on the murderous rampages at Belzec and could not contain my emotion. David, who was accustomed to seeing his father smiling, became distressed.

"What's wrong, Dad?" he asked.

I was not sure how to respond to the innocent inquiry. Unlike other survivors, I often spoke about the Holocaust with my children, knowing it was too important to ignore. My children had a right to know what had happened to their family, to their people. But Karski's book was so graphic, and David was so young. I decided to let him read a couple of pages, and then we'd talk about them.

"Here," I said handing David the open book. "This is what happened to your grandfather."

David read the pages quietly and then cried. I held him in my arms and answered as best I could his questions about how the world could let this happen. I did not have very good answers, for I had been asking myself the very same questions. Where was the world? Where was America? Where were America's Jews as six million were slaughtered?

Concerned with what Gentiles would think, most American Jewish leaders were preoccupied with their own careers; they allowed themselves to be persuaded that keeping a low profile on the Holocaust, even as the smokestacks were belching the remains of Jewish flesh, was the most prudent path. Herbert Lehman; Samuel Rosenman, a lawyer and one of Roosevelt's closest advisers; Joseph M. Proskauer, president of the American Jewish Committee; and Bernard Baruch were among the leaders who failed to use their influence to bring the horrors of the Holocaust before the public.

Rabbi Stephen S. Wise, the acknowledged leader of American Jewry at the time, was concerned that raising the "Jewish" issue would be misconstrued. Like Frankfurter, he feared being accused of putting a Jewish agenda ahead of national interests. When Wise received authoritative documentation about the "final solution," he was persuaded by the State Department not to publicize the information until it was confirmed yet again. Wise was also advised, by another Jewish justice, Louis Brandeis, that "it would make a bad impression on Roosevelt, in the midst of his overwhelming responsibilities... to trouble him with our, in a sense, *lesser* problems" [emphasis mine].

One American leader who did prevail on Roosevelt to help European Jewry was Henry Morgenthau, Jr., then U.S. secretary of the Treasury. He needed some cajoling. Rabbi Irving Bunim, a distinguished leader of Orthodox Jewry in America who witnessed the prodding, reported how Morgenthau radically altered his position vis-a-vis intervening on behalf of the Jews of Europe.

At the beginning of October 1943, three days before Yom Kippur, a group of several hundred Orthodox rabbis from across the country, organized by Peter Bergson, marched up Pennsylvania Avenue, attempting to appeal to President Roosevelt directly. They believed the horrendous stories filtering out of Europe would have a powerful impact on the president, and they wanted to ask him personally to take action against the slaughter of Jews. Unfortunately, the rabbis never got a chance to speak with Roosevelt because his close adviser, Samuel Rosenman, a Jew, told him not to meet with the delegation since the rabbis were not important enough. Instead, the group was allowed to speak with Henry Morgenthau, Jr.

As three of the leaders, Irving Bunim, and Rabbis Kotler and Kalmanowitz pleaded their case, Morgenthau at first appeared distant and reserved. Rabbi Kalmanowitz grew agitated. Pacing back and forth, muttering frantically, he overexcited himself and collapsed.

Alarmed, Morgenthau knelt by the rabbi's side, patted his hand, and pleaded with him not to die. "I'll do anything you want," the secretary promised, deeply moved. He had a previous appointment but postponed it and canceled a prearranged flight. When the emotional Rabbi Kalmanowitz recovered, Morgenthau promised to intercede with the president and the State Department on behalf of European Jews.

In 1990, at the International Leadership Reunion of the United Jewish Appeal held in Geneva, people gave generously and spoke devotedly of commitment to Israel and the Jewish people. Before I pledged my donation, I stood up to say a few words. Rather than give the usual speech about how special Israel was and how important it was to contribute, however, I decided to turn back the clock and ask some questions that had been lying quietly, for many years, deep in my heart.

"Distinguished ladies and gentlemen," I said to the caucus of major givers. "First, I want to thank you for all you do on behalf of the country of Israel and your fellow Jews. I am always impressed by your generosity, your commitment. You give your money and of yourselves so freely that it's truly wonderful to see. But I have to ask you something, a painful question, which I have lived with for decades now: Where were you, as a community of American Jews, during the Holocaust?" My voice became louder as my emotions grew stronger.

"Europe's Jews were desperate for your help. You had means, you had power. As we dropped off, one by one in the labor and concentration camps, or hid in haylofts, behind false walls, in cellars and attics, starving, frightened almost beyond hope, as we survived on forged Gentile papers, we waited daily, even hourly, in the ghettos and camps, for our brethren in America to do all they could to help liberate us. But where were you?

"Today, you help strengthen Israel with time and effort. But where were you fifty years ago, when nothing was done to prevent the extermination of a third of our people?"

The audience was taken aback by my speech and the strong emotion I apparently displayed. There I was, with my Polish accent and the images of the Holocaust in my mind and the imprint of the blows on my body, a living witness among distinguished company, almost all of whom had been old enough during the war to be involved. Gladys, sitting beside me, was self-conscious and upset, for she felt

Elie Wiesel with Sam Halpern.

that my statement may have been too strong. But I had not been able to contain myself. I was compelled to speak by what I recognized at that moment, by a room full of wealthy and powerful Jews who once did so little to help those desperately in need.

I wanted these people to know that time had been a critical element. They had to understand that one day's indifference meant thousands of deaths.

When I was liberated by the Red Army on March 22, 1944, Hungarian Jewry was still alive. My dear friend, Elie Wiesel, has told me that he and his family were only taken from their homes two weeks after Passover. This means that when I was already a free man, plans for the extermination of Hungary's 500,000 Jews were just being implemented. One month *after* I had returned to my hometown of Chorostkow and had begun trying to pick up the pieces of my life, Elie's family was just on its way to Auschwitz and other concentration camps. Had the Allies intervened to disrupt the death camps, how many thousands would have lived? More importantly, had American or British Jews warned Hungary's Jews that the slaughter was imminent, whether by radio broadcasts or dropping leaflets, the victims would have at least been given the opportunity to try to save themselves. Thousands and thousands might have survived.

As soon as I was liberated, I wrote to my Uncle Paul in New York, telling him about Kamionka and the slaughter of Jews. He took this letter to many politicians and Jewish leaders, but got nowhere. With American troops fighting both in Europe and the Pacific, people were not interested in this so-called secondary issue. And many, like Justice Frankfurter, chose not to believe the scope of the horrors. So nothing was done to help us. The world *did* know, but nobody wanted to believe, and so the machinery was allowed to run smoothly. This willful indifference was also a crime.

Contrary to Gladys' fears and understandable reservations, after I made my pledge, my remarks were met with thunderous applause. Many people came up to me afterward. Some were crying; many hugged and kissed me. They knew I had spoken from the heart.

*

After the Nazis' first transport of a thousand people to Belzec, all of Chorostkow's remaining Jews were terrified, yet they were still unsure of what they could do. The next day, the Germans again came into the ghetto and again started killing people. Some members of the *Judenrat* council were among those killed. When people saw that the *Judenrat* no longer had special privileges, they knew everyone was doomed. Whoever could, began to run away. My mother hired a wagon and driver to take her and Arie and some belongings to Trembowla where her brother lived. Relatives from surrounding towns had also fled, and they all crowded into Uncle Dudio's house.

Chorostkow was, at this point, according to the Nazi's plan, *Judenrein.* All Jews had gone to other ghettos, run away to the forests and fields, or been murdered. Sieminski's old farm was still being used by the Germans as a source of food and grain, but there was a desperate need for workers. Curiously, with promises of food in exchange for labor, the Germans put out a call to Jews in hiding to come and work on the farm. Three hundred to four hundred Jews did come out of hiding, and from May until August of 1943 they worked on the farm. My sister-in-law, Eva, was among these laborers. Right before the final liquidation of the farm, the murder of the last of Chorostkow's Jews, Eva ran away to the ghetto in Kopychince. Everyone else on the farm was killed.

Once reunited, my family decided to build an underground bunker beneath the house in which to hide. We knew that before long the Nazis would stage an *Aktion* in Trembowla. Arie and some others began this project, working hard for many days with shovels and pails to carry away the soil. When the hideout was completed, my mother went into it and came right out again. She had already attempted to live in such a bunker in Chorostkow and was unable to stay inside such a dark cave without light and air. "I feel like I'm choking in there," she told Arie sadly. Of course, everyone hoped that the Germans would be defeated before they would render *Judenrein* the few remaining towns with Jews.

On April 7, 1943, about six months after my father had been taken away and murdered at Belzec, the Germans did enter Trembowla, and together with the Ukrainian police surrounded the city. It was early morning, and nobody knew what was about to happen. Was it going to be city-wide *Aktion* or only a smaller roundup? Everyone who could, escaped into hiding. Some wanted to run to the nearby forests but were prevented from doing so by soldiers and policemen stationed all around the city. Arie went into a bunker with about forty or fifty people; thank God, they were never discovered by the Germans. My mother, of blessed memory, refused to go underground, and at fifty-four years of age, she would not even consider trying to survive in the forest. So she, along with about 1,100 Jews that included my aunts, uncles, and cousins, was rounded up. The Germans decided that transporting this group to Belzec would be too costly. Instead, 1,100 people were ordered to undress and then, in underwear, were marched through the city of Trembowla to a little village called Plebanowka, about two kilometers outside the city limits.

My mother had a heavy gold chain and some money with her. She gave these valuables to my little cousin, Herzale, who was about seven years old. When the group passed a small bridge, she told Herzale to hide underneath, instructing him to wait until dark and then find Arie back in Trembowla and give him the packet of money. Herzale did just as he was told and managed to survive until two months before liberation when Anna Bartestka, a woman in town, betrayed his whereabouts for five kilos of sugar.

Ditches had already been dug for the Jews from the Trembowla ghetto. The group was lined up at the edge of the ditches, and each received one bullet apiece before falling into the grave. The soldiers were instructed not to waste any more bullets. A Jew, they were told, was not worth two or three bullets. As a result, some people were not dead when they fell into the ditches. The Germans covered the corpses with dirt. When I came back later after liberation, the local Ukrainian peasants told me that for days they could see the earth moving in this mass grave since many of the Jews had been buried alive. Some of these poor souls may have clawed their way out, but the local residents did not lift a finger to help them; indeed, they may well have finished off any who did manage to escape from the mound of corpses.

A day after the massacre, a young woman from Plebanowka, Nusia Grossberg, who was nineteen years old, came to the site of the mass grave and sat beside it crying all night. Her mother, three sisters, and little brother had been killed and were among the pile of corpses. Nusia wept as the mass grave moved up and down, not caring if the Nazis found her. She, too, wanted to die.

In the morning, a peasant woman taking her cows to pasture found the young woman sobbing by the graveside.

"Run away," the peasant told her. "There's nothing you can do for them. Save yourself. You're young. You can live."

After protesting, Nusia did run away. Today, she lives in Brooklyn with her two children and grandchildren.

The final liquidation of the ghetto in Trembowla took place in July, 1943. After the liberation, only fifty to sixty people from the entire community had survived.

And so our beloved mother was also gone. My mother who had lived only for her family, who worked so hard alongside my father in the store, who would have walked to the ends of the earth to save her children, was no longer with us. I had not even finished saying *Kaddish* for my father when

Monument at mass grave in Plebanowka near Trembowla.

I had to begin praying for my mother. Now, only Arie and I were left. And who knew for how much longer.

*

A major advantage of my job at the *hauptsturmführer*'s was the two-kilometer walk I had to take every day to and from his house. I often stopped to chat with people, to learn as much as I could about the political situation. When I heard one day about the *aktion* in Trembowla, I grew worried. I knew my mother and Arie had run away to Trembowla. I already knew about my father's death in Belzec.

On my daily walk, I made the acquaintance of a Ukrainian man. He agreed to send a letter for me to Ivanofka and allow me to receive return mail at his address. This arrangement was most unusual. Except for a few packages in the beginning, no one in the camps received mail, and so I felt fortunate. I wrote a letter to Jan Gorniak in Ivanofka. Jan was the man who had brought my family flour soon after the start of the German occupation, and I asked him to find out what had happened to my mother and Arie. A few days later I received a reply.

"I saw your brother. . . . I know where he is. I don't know where your mother is." I knew from this last line that my mother had been killed but that Jan did not want to break my heart by coming right out and saying so. His letter went on in a bold fashion. "You might think that you are safe sitting in the camp, that it is only in the ghettos that the women and the old and sick are killed. Don't think that as long as you are productive and work you will remain alive. I have heard them say that they will soon liquidate all the Jews, in and out of the camps. Run away at your first opportunity!"

Jan included a well-known Polish rhyme to underline his point: *Robmy zaid i uciekajmy staid.* Roughly translated, it means: "Let's get in line and then run away." I knew he meant well, and even though I suspected he might be right about an *Aktion* in the camp, I did not take the advice too seriously. After learning that my mother was also dead, I felt determined not to lose more of my family. I wanted Arie close to me. Soon after receiving this letter, I gathered up all my nerve and saluted *Hauptsturmführer* Paul Rebel one morning as he was leaving his house.

"*Herr Hauptsturmführer*," I said respectfully in German, feeling like Esther coming before King Achashveros, knowing I was risking my life with this spontaneous approach. "My mother and father have been killed. All I have left is one brother. You know I'm a good worker. My brother, too, is a good worker. He will do anything you ask of him. Please, *Herr Hauptsturmführer*, I would like my brother to be with me here in Kamionka."

The *hauptsturmführer* was like royalty in the camp. The Jews gave him gold, silver, everything they had. The Germans, Poles and Ukrainians also reported to him. This powerful man governed all the activities at five other camps in the area besides Kamionka: Skalat, Podwolochisk, Chluboczick, Stupka, and Borki. My nervousness was justified. He could easily have killed me for speaking out so boldly. Much to my relief, he laughed after I made my request, saying he had never heard of such a thing. Generally, people tried to find any pretext to get out of the camp, and only a few months earlier my mother had tried to buy me out, a request that Rebel had flatly refused. Now, here was a young shoe-shine boy wanting to bring in his brother. God only knows why the *hauptsturmführer* decided to be nice that morning.

"Only a few months earlier you wanted to get out. Now you want your brother to come here?" he said. "I see no reason to object. Go over to the camp secretary. Have him write the papers, and I will sign them."

When I returned to camp that evening, I immediately went to the secretary. He was a Jew from Tarnopol, whom I knew very well. He quickly wrote the necessary letters on SS stationery stating that my brother was requested to come and work for the SS *hauptsturmführer* of Kamionka. Then he said, "I think you should get a stamp from the *hauptsturmführer*." The secretary was afraid that something would go wrong, and he would be blamed for using SS stationery to make this unusual request. Since I believed it was all in the cause of saving my brother, I summoned my *chutzpah* and with letter in hand went back to the *hauptsturmführer*. After he signed the letter, in a matter of fact voice I asked him to stamp it. I'm not sure why, but he didn't question this request either; he just stamped the letter and handed it back to me.

I was so happy and relieved. I wanted Arie with me because I felt it was too dangerous on the outside. Now, with our mother and father already killed in *Aktionen*, and our eldest brother murdered by the Germans while being held as a Russian POW, I wanted nothing more than for us to be together.

But Arie was fifty-five kilometers away, and there was no telephone or other reliable way to communicate with him. I had some money, though, which I knew would have to suffice.

I went to see the Ukrainian farmer who had already helped me with the mail. I said to him, "Look, I want to pay you very well. I have a letter from the *hauptsturmführer* saying he wants my brother to be brought to work here. Please, go to the Trembowla ghetto and find my brother. Give him this letter from the *hauptsturmführer*, and then bring my brother back here with you."

He agreed but only after I paid him. I had also given him a letter I had written in Yiddish so Arie would understand what I had done and why.

Without much trouble, the farmer managed to find Arie in the ghetto and brought him to Kamionka by horse and wagon. With the proper papers in hand, Arie had no trouble reaching me. We rejoiced on seeing one another, and mourned our parents' deaths. From then on, we slept together and spent all our time together when we weren't working. I was especially diligent in the *hauptsturmführer*'s house, trying to make sure that nothing would go wrong.

Arie and I often spoke of escape. Our clothing was not too shabby, and I was alone on the road each day with every opportunity to flee. Unlike other groups of Jews who were counted upon leaving in the morning and returning to the camp in the evening, my comings and goings were never questioned. There were only a small number of people who could leave the camp unescorted, and I was among them. The others were the four Jewish doctors who cared for the inmates, the SS and their families.

One day, two good friends of mine, Herman Brenman and Izio Hutes, both from Kopychince, came out of camp with me. The Ukrainian guard noticed this fact but didn't stop us. From the day I was promoted to water carrier and wood chopper for the *hauptsturmführer*, the guards had stopped questioning me. My orders were written in German, which they did not understand, and if they asked to examine them, they would have had to depend on me to translate. They knew I was going to the *hauptsturmführer*'s house and thought the other two were also going to work, so they let us all pass. Once we were out of sight of the camp, my friends said good-bye to me and, as planned, used the opportunity to escape. I wished them good luck. Only later on in the evening, when I was about to enter the main gate of the camp, did I realize that if their absence were discovered, I would be shot as the responsible party. Maybe God was watching over me that day, as on many others, because another guard was on duty when I returned; apparently, the guard on duty earlier never mentioned that the inmate who worked for the *hauptsturmführer* had taken two others out with him. Once in the camp, no one seemed to notice the men's disappearance. A few days later, however, Herman and Izio were caught in Skalat and brought back to Kamionka. They never told who helped them escape, despite being severely beaten. Both survived the final *Aktion* of the camp and the war although Izio Hutes died six months after liberation from typhoid fever. My good friend, Herman Brenman, lives in New Jersey with his wife, Mina, his daughter, married son, and two grandchildren. Herman's two younger brothers, Jack and Eddie, were also in Kamionka with us. Jack, eighteen years old at the time, escaped from camp by himself and arranged for a horse and wagon to return to Kopychince. There he waited for his fourteen-year-old brother, Eddie, whom I also took out of the camp with me. The three brothers survived the war in a bunker in Kopychince. Jack lives with his wife, Sophie, in New York and has three children and five grandchildren. Eddie and his wife, Sally, and their son live in New Jersey.

Arie and I often spoke of escape. The simple reason we did not try, until the very end, was that we did not want to save two lives at the expense of scores of others. We had seen what often happened when other Jews escaped and their flight was discovered. Once, a *landsman* from a town not far from Chorostkow, ran away while working on the road. The next day, *Hauptsturmführer* Rebel came into the camp and ordered everyone into the yard. It was raining and very cold, but we were made to stand there, without moving, from five until seven o'clock in the morning. Then Rebel stood in front of us in the center of the yard, facing the inmates.

"A man ran away today," he thundered. "You will all pay the price."

We were frightened for we knew how the Germans punished.

"You, you, you, and you," the *hauptsturmführer* pointed at four Jews randomly. "Himmel commando, shoot them!"

A Ukrainian police officer, only too happy to oblige, dragged the men from the line and shot them right in front of us with one bullet each to the head. They wanted to frighten us, and they succeeded.

"If any of you think of running away, the blood of your fellow Jews will be on your head," the SS officer screamed at us.

These monsters actually had the audacity to blame us for trying to save our lives. In the end, no matter how twisted this logic was, Jews *would* die if we ran away, and I said to Arie that I would never consider escaping: "I will not have others killed because of my decision." Arie agreed. He too did not want to live with the death of other Jews on his conscience.

Other Jews did their part to help each other. One day, a friend of mine, Moshkele Feingold, also from Chorostkow, was not working to the liking of Miller, the SS *scharführer*. Miller started to beat Moshkele, and when he had enough, took out a gun to shoot him.

At that moment, Mr. Zuckerman, one of the Jewish *kapos*, came over to the German and said, "You're going to waste a bullet on this Jew? Give him to me. I'll finish him off myself."

The SS officer smiled with sadistic pleasure and said, "Fine, take him." They loved seeing one Jew hit another. Zuckerman then fell upon Moshkele with such ferocity that the German laughed with satisfaction and walked away. Zuckerman kept it up, blow after blow, until poor Moshkele looked as though he was practically dead. We who were watching were horrified. It was one thing for an evil German or Ukrainian to treat us so savagely, but for a Jew to be beating a Jew was too painful and humiliating to witness. But as soon as the German officer was out of sight, Zuckerman stopped. Taking one last look around to make sure none of our enemies was watching, he said: "Here, hurry, take him into the bunker and clean him up."

By taking charge of Moshkele's destiny, by beating him rather than letting him be shot by Miller, Zuckerman actually saved a man's life. When I realized how he had manipulated the situation, I was proud and grateful. Zuckerman had risked his own life for Moshkele's. Of course, I was sorry that Moshkele had been beaten, but I was happy that he was still alive. Today Moshkele lives not so far from me in Weehawken, New Jersey.

One day in December of 1942 while I was working at the *hauptsturmführer*'s house, a pig was killed. It was fat and would provide many delicious meals for the Germans. After all the meat was cooked, it was put away in the icebox. I asked the *hauptsturmführer* if I could take the water in which the pig was cooked over to the camp. There were little bits of meat still floating in it, and I knew that even if only a few people got these morsels, the broth would provide more nourishment than many had had for weeks or months. The *hauptsturmführer* agreed, and I carried two large pails of this liquid to camp. It was very hard carrying these heavy pails, but I was happy to be helping others. Every day that I worked in the *hauptsturmführer*'s house, I thanked God for the privilege of helping others survive another day.

*

Aside from hard-core life and death matters, working at the *hauptsturmführer*'s house also had pleasurable, even comic features. One such experience involved my work with the horse Rebel received from Mr. Neirla, the head of the *Judenrat* in Skalat, a ghetto and labor camp about fifteen kilometers away from Kamionka. Neirla was the man who had taken my mother's money when she tried to get me out of Kamionka, money that he had then returned when he could not secure my release.

In order to maintain good relations with the Jews of Skalat, Neirle often brought the *hauptsturmführer* gifts, and one day he arrived at Rebel's house with a beautiful chestnut horse. The animal was less than two years old and was still a little wild. Only a practiced rider could stay on him. While many SS officers were excellent horsemen, Rebel was not. Whenever he tried mounting the horse, he would be thrown to the ground. A horse knows right away who is boss. If the mount feels that the rider is not in charge, it will try to throw him. But if the horse feels the rider knows what he's doing, the animal will comply. Then, both horse and rider can have a good time together.

Despite Rebel's knowing that he could not enjoy this horse to the fullest by taking it on long, brisk rides in the forest, the *hauptsturmführer* loved and wanted to keep it. He came up with a good solution for riding this young, spirited animal.

"Do you know anything about horses?" he asked me.

"Yes, *Herr Hauptsturmführer*," I answered immediately, realizing the opportunity that was about to come my way. "I've been near farms all my life, and I've been riding horses since I was a little boy."

"Good," he said. "Then everyday you will go to the stable, take the horse out for a ride, and tire him out. I want him kept in good shape."

"Yes, sir," I responded happily.

"After an hour or so, you will bring the horse to me."

"Yes, sir, *Herr Hauptsturmführer*."

I walked everyday to the stable where the horse was kept. It was quite far and would take me a while to get there. Being out of the house and walking by myself, I felt almost like a free man.

When I got to the stable, I took Chestnut, as he had been named, out for a ride. We would gallop hard and fast together. We would trot and then saunter through beautiful fields and forests. I would stare up at the sky and pray to God, with all my heart, with all my soul and might, that He redeem his people Israel before too few of us remained. I would immerse myself in the physical sensations of the ride, breathing in the beautiful horse's smell, feeling his hair grow damp with sweat. It was an earthy, simple, sweet experience. The contrast with what was going on only a few kilometers away in Kamionka was almost too painful to bear. I willed myself not to think about it for minutes at a time to replenish my soul with the serenity of the ride and its sense of normalcy.

After an hour or so, the horse was wet and tired. When I then brought him to the *hauptsturmführer*, he was less frisky, and Rebel was able to ride him. The ploy worked, me tiring out the lovely horse in order for the *hauptsturmführer* to get his pleasure, too. Everyone was happy.

Rebel had a number of other horses in the stable, but they were older and not as beautiful as Chestnut. Sometimes the *hauptsturmführer* would take out an older horse, one that was way past his prime and no longer made life difficult for the rider; but when

Rebel wanted to impress a young lady or other important SS officers, he would ride Chestnut, but only after I had tired him out.

My being able to provide this service made the *hauptsturmführer* like me. I knew so much of what he needed: I cleaned his boots, I chopped his firewood, I carried in water from the well, and I tired out his horse!

Of course, when I was wildly galloping with Chestnut in an open field or thick forest, I thought of running away. Who wouldn't have, in my situation? However easy it would have been for me to escape, I did not. I could not stand the thought that others might die because of a selfish act of mine; then too, I had no place to go. It might be argued that in the end almost everyone was killed, and so my escaping would not have made a difference. It is true that almost everyone was killed. But that was because the German barbarians were obsessed with their notions of racial purity. No one was killed because Sam Halpern decided to look out for himself alone. For me that has made all the difference.

After the war, many people, especially American Jews, including some members of my own family, asked me why we never fought back. Why, for instance, when the learned, kind Dr. Bloch was being shot, didn't we start a rebellion and try to save him? Why did millions of Jews in Europe go passively to the camps and then to their deaths?

This logical question deserves an answer. Perhaps a story about the camps will help suggest an answer. When I was first brought to Kamionka, there were Russian prisoners of war whom the German army had captured a few months earlier. To make room for the transport of Jews, some of the Russians were sent to other camps and others were killed. Killing POWs was against the Geneva Convention, but the Germans were beyond abiding by any rules of civilized conduct. They had become utterly savage. With my own eyes I saw the execution of POWs. Having been raised so close to the Russian border, I understood Russian and listened carefully to what the Russian POWs were saying as they were being selected for death. One man, about forty-five years old, was considered too old for a labor camp and so the Germans decided to shoot him. He stood tall and looked straight into the eyes of the German soldiers: "I have three sons in the

Red Army. They are on their way. Remember, you will pay for this."
And then the Germans shot him.

There was nothing the Russian could do in the face of many armed
German soldiers. Polish soldiers, whose army had been swiftly
defeated at the start of the war, faced the same situation. I saw four or
five German soldiers control a thousand Polish POWs. Later on in
Kamionka, a small number of Germans did whatever they wanted with
Russian soldiers, men who had been trained to fight battles. High-
ranking officers were reduced to powerless, ordinary men when confronted with the lowliest German soldier and a gun. When the tide
turned and the Germans began losing the war, I beheld the same sight
in reverse: hundreds of mighty German soldiers, who only weeks
before took life or saved it as their mood dictated, were now herded
about passively by a few Russian soldiers with weapons.

These soldiers had all been trained to fight, to use firearms, to survive under the harshest conditions. If they could not resist imprisonment, how were we Jews—a civilian population, with little or no
firearms experience and no weapons, a tribe of merchants, artisans,
scholars, women and children, all weak from starvation and exhaus-
tion—able to rebel against a well-equipped army? If you are under the
gun, there is little you can do.

Certainly, there were a few, wonderful exceptions. The Warsaw
Ghetto uprising, the first of its kind among a civilian population in
Poland, is the most famous. Even in Warsaw, however, organizing to
fight did not take place when there had been half a million Jews in the
ghetto. Only when almost the entire ghetto had been liquidated and
death was at hand did a few thousand remaining residents—right-
wingers, leftists, Bundists, religionists, atheists, Jews of every political
and religious stripe—band together, under the leadership of Mordechai Anielewicz, to fight since they knew their days were num-
bered. They realized they would not be able to beat the German army.
But if they were going to die, they would at least take some Germans
with them.

Those of us in Kamionka who were young and still strong would
have been more than willing to fight in an organized fashion if we
thought we had the slightest chance of making a difference. For
months after learning of the German defeat at Stalingrad, we waited

for partisans who were rumored to be in the vicinity. It would have been a great honor, a tremendous opportunity, to join them, to fight to save the lives of innocent Jews and non-Jews under German occupation. We had heard that the partisans liberated a camp not far from ours. Many Jews had joined their ranks immediately. In the end, though, the partisans did not come near Kamionka until the camp had already been liquidated.

One night in April 1943, Ladovsky, Rebel's Jewish chauffeur, came into my barracks and woke me up. He had just returned from Warsaw with Rebel where they had gone to purchase supplies. In Warsaw Ladovsky had heard about, and actually seen, the uprising during its second day.

"Jews," he told me, "are killing Germans! I saw it with my own eyes, German blood being spilled!"

"Thank God I lived to see the day," I said to him and jumped off my bunk.

The two of us began to sing and dance, crying and laughing, beside ourselves with joy. After two days of successful fighting, Mordechai Anielewicz said that killing German soldiers proved that they, too, were vulnerable, that the Germans were not invincible. Like Jews, they could bleed, and this resistance saved Jewish honor. Of course, within a few weeks the Germans had overrun the ghetto, killing almost everyone inside, and shipped the survivors to the death camps. But the thought of Jews defending themselves thrilled us beyond description. Even though we knew there were Jewish soldiers fighting in the Allied armed forces, we had become accustomed to feeling helpless under German occupation.

In camp, I had a friend named Bumek Katz. He was from Chorostkow, and his father, a wealthy man, had been taken away to Siberia years earlier by the Russians. His mother and two sisters remained in Chorostkow until the *Aktion* that liquidated the shtetl. His mother and older sister had been taken away to Belzec, like my father, and only his little sister, Janina, managed to hide under the doorway to their house and evade the transport.

The day after the *Aktion*, the few hundred remaining Jews came out of hiding. Among them were little Janina, my brother Arie, and my mother. Janina, who at this point had no one to look after her, fell under the care of the *Judenrat*, who decided she would be best off in Kamionka near her brother. This relocation was easily arranged for the right sum of money, and Janina was brought to live with the group of about sixty Jewish women who were housed separately from the men. The women's barracks were outside the barbed wire fence, but they were closely guarded by Ukrainian police. The women were responsible for running the camp laundry.

Even though Janina was supposed to work like everyone else, there was only so much she could do. She was just eleven years old and was traumatized, terrified, and weak. The women in the laundry sheltered her as much as they could, but after a while everyone realized the danger Janina faced. At any moment the Nazis could kill her because she wasn't productive. We decided that Janina could only be saved by getting her out of the camp and hiding her with a Christian family.

One evening, Bumek and I took Janina about two kilometers from Kamionka to the home of a Ukrainian farmer. We told him that her family, which was known to have a great deal of land and money, would pay him generously after the war if he hid the little girl. He agreed. Our timing could not have been better since about twelve days later, on July 10, 1943, Janina's brother perished together with all of Kamionka's Jews. Janina would certainly not have survived the *Aktion*.

In March 1944 when we were liberated, Arie and I walked fifty kilometers to this farmer's house and found Janina was still there. She was alive and healthy, living as a shepherd girl tending geese. Wearing an old torn dress, barefoot, with hands rough from working, she looked like a poor peasant. Although only nine months had passed since I last saw her, it felt like an eternity. When Janina caught sight of me, she stopped what she was doing and ran over. She asked right away about her brother, Bumek, but I didn't have the heart to tell her that the Germans had killed him. Instead, I said he was in the Russian army, fighting on the front. I told her that right then I was busy but would come back to take her to Chorostkow.

I told the Ukrainian farmer that not only would Janina's father pay him well for looking after the girl when he came to pick her up, but that Janina's brother was an important officer in the Russian army. I wanted to scare the man into taking extra special care of her.

In the meantime, Janina's father had written a letter from Siberia addressed to the mayor of Chorostkow. The mayor, not knowing to whom to give the letter since no one in the family remained in town, turned it over to us. How I rejoiced when I realized that Janina had a living relative! I wrote back to her father right away: "Come home, your daughter is alive!"

Very soon after, her father arrived in town from Russia. He went to the farmer's house, gave him the little money that he still had, and took Janina with him. Later they moved together to Curacao where Janina still

Yanina Katz in Curacao. She was helped by Sam Halpern.

lives with her son, daughter, and grandchildren. She also owns a large, elegant department store in downtown Curacao called Casa Janina. We have remained good friends, visiting and staying in touch. I know that if Arie and I had not looked for Janina again after the war, she would have remained on that farm, a Ukrainian peasant girl, cut off from her roots and her people. She would have been lost to the nation of Israel forever.

July 9, 1943 was a Friday, and I went to work at the *hauptsturmführer*'s house as usual. I had seen many German officers in the house that day, which was not unusual, and paid them little attention as I went quietly about my duties. I chopped wood for the stove and fireplaces, brought in buckets of water from the pump, and shined the *hauptsturmführer*'s boots to perfection. When I came into his room toward the end of the day with a pair of boots, he screamed at me, "Get lost. Don't you see that Katzman is here?"

Katzman was the notorious SS general in charge of *Aktionen*, liquidations of ghettos and camps in the Lvov region. His reputation as one of the biggest murderers preceded him. I knew that if Katzman had arrived in Kamionka from Lvov, three hundred kilometers away, the Jews were in trouble. To this day, I do not know whether Rebel was warning me that I should try to save myself or if he was simply nervous with such a powerful SS man in the house and wanted me out of the way to prevent trouble. He may have been worried because there I was, a Jew, working for him in his own house without the required yellow square and with a normal haircut, and even with decent looking clothes on my back. I honestly cannot say I know what Rebel's motivation was, but even if, to give him the benefit of the doubt, he wanted to warn me about the imminent threat of the *Aktion*, it would still not erase the thousands and thousands of murdered Jews for whose deaths he was directly responsible in the many labor camps under his jurisdiction.

I promptly left the *hauptsturmführer*'s home and walked back toward camp, stopping first at the Jewish doctors' houses right down the road. I told Doctors Lachman, Reichenberg, and Meibloom what Rebel had said. Although they were all Jews and charged with caring for the camp's inmates, they also treated the SS officers and their families. In fact, Reichenberg was Rebel's personal physician. These doctors were therefore allowed to live outside the camp although they, too, had to wear the yellow patch identifying them as Jews. The doctors knew me from my daily walk and befriended me since I was still rather young. They would call me Halperco, meaning young Halpern.

After analyzing Rebel's statement, "Get lost. Don't you see that Katzman is here?" they all agreed that the end had come, that there would be an *Aktion* the next day. I was still young, and I felt that these men in their forties could see into things I could not. They told me that everyone would have to escape to save themselves. They asked me to tell Mr. Koltz, the *lagerführer*, the Jewish elder or manager of Kamionka, as soon as I returned to camp and warn him of the imminent threat to all Jews there. I did as I was told. When I returned to camp, I rushed to see Koltz and delivered this message: "The doctors say you should open up a gate in the back of the camp to let people run away. Tomorrow there will be an *aktion*. Katzman is here."

Koltz did not believe me or the doctors, however. He said, "The *hauptsturmführer* would never be involved in something like that, and he certainly would tell me if Katzman was a threat." Koltz insisted that the Germans could be trusted, and he was assured that nothing like an *Aktion* was going to happen. "Our work is too important," he insisted. "The German war effort still needs us. The highway to Kiev must be maintained."

I knew Koltz was from Berlin. Like many Germans Jews, he was quite gullible. In this instance, though, I believed his stubborn disbelief in my report and the doctors' warning was not mere naivete but a *desire* not to acknowledge what could happen. This self-delusion was not so apparent with Polish or Russian Jews. In Hebrew there is a saying, "*Kabdeyhoo v'chashdehoo*," ("Respect him and suspect him"). This best sums up the attitude among Eastern European Jews. Koltz then told me that I better not cause a panic among the Jews, but I said: "Look, Koltz, I'm doing what the doctors told me to do."

As I was trying to convince him of the danger, Itzhak Goldfliess came in. He had just returned from working on the road. A German road building engineer, Mr. Kirschner, who liked Itzhak because he was such a good worker, told him that an *Aktion* in which all Jews were to be killed was planned for the following day.

Kirschner was chief engineer for the Otto Heil construction company. He worked the laborers hard, demanding perfection under extremely difficult circumstances. With his German mentality, Kirschner could simply not understand when someone was unable to work well, whether because of age, weakness, or ill health. A person who was not working hard drove him crazy. Out of frustration, more than ideology or sadism, he would beat that person, but he was not involved in any mass murders as far as I know and, unlike the Ukrainian overseers, Kirschner always let his people rest at least half an hour, sometimes three quarters of an hour, every day. He would say, "Rest, so you can work." Anyway, he helped save Jewish lives with his clear warning to Goldfliess.

"Mr. Koltz, that means you too," Goldfliess said earnestly. "You've got to run away."

But Koltz did not believe either of us. He thought that because he had a position of leadership and power, just like the *Judenrat* in the cities and towns, either he would be spared or at least would be given ample warning of an impending *Aktion*.

It was beginning to get a little dark, and Goldfliess and I, who believed the warnings, stopped asking questions and trying to persuade Koltz. Already we had noticed that certain men were not around the camp. Zuckerman, the *kapo*, for example, had not returned since early morning. It soon became obvious that he and others who were able to move more freely in and out of the camp had already fled.

Another ominous sign was the clearing out of Kamionka II. Kamionka I and II were about five kilometers from each other. There were about three thousand inmates in number I, and about two thousand in II. The inmates in Kamionka II worked almost exclusively in the stone quarries and road building. The Jewish leader in Kamionka II was Shaye Moser. After the day's work, all the inmates from Kamionka II were ordered to march to Kamionka I. On the way, Ukrainian policemen and SS officers mercilessly beat the men. Shaye Moser, protective of his people, protested this vicious treatment, and without much ado he was shot on the spot. When we heard about Moser's murder, we knew the end had come.

We who were still inside knew what needed to be done. First, we spread word through the camp that an *Aktion* was planned for the following day and that everyone should try to escape. When it was dark, we cut a hole in the wire fence, thankfully not electrified as in the large concentration camps, just big enough for a man to crawl under. With the police and soldiers patrolling the front gate, it was rather easy for us to get through the fence in the back of the camp undetected and escape into the corn fields not far away. Since it was summer, the corn was high, and it would provide safe cover, at least for the night. Although I had decided on escaping, I also thought it would be best to stay close by, in the corn field, just in case it all turned out to be a false alarm. If there was no *Aktion*, I reasoned, I could always sneak back into camp and perform my duties at the *hauptsturmführer*'s house while I waited out the war.

Of the five thousand Jews in the two camps, only about three hundred escaped, and of these, only thirty-six survived the war. The rest were killed by the Germans and Ukrainians. Everyone in Kamionka who chose to escape was able. We were all given sufficient warning, and everyone was told where the hole in the fence was. Of course, many were too sick, weak, or old to get past the fence or would have been unable to sustain themselves once outside. The world beyond the fence may have meant freedom, but it did not mean safety. The Germans and their informers were still everywhere, and the Ukrainians were still involved in killing Jews. Life on the outside was one of constant fleeing and hiding, always with the imminent threat of capture. Many inmates were just plain afraid. Some who decided to stay in camp began to pray, and as I went under the fence, I could hear their prayers in Hebrew calling out to their Maker.

I ran into the corn fields and stared at the stars blinking overhead. I was about two hundred yards away, close enough to hear everything that might go on in camp, far enough away not to be seen. I wanted to stay awake, afraid that something of importance might happen at any moment. I tried to keep my eyes open, but all my efforts were in vain. Wondering where Arie had run off to, I lay down among the corn stalks and fell asleep. I was awakened at four o'clock that morning. It was *Shabbat*, and I remember thinking that the Germans always liked killing us on our *yamim tovim* (holidays). By the sounds of the SS surrounding the camp, their final liquidation of camp inmates had begun.

Rebel did not want Kamionka liquidated and resisted just a little at first. His opposition was not the result of some sudden burst of humanitarianism, of course. Rather, with the end of the camp would come the end of his little kingdom, and if he were no longer needed to run this conglomeration of death camps, his chances of being sent east to the Russian front were much greater.

Because of what had recently occurred at a camp about twenty-five kilometers away where the Jews joined partisan groups that preceded the advancing Russian army, the Germans were determined not to give their enemies any more soldiers. The Germans were afraid of the partisans because of their fighting power and, more importantly, their wrath. The Germans also wanted to destroy all evidence of their evil by exterminating the witnesses.

Being only two hundred yards away, I was able to hear everything that happened in camp. Right away, the Germans began to shoot. They ordered everyone out of the lice-infested barracks, and people were shot as they stepped outside. I wanted to stand to see what was happening. I also wanted to flee. I knew that if I moved, they would see the corn moving, and that would have meant the end for me. Some of those who were hiding in the fields stood up and were immediately shot. I heard them moaning all around me. So I lay there, in the high corn, as quietly as I could and moved as little as possible. All day long

In July 1995, while visiting Kamionka with my family, I met with the mayor and made arrangements to erect a monument to the victims in Kamionka camp.

I prayed to God to save me and protect Arie, who had also run away. I suspected that, like me, he was lying low somewhere nearby, waiting for the *Aktion* to be over. I heard the Germans bark orders in their gruff voices, telling people to stand here, to stand there. I even recognized some of them. Then I heard shots. Koltz was indeed not killed that day but was taken away to Tarnopol, only to be killed a few weeks later at another *Aktion*.

Group after group of Jews interned at the Kamionka labor camp, thousands altogether, were killed that summer day. Throughout the gunfire and despite the screaming, I could hear a violin playing and a woman's beautiful voice singing German lieder in the background. Among the few women imprisoned at Kamionka was an exceptionally good violinist and singer. Rebel liked her playing and singing, and he gave her extra food whenever she performed for him. Throughout the *Aktion* she was ordered to play the violin and sing songs requested by the *hauptsturmführer*. This "master race" had perfected the art of sadism. They tortured her by having her provide background music for her people's slaughter. And then, right before they were all through with their murders, Rebel had her killed.

The Germans and Ukrainians then piled all the dead bodies into a large ditch constructed in the camp and set the bodies on fire. I could feel the heat of the blaze. I could smell the flesh being consumed. Tears ran uncontrollably down my face. My poor *mamale*. My poor *tatale*. *Am Yisrael* reduced to this. Burnt corpses without graves. I didn't even try to stop the tears, and in spite of them, or because of them, I began to whisper aloud to myself the Mourner's *Kaddish*.

After the fires died out, I heard the Germans order their men to bathe and eat and rest early. They would have another full day tomorrow, but for now their day's work was over.

On July 10, 1943, *Zayin b'Tammuz*, Kamionka was completely liquidated.

At a gathering of the survivors of Kamionka, left to right, Jack Brenman, Emil Gottlieb, Sam Halpern, Herman Brenman, Eddie Brenman, Ziggy Gottlieb, Izador Halicher, Arie Halpern, and Abus Zaidman.

The Hayloft

I waited for the Germans to finish their slaughter. And then I waited some more. Once the sun had completely set and the stars filled the sky, once I could no longer hear German orders being barked and boots pounding the dirt, I decided to leave the corn field. I felt compelled to run far from this place, which reeked of blood, bullets, and charred flesh. I also feared that German soldiers might come into the fields surrounding the camp with their large, vicious dogs in search of those who had run away before the *Aktion*. Or maybe they would start randomly shooting rounds of ammunition between the high stalks of corn to scare us out of hiding.

At about 10 o'clock at night, I stood up slowly, stiff from sitting in one position for over twenty-four hours. I was fine, thank God, but with all the killing around me, I had an irrational need to make sure I was intact. A sense of disbelief surrounded me: had I really escaped the slaughter? Were the hundreds of men I shared barracks with, the thousands I saw every day in and around the camp compound, all dead?

Slowly, cautiously, I made my way through the corn field and, after about fifteen minutes of terror, came upon the farmhouse of the Sapun family. They were Ukrainians, and I was not at all sure of the reception I would receive as an escaped Jew from Kamionka. Despite hunger and thirst, I sneaked into the barn where hay and corn were stored and stretched out to rest for a while. After the frantic twenty-four hours I had just endured, I fell asleep immediately. It was not a deep sleep, though, and on Sunday morning when the woman of the house came into the barn, I woke. I decided to present myself and ask her for food.

I stood up slowly in the hay, and when she saw me, she became frightened. I told her she had nothing to fear, that I intended her no harm. Like many local people, she was not certain whether runaway Jews would take revenge any way they could on the Gentile population. After all we had suffered, I think they half expected us to wreak violence on their property and lives. Of course, we didn't. I was still focused on survival, not revenge, and besides, I wasn't violent by nature.

I asked her to tell me everything she knew about what had happened to the Jews of Kamionka. She had heard that everyone had been shot and then burned. The bodies were doused with gasoline, and rubber tires were thrown on top to help keep the fire going. The fire had burned for hours, the smell and ashes drifting over the entire area. Some local farmers had been recruited to cover the mounds of burnt corpses with earth. Then she told me I could not remain on her property. When one of the doctors from Kamionka had run away, she explained, a Ukrainian neighbor agreed to hide him. Somehow the Germans had learned about the offer, and when they came into the house, they killed not only the doctor but the farmer and his family.

She said, "I'm too afraid to keep you."

She ran out of the barn and into her house, only to return a couple minutes later with bread and some milk in a bottle. "Here," she said to me, "take these and please go. I'm so afraid I'll be killed."

I took the drink and food and thanked her. I understood her fear and never judged anyone harshly who was unwilling to jeopardize a family by hiding Jews. Those who did take the risk were saints; those who did not were merely human.

I decided right then that I would return to the village of Ivanofka, about eight kilometers from Chorostkow. Through many years of business, I knew quite a number of Christian families there and felt that I would have a better chance of finding someone willing to hide me in Ivanofka. I decided to try the Gorniaks first. After all, hadn't Jan Gorniak written me in camp, urging that I run away, and hadn't the family generously provided mine with a sack of flour? Later on, when Jews had been confined to the ghetto, Jan drove through town on his way to collect firewood from the forest and stopped to ask Arie how he was doing. By then, most Gentiles avoided Jewish acquaintances for fear of 'offending' the Germans. The day Jan stopped his wagon for Arie, my brother explained my family's situation:

"It's pretty bad," he said. "My brother is in the labor camp. . . . I'm planning to run away because I think they're going to try and kill all the Jews. Why don't you come inside for a moment?"

Jan entered the house, and Arie gave him feather beds and pillows along with other bedding articles and clothing.

"If I'm alive after the war," Arie said, "and if you want to then, you can give me back some of this clothing if I need it. If I'm not alive, since you are such a nice man to have stopped to talk to a Jew in the ghetto, to have helped my family in other ways, too, then better these things should stay with you than one of these others who run around here."

Jan quietly took the items, not fully understanding the young Jew's motivation. How clever Arie was; later, after the war, having some of these items made an enormous difference in our lives.

From the Sapun house it was quite easy to walk into the fields of tall vegetation, and I soon lay down to rest some more. I had time. I knew I would have to walk mainly at night when few people were out and the darkness would provide additional cover. I remained in a near-by field until dusk and then slowly, like a spy on a secret mission, made my way through the dense foliage. I did not know in which direction I was walking, but judged, from Kamionka's location and its relation to the farmhouse, where I needed to be headed. That night, I walked through the fields until dawn. As soon as I heard farmers and their families beginning morning chores, I found a hidden spot in a field and slept.

On the second and third nights as I started on my trek through the dark, I approached a Ukrainian farmhouse. Knocking softly on the kitchen door, I waited for the woman of the house.

"Will you sell me a piece of bread?" I would ask when she arrived, holding out the few zlotys I had received in one of the packages from home and kept with me throughout my time in Kamionka.

On both occasions, the women refused my money; in fact, they never even acknowledged the offer. The women simply gave me bread and milk. These peasants wanted to help a starving man, but they were afraid to get more deeply involved. So they spoke little. They didn't ask if I was a Jew. They didn't ask me where I had come from or where I was going. It was clear to anyone who bothered to notice that I was a Jew from a labor camp. I was so thin and dirty at that point, where else would I be from? By not asking any questions, though, they could pretend not to know. Then they abruptly closed their doors when I turned and walked away to find refuge in the fields.

In the early morning of my second day of walking, I had to cross a road to get from one field to another. Just as I was running across, I saw a Ukrainian man on a horse just a few yards away. He saw me too and came galloping over. I was so frightened I froze.

"You a Jew?" he asked gruffly.

"Yeah," I said, knowing it was futile to lie. I was obviously a Jew. And how could I run? I was on foot; I was weak and disoriented. He, on the other hand, was tall and strong, he was from the area, and he was on horseback.

"Come with me to the police," he said.

I knew that if I let him take me to the police, they would kill me. After all I had managed to live through, my life would be over. A change of mood came over me, and I decided to resist. I would fight him physically if need be; I would try to run away. I had nothing to lose. If I won, I could continue running. If I lost, he would take me to the police. Then suddenly he said:

"You have any money?"

"A little," I replied.

"What else do you have?" he continued.

"Here," I said, reaching into my pocket, "I have this lighter."

Only a few days before, a German officer visiting the *hauptsturmführer*'s house had given me this nice German lighter as a tip for shining his boots. It worked well and was an impressive piece.

"You need this?" I asked. "Take it, it's yours."

The Ukrainian leaned down from his horse and took the lighter from my hand. As he was admiring it, I ran into the corn fields with his tacit consent. Without exchanging a single word, he had agreed to let me go. I have often thought of how the small things along the way saved my life. In this instance, it was a lighter. At other times, it was befriending a doctor or knowing how to ride a horse.

After this incident, I was more careful about crossing roads. I was not sure if I was headed in the right direction. I did not have a compass, and I could not ask anyone. In fact, I deliberately avoided everyone. I walked into the field and felt lost. Should I go right? Should I go left? Where did the nearby village lie? I avoided any villages and the risk that I would be turned over to the Gestapo or local police. Where was Chorostkow? Trembowla? Ivanofka? As I was struggling with these questions, a brown sparrow flew by me. It was flying low and slow, and I could see its delicate wings catch the wind and its small eyes looking out, as if stealing a glance at me. Not knowing what else to do, I decided to follow the bird. For a number of hours I ran and stumbled through the fields following the flight of the little bird, not knowing where she was taking me. Irrationally, I felt a bond with the bird and thought she had come to guide me. After an exhausting run, I lost track of her. It was as if she suddenly soared straight up into the sky.

At this point I was at the edge of a field. Timidly, I poked my head out from between the high stalks of wheat and saw that the bird had led me to a highway with which I was familiar. From this point, I could not only find my way to Ivanofka but could easily target the Gorniak's home. If they would not shelter me, I would go to the next family on my mental list. Remaining in the fields, I followed the highway all the way to my destination. This time, the companionship of a delicate, low-flying bird saved my life.

*

On Tuesday, July 13, after three days of walking through fields and forests, much of the time in the rain, I arrived at the Gorniak farm. It was already late in the evening and I walked through the backyard, passing a large vegetable garden beside the house. Since it was summer, the garden was filled with tomatoes and cucumbers, beets and potatoes, delicious vegetables I had not seen or eaten in a very long time. When I walked a little closer, I could see Jan Gorniak, bless his memory, standing in the front yard. I knew Jan well, not only because he was a good friend of my older brother, Avrum Chaim, but because we had done business together before the war. My father often hired the Gorniaks to transport wheat from our store to the train. In addition, his mother, Tatyana, had gone to school with my mother. The families had known each other for quite some time.

Jan Gorniak and his wife Josefa.

I approached the house cautiously. Jan saw me. He held up his hand as if to say, "Don't talk." He pointed to the barn and indicated that I should go up into the hayloft. I was a little suspicious, considering all I had witnessed. Not surprisingly, I trusted no one.

"Hurry, into the hayloft," he said.

I obeyed. From the urgency and care in his voice, I knew I was in safe hands. Above the horses and cows, I scampered up a narrow ladder and in the dark buried myself in the fresh, sweet-smelling hay. It had been sixteen months since I had slept on anything soft. I didn't care about my hunger or about how long they would let me stay. I was dry and about to fall into a deep sleep. "Aah, this is wonderful" I moaned to myself when suddenly a hand grabbed my arm. Oh God, I thought. A trap. I should not have trusted Jan. I will be turned over to the Germans and then shot. I was about to begin saying the *Shma Yisrael* when I opened my eyes.

"Who's this?" a voice asked. It was so dark I could see only the outline of a face, but the voice! The voice I knew so well was music to my ears.

"Arie," I cried. "It's me, it's me."

"Shmerele," answered the beloved voice of my brother.

Without discussing where we would go after escaping into the fields surrounding Kamionka, both Arie and I had decided not only to return to the Chorostkow area but to the Gorniaks. I grabbed him in my arms, and he held me; we cried with joy and relief.

"If God spared us," I said to Arie, "and we lived through the atrocities at Kamionka, and now, without discussing our intentions, we both made it here to the Gorniak's and are now together again, I hope to God that we will make it through this war." We dried our tears and settled into the luxurious hay.

Tatyana Gorniak, bless her memory, came up the stairs to the hayloft. Tears were pouring down her soft face. She sat before us and spoke.

"Thank God you children are here," she said, taking our hands in hers. "Last night your mother came to me in a dream and asked me to save you. I promised her I would. Thank God you came here. I will do all I can to fulfill her wish and my promise."

Only then did Arie understand why Jan had asked that morning "Where is your brother?" when he arrived in the yard. Arie had answered that he didn't know where I was but that we had both run away from the *Aktion* at the camp. That is why Jan was standing outside his house that evening: he was waiting for me. Tatyana cried some more; Arie and I choked back tears. Who could understand the workings of the world, why we had come together at this merciful house, and how our mother, God rest her soul, had visited Tatyana with a request, knowing her sons were on their way.

Tatyana Gorniak and her children.

Tatyana brought lots of food for us: fresh potatoes, fresh bread, borscht, and sour cream. This was the kind of food I had not even seen, let alone eaten, in more than two years. It was the most delicious feast of my life. It is hard to describe how I felt eating that tasty, lovingly prepared food. The spirit of God had been mixed into the bread, and with each bite our souls and bodies were strengthened.

Then Jan came up. "It is a horrible and tough war," he said. "We must help each other." These glorious phrases were full of promise.

When I arrived at the Gorniak doorstep, I expected that if I were lucky, this good family might hide me for a day or two. Or, I thought, they might give me bread but tell me to keep moving. Or, considering the risks to their own lives and their children, they might refuse to help at all and just order me off the property. In the Netherlands, Belgium, and France when Jews were found hiding in Gentile homes, the Jews were killed and the Gentiles beaten, but in Poland, sheltering Jews was dealt with much more severely. The Jews were killed as well as the Gentile family, and the house and farm were then burned to the ground. The law requiring this awful punishment was put into effect in Poland because while the Germans considered Western European citizens human, they deemed Poles less than human, not just above Jews who were considered subhuman.

Josefa, Jan's wife, and the younger brother, Michael, came to greet Arie and me. The entire family hugged and kissed us. After two and half years of being called animals and treated sadistically by Germans and Ukrainians, the affection of these Gentiles was incredibly moving. With these simple acts they invited Arie and me back into the brotherhood of man, into the human race. When they embraced us, I knew we were among a family of angels.

Then Arie told us about what had happened to him as he made his way through the fields and villages. Two days earlier, on Sunday, he was passing through the village of Welawcze. He had left the fields for a while and was walking down the main street of the village when he saw a group of Ukrainian policemen standing around talking. He knew that if he walked by, they would immediately notice him. Gaunt, dirty, and unkempt, his appearance betrayed his identity as a Jew or someone right out of a concentration camp. If they caught him, they would no doubt kill him themselves or happily turn him over to the

Gestapo. He might then be killed or sent to Auschwitz or one of the other large death factories still in operation.

He stopped in his tracks, not knowing what to do. He was reluctant to turn back, for he was only about two hundred feet away, and he suspected that one or two of them might already have noticed him. Turning around and walking quickly in the other direction might arouse suspicions.

While trying to decide what to do, Arie noticed a Ukrainian priest coming down the street. He went over to the priest and, as was the custom in those days, took the priest's hand and kissed it. Then he looked straight into his eyes and asked, "Can you tell me where I might find the road to Trembowla?"

The priest looked at Arie, knowing right away that this disheveled young man was a Jew, and they linked arms. The two men walked together, arm in arm, through the town, past the policemen. When they reached the outskirts, the priest unlinked his arm and said to Arie, "Go with God."

There were Ukrainians and Poles who risked their lives to save Jews, and there were others, like the Ukrainian neighbor who betrayed my wife's cousin although they had known each other their whole lives. Thank God the Gorniaks were righteous, God-fearing people who, like the priest, made the moral choice to try to save two Jewish brothers from certain death.

Twice a day, early in the morning and once in the evening, Tatyana or some other member of the family would bring a covered pail of food into the barn. She made it look a little sloppy so none of the neighbors would suspect that the mess was for humans. She wanted them to think the pail contained table scraps for pigs.

Michael Gorniak, who was fourteen at the time, also slept with us in the hayloft. We were forever insisting that he return to the house.

"Go," I would say to him almost daily. "You have a nice bed in the house. It's warm there, not too hot and cold like here. It's too unpleasant for a boy your age. Go."

We tried to convince him that we had endured much worse at Kamionka and that compared with the camp, the hayloft was heaven, but he would not be dissuaded. He always responded to our entreaties by saying, "If you can sleep here, I can sleep here."

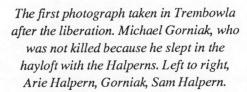

The first photograph taken in Trembowla after the liberation. Michael Gorniak, who was not killed because he slept in the hayloft with the Halperns. Left to right, Arie Halpern, Gorniak, Sam Halpern.

Hungry for news from the front, one of the family members would make the eight kilometer trip to the city every day to buy newspapers. Sometimes there were no Polish papers available, only German ones. Most people considered buying the German papers too dangerous since everyone knew that the average Pole understood no German, unlike many Jews. So if a Pole bought a German paper, he was practically announcing that he was hiding Jews. Jan didn't care, however. He wanted us to keep up with the news so badly that when he had no choice, he would buy the German papers. Arie and I would pore over them for hours, analyzing, often by what was not said, how the war was going.

When I arrived at the Gorniaks', the Russian front was about two thousand kilometers away. The German army was deep into Russia, not far from Moscow. Then they began to be pushed back. Every day we consulted a map to track the retreat of the German army, the advance of the Russians. We calculated how far the Russian front would move. We were often wrong and would correct our optimistic estimates with each newspaper article we carefully dissected. Sometimes the Russians were able to move three hundred kilometers in a few days, and sometimes they managed only ten kilometers in three months. It all depended on the terrain. Rivers and mountains could slow them down. We tracked them as closely as we could, knowing the Russian army was our ticket to freedom, to life.

When we weren't keeping up with political and military fronts, we prayed to God, reciting as many of the prayers as we could by heart. We had two pages from a *siddur*, of Psalms, that Tatyana had received at the local grocery store. The war had resulted in a tremendous paper shortage, and Jewish prayer books were commonly used in the packaging of all sorts of goods. One day Tatyana had bought some sugar, and when she came home immediately recognized that the paper it was wrapped in was from a Hebrew book. She gave the sheets to us, and it was these *tehillim*, these psalms, that Arie and I said two or three times every day.

In between, we would play cards. Often the days dragged by slowly, and sometimes they passed quickly. It all depended on the news. Good news from the front helped speed the day along. Bad news made every minute seem like an hour, every hour an eternity.

While we were grateful for the care and attention the Gorniaks gave us, we were also in constant fear and pain. Having so much time every day, with so little to do, provided us with the opportunity to think about the loss of our parents, older brother, and other relatives and friends. I was acutely aware of how close to home I was living, of how everything I had once known and loved had been destroyed by the Germans.

Man is born to labor, to use his mind and body to produce, and I came from a long line of hard working people. Being confined to the hayloft for weeks on end therefore proved stressful for me. I wanted to get out into the world, to use my hands, to use my head to create. But I was a prisoner still, under constant surveillance. The slightest miscalculation could cost the lives of everyone I lived with. So I learned to practice patience, passively to watch the sky turn from bright blue to dark black. I stared at the stars and hoped that one day I would walk out of the Gorniak barn a liberated man, able to throw myself into a productive life filled with joy, safety, and laughter.

Notwithstanding the risk, Arie and I, desperate for some physical activity, would sometimes come down from the hayloft. In the barn, we cut straw for the horses. We needed the exercise, to use our muscles, to sweat. Jan would never have dreamed of asking us to help on the farm; it was far too risky, but we wanted to contribute something to this household whose hard work and courage were keeping us alive.

Even Tatyana Gorniak's deaf, mute brother, who lived with the family, looked out for us. He would come around to visit and bring us some bread. By caring for us, by indicating with his hand held over his mouth that he could not speak, he let us know that he would never tell anyone that we were hiding in the hayloft.

The family's extreme care for our welfare was made clear early on. Just before we arrived, one of Jan's two horses had died. With only one horse, he could not be as productive on the farm as he needed to be. When my brother and I learned of this situation, we gave Jan what money we had so he could replace the horse. A while later, Jan needed some more money, and when he came to us for help, we told him that we had nothing more to give, that we had already given him everything. When Tatyana heard about this, she became upset. She felt we should not be without money since at some point we might have to leave our hide-out. She therefore borrowed money from her uncle in order to repay us and scolded us that we were never to be without funds. After all, the Germans could search the farm any day, and we would be forced to flee.

Another time, a command was issued from the German government that all farmers had to give one sack of grain to the army for every acre of land they owned. The problem was that Jan did not have enough grain. When we discussed the decree, he said he didn't know what to do.

"If you don't give the proper amount of grain, they're going to come looking for it. Then they'll find us," I said. "Go to your neighbors, borrow some, and tell them you'll return it later at harvest time."

Jan agreed and borrowed grain from his neighbors, but we found out, in time thank God, that the Germans were coming to inspect the barn anyway. That morning Arie and I ran off to Father Lubovich's barn. He was the Ukrainian priest, the father of my school friend, Piotr, with whom I had once done a great deal of business. The priest did not see us, but we knew exactly where he stored his many sacks of grain, and among them Arie and I sat for hours. We knew we could trust the priest since Tatyana had confessed to him that she was hiding the Halpern boys.

"Don't tell anyone else," he counseled her. "And if you're ever in trouble or they are, if you don't have enough food for them, send them to my house."

We knew the priest was a righteous man, a good friend, a God-fearing Christian. Thank God for these people. They saved our lives and those of a handful of Poland's three million Jews. After dark when we knew the Germans must have completed the inspection, we crept out of the storehouse and quietly made our way back to Gorniak's barn.

There was a custom among the Jews of Galicia to eat wide noodles with cheese before *Tisha B'Av*. Because I had already figured out a way to keep track of the Jewish calendar, I knew that Tisha B'Av was approaching. I knew I would fast and recite by heart the few lines of Jeremiah's *Lamentations* I remembered. "How does the city sit solitary/That was once full of people! How has she become a widow!"

What I did not expect was the plate of wide noodles and cheese that Tatyana Gorniak brought up to the hayloft before sunset on *erev Tisha B'Av*. Somehow she, too, knew that the day of mourning for the lost Jerusalem was about to begin, and, knowing our tradition, she decided—like a devoted mother—to prepare the traditional repast. This act of kindness meant so much to me. Not only were the Gorniaks risking their lives in saving ours, not only did they treat us like friends, but they showed respect for our spiritual traditions. That *Tisha B'Av*, despite the war still being waged all around us and the losses we had suffered in our family, Arie and I felt privileged and grateful.

Jan Gorniak was often able to procure pure grain alcohol. Many nights I would make vodka for him from the alcohol. I was an old hand at this process, which I had learned at the distillery during the first Russian occupation of Chorostkow and Trembowla. Sometimes during the day, Jan would invite German soldiers into the house, and together they would drink the vodka I had made. Jan tried to keep on the good side of the local Germans. He knew they were more likely to give the benefit of the doubt to a farmer in whose house they had eaten good meals and drunk vodka. He also wanted to appear as if he had nothing to hide.

Nonetheless, a rumor began circulating in town that the Gorniaks were hiding Jews. Jan dealt with this complication by removing a substantial part of the roof so that everyone could see he had nothing but hay in the barn. Then he rebuilt the roof. Throughout this process Arie and I remained tucked away in the barn downstairs. When the new roof was completed, we climbed back up the ladder to our more permanent hiding place.

At Christmas 1943 and New Year's of 1944, the Gorniaks threw family parties. After nightfall, Arie and I crept over from the barn and joined the festivities in the house. We drank the vodka that I had made and sang Polish songs. We ate the delicious food Tatyana and Josefa had prepared for the holidays. We celebrated life and looked forward to the end of the horrendous war.

Some Polish and Ukrainian families saved Jewish lives for money. It was a business transaction: so much money for so much time, so much money for so much water and food. But this was not the case with us and the Gorniaks. They saved our lives out of friendship rather than monetary compensation. The Gorniaks were wonderful, brave people.

In January 1944, about two months before our liberation, a group of Ukrainian ultra-nationalists came to the Gorniak farm, and for no reason other than that the family was Polish, they murdered Piotr Gorniak, Tatyana's husband, and her deaf-mute brother. The Ukrainians were simply bloodthirsty. In the beginning of the German occupation, Ukrainians had been recruited by the occupying army as important aides in transporting and eventually annihilating Jews. Now that there were no more Jews in the region, these same men decided to focus their attention on the Poles, whom they hated as well. They chose the Gorniak farm to vent their venom. That night they descended like a plague, and a wonderful family lost two men to the Ukrainian thugs.

As usual, we were in the hayloft and heard the Ukrainians enter the yard. We were very frightened, thinking that somehow they had found out about us and come to kill us, but they entered the house rather than the barn. Then we heard screaming and Piotr Gorniak, Jan's father, begging for his life and that of his brother-in-law. Then shots rang out.

I cannot find words to describe how terrible I felt. Even today, I feel the pain of that moment, the helplessness and rage. It was like hearing my own family being killed. I wanted to run out of the barn and strangle the Ukrainians with my own hands. I wanted to grab a

Aunt Sheindel, whose hiding place was betrayed for 5 kilos of sugar.

rifle and shoot them. But I could do nothing. If we were all going to remain alive, I had to stay still. It was the worst feeling in the world to sit there quietly, hearing butchers slaughter good, innocent people.

After the shooting, Tatyana came up to the hayloft. She had been crying, and we didn't know what to say to her. I half expected her to say something like, "See, I'm saving Jewish lives, I'm trying to do the right thing, and they're killing us." Instead, she looked lovingly at Arie and me and said:

"Thanks to you, my son Michael is alive." She paused. "If he had been in the house, they would have killed him as well. Thank God you are here, and he sleeps with you."

Had Jan not been away from the house that night on some farm business, he too would have been killed.

A few days later, disaster struck again. The Germans had posted notices all over the district offering a reward of five kilos of sugar for anyone who revealed where Jews were hiding. On January 4, Tatyana came into the barn wringing her hands and crying. "Oh, oh, terrible things have happened. Eight people have been killed, betrayed by Anna Bartestka for sugar."

All eight people were members of my family who had been hiding nearby: Aunt Sheindel and her two children, Herzele and Pepa; my cousin Moshele Wolfson and his two children; and my cousin Naftali Krautshtick and his daughter. They had been living in a field of potatoes. There, farmers had dug enormous ditches used as storage bins. These fields were far from the village and considered relatively safe. My cousins would spend the day in the fields and at night sleep in the storage bins.

Once or twice a week, one of the local farmers dropped off bread and milk. My family had survived until two months before liberation with the help of Ukrainian and Polish farmers. Mrs. Balutchka, one of the farmers who delivered food every week had been a school friend of my cousin's and was committed to saving her, her children, and the other members of the family who had gone into hiding with her. All eight were executed by the Gestapo.

We were shocked by this horrible tragedy, the loss of eight lives for about ten pounds of sugar, and tried to be even more careful, knowing that there could be many others in the area looking for a way to claim the German reward.

Sixteen young Jewish boys were also being hidden in the nearby village of Wigdorowka. They had also managed to survive through the worst of the war years until they, too, were discovered by the Gestapo in early March of 1944, just weeks before the Russians took possession of the region again.

One month later, in February, Jan Gorniak came home with a German newspaper. He had not been able to find a Polish or Ukrainian paper and was desperate for news. He brought the paper into the barn for us to translate. We descended from the hayloft and were standing by the cows. We had just finished reading the main news item about how much territory had fallen into Russian hands and how the front along the border had been pushed westward. We were smiling and slapping each other on the backs when all of a sudden we heard Marisha, Jan's three-year-old daughter, call into the barn.

"Tato, policeman. Tato, policeman."

She was only three years old but knew that a policeman on the family property was not good news.

Jan threw the barn doors closed, which gave us a couple minutes to scramble up to the hayloft. Once Arie and I were safely hidden, Jan opened the doors. There stood a local Ukrainian policeman. Jan looked as if he were grooming a horse and in a casual, friendly voice called to the policeman, "How are you?"

The policeman stepped into the barn, "Fine, fine, and you, how are you, Gorniak?"

"Wonderful," Jan said. "My horse is in good health this season, and the cows are giving excellent milk. What more can I ask for?" He patted his horse on the nose and then said, "Come inside. Let's have a drink," and he led the policeman out of the barn. As they walked toward the house, Jan yelled to his wife, "Go prepare a nice lunch for the officer."

The policeman said to Jan. "I want you to take me to the neighboring village. Okay?"

If it were not war time and if Jan were not afraid, he might have resisted this imposition on his time and horse. He might have even refused outright. But Jan was in no position to refuse. Not only did he say yes, but he went even further.

"Of course I'll take you," he said. "But before we go, you have to eat and drink in my house."

They went into the house, and Gorniak opened a bottle of vodka and after an hour of eating and drinking heavily, he took the policeman ten kilometers to another village. In this way, Jan not only made sure the officer would not be back soon to snoop around the farm, he made the officer feel that Jan was a friend.

That afternoon we owed our lives to little Marisha. Her cleverness had saved us. Sweetly, innocently, she had called out to her father as if to tell him that a friendly visitor had just arrived. But with that one word, "policeman," she had given us the time to hide, which is why we are alive today.

Unfortunately, Marisha is no longer alive. Thank God, however, she had two lovely children, whom I visit whenever I am in Poland. I am privileged to be able to help them. The Gorniaks saved my life. They treated me like a member of their own family. Until today, all their children and grandchildren call Arie and me "Uncle" and Gladys and Eva "Auntie."

On March 22, 1944, Russian tanks moved through the area. The German Army had already retreated days before. The war was far from over, it would be another fourteen months before Germany surrendered to the Allied forces, but for us this was liberation day. Under the Russians, we could come out of hiding and begin anew.

Arie and I walked out of the Gorniak barn into the light of day. It was an overwhelming feeling to breathe the fresh country air and stare at the sky without fear of being murdered. We looked around us and then at one another. We had survived, and we were together.

It was one day after the vernal equinox, the official inauguration of spring, and like the natural world around us, we began a journey of rebirth. Tatyana Gorniak cupped a hundred zlotys in her hands, she blew on them as if to imbue them with extraordinary powers, and then pressed them into our hands.

"God should give you luck," she said, with tears in her eyes.

Before the war, a hundred zlotys were worth something. At that point in the war, though, they were practically worthless, perhaps equivalent to ten cents today, but they were all she had. The zlotys were a symbolic gift, which meant a great deal to us.

Before we left, the Gorniaks told us that if the Germans were to break through the Russian lines again, we should return to their home as fast as possible. You cannot imagine how important this invitation was to us, to know that this family cared so much about us that they were already making contingency plans in case this horrible turn of events occurred.

Arie and I decided to return to Chorostkow to see if we could find any family and friends who had survived the German occupation. Our town was only a few kilometers away. For the first time in more than two years, we were free to walk the roads and say hello to a passing farmer or watch the sun move across the sky, or merely amble along without being beaten by vicious guards. Full of expectations, we walked the road we knew so well. Finally, after years of horror, death and destruction, we were free men heading home.

After Liberation

We walked for two hours to reach Chorostkow. On the way, we were stopped by a group of Russian soldiers who demanded to see our papers. Papers? I hadn't had proper documents since I was taken to Kamionka.

"We are Jews," I explained to the Russian soldiers. "We have just spent eight and a half months hiding in a hayloft. We are camp survivors. All our papers were taken away from us a long time ago by the Germans."

They did not comprehend our predicament and took us to the local military headquarters. There, the captain in charge listened to our story. He himself was a Jew and understood.

"But you must have documents," he insisted. "The next group of Russian soldiers you meet on the road may kill you. They may think you are spies or German soldiers attempting to run away."

He took the necessary papers from his desk and slowly, carefully filled out our personal information. Then he sent us on our way.

When we finally got to Chorostkow, everything looked different. Most of the Jewish homes in the center of town had been leveled as were the small synagogues. Only one wall remained of the Great Synagogue. Some of the Jews who managed to survive the German occupation returned to find their homes still standing.

But our home was gone, which hurt us very much. Arie and I were more concerned about people than buildings. We knew our parents were no longer alive, but had other relatives survived? When we first walked into Chorostkow, I stopped an elderly Polish man on the street.

"Are there any Jews in town?" I asked him.

"Oh," he said, "there are many, many Jews in town."

Many, many Jews! How happy I was! There had only been two thousand Jews to begin with in Chorostkow, and now I was being told that there were many in town. There was a good chance that among those many, many were friends and family members.

Arie and I quickened our pace and began to look for Jews. I did not see anyone, neither Gentile nor Jew, and began to wonder if anyone was really there at all. We kept walking up and down the stone streets when suddenly I heard voices coming from the home of Baruch Stein, our dear friend for many years. As I approached the house, I heard Yiddish being spoken. I did not hesitate. I did not even knock. I just opened the door and entered. And inside I indeed saw Jews. Everyone who had managed to return to Chorostkow—a total of 26 Jews—was living together in that one house. I asked right away if anyone else had shown up. They pointed to me and Arie. That's all. To the Polish man who had claimed that many, many Jews were in town, twenty-six was a large number. Even after the slaughter of millions, the local population was still so anti-Semitic that a couple of dozen Jews was perceived as too many.

None who survived and were living in that house were relatives of mine. Some were friends, most were acquaintances. Among the survivors were two sisters, Mathilda and Eva Krenkel. Our family and theirs had been close friends for many years. Over time, Itzhak Goldfliess married Mathilda, and Eva later became my sister-in-law, marrying Arie.

Arie and I stayed in that house for a few days. Then someone came and said that the Germans were returning. We all became frightened, and I went and spoke with a Russian soldier. I asked if it were true that the Germans were coming back.

"I don't think they'll make it back here," he said, "but if I were you, I wouldn't stay. It's still not so safe. Go east, into Russia itself."

We decided to follow his advice but before running away from Chorostkow, we went to see the Polish man with whom Arie had entrusted some clothing and bedding during the war. We asked him if we could have some of the clothing back, and he said that he had given most of it away for food, but he did have my father's black coat with a satin collar—the kind of black coat Hasidic men usually wore on *Shabbat*. He also gave us a pair of black striped pants that had once belonged to our brother, Avrum Chaim.

Arie put on the pants, which were considerably nicer than the ones he was wearing. Then we walked and hitchhiked some sixty kilometers to the Russian border. The trip was dangerous and harrowing because in pockets here and there, the Russians and the Germans were still fighting over every kilometer of land. The Germans were stubborn and unwilling to accept defeat on any level. Luckily for the Allied forces, the Russians, who had suffered so much on their own soil—losing millions and millions, both soldiers and civilians, to the German army—were fighting ferociously with a thirst for revenge. Had the Allied forces on the west been forced to fight Germany alone without the Russians devouring them on the eastern front, the war would have taken much longer and been costlier in British and American lives.

Once we arrived at Podwolochisk, the town right over the border, we decided to sell the coat. Arie went to another village, about two kilometers outside of town. He wanted to barter the coat for something that might be of value to us. At that time there was little money available, and it was practically worthless. But a sack of wheat could be bartered for a pair of boots. Arie went around from group to group with the black coat and satin collar in hand, but there were no takers.

"Who wants a Jewish coat?" the peasants asked.

Arie was becoming discouraged but decided to try one more farmer.

"Would you like to have this coat?" Arie asked the farmer.

"A Jewish coat? Who wants a Jewish coat? But I'll give you two liters of alcohol for your pants."

Without hesitation, Arie answered, "It's a deal."

There had been an alcohol factory in Podwolochisk. When the Germans retreated, the place was looted. The population took as much alcohol as they could. This item was plentiful, at least for a time. Arie thought it could be useful to us as well.

The farmer gave him the alcohol, and Arie handed over his pants. Then he asked, "Can you give me an old pair of pants to go home in?"

The farmer searched through a nearby sack and found a dirty pair filled with holes. But they would do, and with the alcohol in hand, Arie walked back to Podwolochisk to meet me.

I was able to turn the two liters of pure alcohol into four liters of vodka.

With this vodka, we were really able to bargain. We went to a Russian soldier and said, "We'll give you a bottle of vodka for a suit from the army."

The soldier agreed. Next we took the suit to a farmer who gave us bread and eggs for the suit. Then we went to another farmer with some vodka and traded that for a watch. With the watch, we went to a jeweler in town who gave us rubles. Another farmer gave us some fruit for the vodka, and with that we were able to get some butter. The butter was easy enough to sell to housewives, and again we had some more rubles. For three weeks, Arie and I hustled—we traded items back and forth, accepting anything we could determine had a tangible value, and turned it into rubles. In the end, after three weeks of non-stop activity, we had accumulated a good quantity of rubles.

Jews from many towns in eastern Galicia had run away to Podwolochisk. The town was right over the Russian border, and we all felt the border was secure, at least for the time being. Some people, of course, ran deeper into Russia, but many, like us, were reluctant, having had a taste of life under the Russian government after its occupation of eastern Poland in 1939. Certainly we preferred the Russians to the Germans, but in case the war came to a swift end, we wanted to keep our options open. We did not want to get trapped in Russia.

Once we arrived in Podwolochisk, we saw that, just as in Chorostkow, many Jews remained together. They all slept in one room, which was not terribly clean. It was not at all private. Many people had run away from concentration and labor camps, and they were still in a state of shock. I was a free man and felt strongly that I did not want to live under these conditions one hour longer than was absolutely necessary. I told Arie that we were going to take the money we had and rent a room. Instead of living a hundred people to a room, we rented one room in an apartment.

Louis Fried and his wife and little girl from Chorostkow joined us. The Hesheles family from Skala on Zbrucz, whose parents had passed away, lived there with us, too. (Today, Victor and his family, his sister and her family, all live in Brooklyn. And Arie and I lived there.) A total of eight people came to the rented room in Podwoloc. Everyone had his own bed, except for Arie and me who shared a double. It was far from ideal, but it was clean and orderly and certainly manageable.

About two weeks after liberation, the holiday of Passover arrived. There were no *matzot*, no *haggadot*, and no kosher wine, no kosher shank bone, no *haroseth*, no *karpas*, no *maror*. But, thank God, there was plenty of freedom. Our first Passover *seder* after being delivered from Nazi bondage was a glorious event. On the outside, the celebration was extremely modest and brief. But on the inside, this Passover was incomparable. We received a few *matzot* from Jews in a neighboring village. We prepared potatoes and borscht. Arie and I, and the few other friends who shared a room, thus conducted our first *seder* after liberation.

Only sixty kilometers from the front lines, unsure if the Germans would break through and capture this territory and possibly endanger our lives once again, we were intent on celebrating the all-important holiday of Passover, remembering how we were slaves in Egypt and how God delivered us from that hell and brought us to the promised land of our ancestors. Not only did we recount the story as if we had been slaves in Egypt and then redeemed, we knew we had been slaves who had really been redeemed. Bondage was our recent experience, deliverance our most trusted ally.

All the songs, *Dayenu, Avadim Hayeenu, Chag Gadya*, took on new meaning as we sang the ancient verses and rejoiced that we had lived to see this moment. "Next year in Jerusalem!" we called out at the end of the *seder*, expressing the ancient longing to return as a sovereign nation to the land of our ancestors. Knowing that Jews were trying to make this dream a reality, while so many others remained tortured in European prisons and concentration camps, provided us with solace and hope.

For the entire week of Passover, Arie and I ate only potatoes and borscht. Other than the meager pieces we had managed to get for the *seder*, there were no more *matzot*. There was nothing else to eat that was not *chametz*. But being free men, we were certainly not going to forget the affliction of our people, both in Egypt thousands of years earlier and in the death factories of Auschwitz and Chelmno today.

After the holiday, we decided to return to Trembowla to see if anyone else had come back. We also wanted to know if we could establish our lives there again. The German threat was over by then, and we bought ourselves nice suits. With money in our pockets, we returned to Trembowla.

The Jews in the town were as we had left them—with nothing of their own, they approached the local Poles and begged for food. We tried to help as much as we could. We also went to see the Gorniaks and emptied our pockets to help them.

Since the war was still being waged, every man between the ages of eighteen and fifty-four was being called up to fight. Poles, who had not had the opportunity to defend their country under the German occupation, were now rising to the challenge of throwing the oppressive conquerors off their soil. I, too, being a young man in my twenties, was called up to fight.

The day before I was scheduled to report to the train station to join a Russian regiment, I discovered that Mr. Pekar, the director of the distillery from 1939 to 1941, under whose guidance I had worked, had returned to Trembowla. He was again director of nine alcohol factories and had come to get everything running and in order again. The war between Russia and Germany was still raging, and alcohol was desperately needed to make rubber. The rubber was then used to make tires and various weapons.

I had not seen Mr. Pekar in thirty-three months. He had been a chubby, middle-aged man before the war but was now skinny and old. In only two and-a-half years, he looked as if he had aged a decade. When he saw me, he was warm and friendly.

"What are you doing these days, Sasha?" (Sasha was his nickname for me.) "How is your family," he asked, adding gently, "did they survive?"

I told him that my mother and father and eldest brother had been murdered by the Germans, and only Arie was still with me.

"What are you going to do now?" he asked.

"Tomorrow I have to go to the army," I answered.

"Uhuh. Tell me, Sasha, is Bilgreier still alive?" Herman Bilgreier had been the factory manager until 1941. After the Germans occupied the town, they retained him even though he was Jewish because they, too, needed to continue manufacturing alcohol. Bilgreier was the only man left who knew how to run the factory. With his son Dolek, Herman lived on the top floor of the distillery. When the Germans retreated, ten days before the Russians re-occupied, Bilgreier and his son were killed by Ukrainian partisans.

"No, Mr. Pekar," I had to say, sadly. "Bilgreier is not alive. He, too, was killed."

"So then," he replied, "from this moment on, Sasha Galperin [this is how he always pronounced Halpern] is manager of the alcohol factory."

I could not believe my ears. This was a tremendous appointment. Mr. Pekar explained to me that managing the distillery was as important as fighting on the front. Rubber was essential to the war effort.

"Listen," he interrupted my joyful thoughts. "Go to the factory now and begin to organize so we can start production as soon as possible. I want you to do whatever is necessary to make the alcohol."

"Yes, Comrade Pekar," I said and immediately went to the factory to survey the damage.

The factory was in a terrible state. There was garbage everywhere. All the machinery was gone. Only the heavy pieces that had been bolted to the floor remained. Everything inside was gone. How was I to make alcohol for Mr. Pekar under these circumstances?

Potatoes and wheat and yeast were available for money. But the machinery? Even if the money was there, from where would all the machines come during war time? I had an idea, though—a way to get the equipment back.

I took four young men and gave each a borrowed horse and a bugle. As they made their way through the streets of Trembowla and other neighboring villages, they loudly announced to the residents:

"Sasha Halpern is manager of the distillery. He wants to thank you for being kind enough to save the factory machines from the Germans. He has a list of who took what from the factory, he knows exactly where each piece is, and he would like for you to bring them back now so the factory can resume production. Everyone who returns the machines promptly, will be rewarded handsomely.

"Whoever does not cooperate and does not return the machines, they should know the government will come into their homes and take the machines away, and those individuals will be punished."

The bluff worked. Of course, I had no idea who had what, but I guessed that the local population had "looted" the factory floor. In four days every machine part was returned, thousands in all. People had become afraid that the punishment might mean death. The entire population decided to cooperate rather than risk punishment by the Russian government.

The only items not returned were the enormous leather belts used to run the wheels of the machines, having long since been cut up for shoe soles and pants belts. To get the factory back in working order, I needed to find new belts, which would not be easy since there was a severe leather shortage. At first I could not locate any at all, despite searching throughout the neighboring towns. Finally, I learned that in Chernowitz I would be able to purchase the belts on the black market. I traveled all the way there and returned triumphant.

In a matter of three weeks, I had the factory on line. Mr. Pekar was as pleased as could be, and I, too, could not have been happier. With vodka, I was king; with vodka, I could do anything.

In addition, the other managers always came to Mr. Pekar, asking for things, large and small. They called on him to provide everything they needed for the factory and sometimes for their personal use. I was the exact opposite. Not only did I arrange to get the factory up and running entirely by myself, not only did I not need his assistance in providing for myself personally, I actually helped him get settled after nearly three years of absence from Trembowla. I found him an apartment, furniture, and a car. He was not only indebted to me for my efficiency and help, but before long I was his favorite manager.

I had a friend, originally from Moscow, who was made manager of a nearby brick and cement factory. When the friend visited me, he would say: "Sasha, you're much better off than me. It's better to be a watchman in an alcohol factory than manager in a brick and cement factory. Who can drink cement? Who will trade for it?" He was right. With vodka, I could make friends with important officials. I could get goods on and off the black market. I had influence. For example, a few days after Mr. Pekar gave me the job of factory manager, I went before the local draft board to request twenty men to work for me. I already had many men working at the factory, but I wanted these additional employees so that production could be brought up as fast as possible.

Soon, I developed a reputation for running a tight, efficient operation. An article was even published in a Moscow newspaper praising a certain young and energetic manager by the name of Sasha Galperin who had brought up production in the alcohol factory with tremendous speed! A factory's normal output was five hundred liters of alcohol a day, but in my factory we were producing fifteen to sixteen hundred liters. The key to my success was not limiting production to a single eight-hour shift. I decided to keep the factory running twenty-four hours a day. With three consecutive shifts, I tripled production. Ninety percent of the alcohol was sent to factories in Moscow and Kiev for the war effort. The remaining ten percent was kept locally and made into vodka.

Soon after we returned to Trembowla, Arie became ill with typhoid fever and was hospitalized for three weeks. After he recovered, he began to work with me in the factory as an accountant. Then, about five months later, a Russian law was enacted that made it illegal for two relatives to hold high positions in the same factory. The authorities were worried about corruption and theft. Although Arie had to leave the alcohol factory, he managed to get a job as an accountant in another factory. He, too, was earning a good living, had a prestigious job, and, under the circumstances, was doing as well as could be expected. We felt fortunate.

The Ukrainian policeman from Chorostkow, Ivan Ratinsky, who had offered to hide me before I was sent to Kamionka and who, I later learned, had indeed saved the lives of three local Jews, used to visit the distillery in Trembowla. For him, I always had an extra bottle or two of vodka. I made a point of giving vodka to those Gentiles who had saved Jews. It wasn't much compared with their gift of life, but vodka was then a fairly valuable commodity that could be bartered for food or other essential items. I just wanted to do something nice for anyone who helped save a Jewish life. I felt I owed them something.

Later on, Ivan Ratinsky was arrested by the Russian authorities and sent to Siberia. As I mentioned earlier, he had been a fierce Ukrainian nationalist and so had killed many Russians in an effort to wrest territory from Russian control. People said he had killed scores of Russians with his own hands, which shows that the same individual is capable of both great and terrible deeds. Ratinsky was rewarded for saving Jewish lives with vodka and the esteem with which all Jews treated him. Then he was punished by the NKVD for the barbarous murders of Russians that he apparently committed.

As manager of the distillery, I was issued a pistol, which I wore at all times in a special holster. One day as I was walking through Trembowla with Jan Gorniak, I saw Anna Bartetska, the woman who had betrayed the eight members of my family for some sugar. I recognized her immediately and walked right over to her. She tried to walk away, but I blocked her path.

"I'm going to kill you," I said to her, taking out my pistol. "Everyone here knows you betrayed my family for five kilos of sugar." I held my pistol higher, aiming at her heart.

Jan grabbed my arm and pulled me back. He was seven years older than me, stronger and, like my older brother Avrum Chaim, his childhood friend, an authority figure for me.

"Shmercio," he said to me sternly, "you lived through such a terrible war. You want to go to prison for killing her? For this piece of — —? Don't ruin your life for her. Let her go to hell." He spat on the street by her feet and pulled me away.

I let him overpower me because he was right. I had not lived through so much to wind up in prison for killing an awful person, no matter how much I felt she deserved to die. A couple of days later when members of the local Russian NKVD made a visit to the distillery, I mentioned the incident to them.

"You know," I said to the chairman of the NKVD, "everyone in town knows this woman showed the Gestapo where my family was hiding in the fields. She betrayed them for some sugar. I wanted to kill her right then and there on the street but was prevented by my good friend."

"Don't worry," he said to me. "We'll take care of her."

Two days later she was arrested by the Russians for collaborating with the enemy and was then sent to Siberia. I know some people would say that revenge is not the Jewish way. I was not looking to avenge the deaths of my cousins and their children, though. I just wanted her to be punished for what she had done.

A related incident happened not long after this one. Its roots, though, were in the early days of the German occupation of Chorostkow. As I said earlier, some local Ukrainians thought the German invasion was a wonderful opportunity to express hatred for Jews. Two days before the Germans even entered Chorostkow, a Ukrainian, Mikola Werbowetzky, had killed a Jew named Halpern (who was unrelated to my family). Everyone knew about this murder, and soon after the Soviet Army arrived, the man was arrested and taken to a jail in Chortkow.

Three months later I was summoned to appear before a military court to testify about the matter. Although the trip was long, I knew I must go. I borrowed a motorcycle and in the pouring rain drove forty kilometers to the court in Chortkow.

When I went inside the jail, I saw a changed man. Werbowetzky was still a young man, but after three months in jail he had grown a beard and his hair had turned white. I almost did not recognize him.

"Why did you kill Halpern?" I asked.

"Because they said we could kill the Jews," he answered.

"Did Halpern ever do anything bad to you? Did you have a grudge against him?"

"No," he said. "He would come to me, and I would sell him eggs."

"So why did you kill him?"

"They said you could kill Jews. I had a rifle. So I killed him."

Since Werbowetzky readily confessed to the crime, the Russians declared there was no need for a trial, and I never testified. The next day, Werbowetzky was hanged in the public square.

*

On New Year's Eve, 1945, we had a party in Trembowla. I had brought some bottles of vodka home from the distillery, and they were soon emptied by our high spirited friends. We forgot our problems and for hours celebrated the new year. Exactly at midnight, after quite a bit of eating and drinking, we stood up and began to sing *"Hatikva,"* the

Zionist hymn of hope. The words and melody expressed our longings. Everyone stood and began singing, verse after verse. This song represented the redemption of our people and the land of Israel, our salvation and faith. We sang so loudly that the walls of the room practically shook. For a few minutes we were joyfully transported to the land of Israel. We could almost feel the hot sun on our faces, the pebbles beneath our feet, and see the dome-like sky, which seems so much closer in the Holy Land.

The next day I was summoned to the commissar's office. The stern look on the man's face told me the news I was about to hear was not good.

"Comrade Halpern?"

"Yes, comrade."

"Please sit down."

I obeyed.

"It pains me to do this," the commissar proceeded, "for you are a hard-working young man and a good manager, but I have to put you under arrest."

"What have I done?" I asked respectfully.

"You are being charged with subversive activities."

I knew that under the Communists, a charge of subversive activities meant a long jail sentence, exile to Siberia, or even death.

"What exactly did I do?" I asked.

"Well, what were you doing last night?"

"Last night I was at a New Year's Eve party."

"And what did you do there?"

"Drank and ate and sang."

"What exactly did you sing?" he asked.

"Oh," I answered. "Many songs. Some Polish, Russian, Yiddish, Hebrew."

"That's it. Why did you have to sing a Hebrew song? It's nationalistic and anti-Communist. Some might say this makes you an enemy of the people, a charge punishable by death."

I blamed the song on all the vodka I had consumed and argued that the song did not reflect some deeply held conviction on my part. I argued that I wanted nothing more than to be a productive Soviet citizen, working for the good of the collective. I even translated some phrases from the Hebrew pioneering songs, selecting those verses written by socialists celebrating the new world order.

My good relations with the local officials and effective management at the distillery helped to tip the scales in my favor. I was released with a stern warning never again to engage in Zionist, anti-Communist activities. I knew that in the future I would have to be more careful.

On Friday afternoons, many people came to the factory, hoping to buy alcohol. They arrived in cars or horse-drawn wagons and even on foot. One Friday as I was walking through the factory, I saw among the usual group of fifteen or so people, a clean-cut young man who was dressed in a fine, leather coat. He had already received vodka and came over to me to sign the requisition. After I handed it back, he whispered to me, "Amcho?"

I replied, "Ken" (yes in Hebrew), not at all surprised that this man, who looked a little Jewish, was trying to find out if I was also a Jew by using the amcho password (which means "our people").

He continued. "I have here a requisition for two hundred liters that you have signed, but I did not come all the way from Lvov just to return with two hundred liters. With that amount I cannot make a living."

He paused to see how I was taking his pitch. I was calm. I had nothing to lose by listening.

"You just sold me the alcohol at the going price of one ruble and seventy kopeks per liter. In Lvov, I can sell a liter for twenty rubles. Whatever profit there is to make, I'll split half and half with you," he said and waited for my response.

The profits he was offering were too great to turn down. "Okay," I said. "What did you bring with you to transport the vodka back to Lvov?"

He had come prepared with a thousand liter barrel hoisted on a truck. I had this barrel filled, and the young man immediately paid for the entire load and then gave me half the profits he expected to make on the additional eight hundred liters I had agreed to sell to him.

That year, Passover fell in March. I remembered all too well the *seder* we had the year before when we ate potatoes all week, told the story of bondage, and thought so painfully of all the little children who were not there to search for the *afikoman*, all the fathers who had been killed and all the sons, mothers, daughters and wives who were gone. This year, I was determined to make up for the loss and pain of the previous year.

Since Arie and I had good jobs and were doing well financially, we lived in a large, beautiful apartment. A couple, Mr. and Mrs. Wolf Kahane, and their daughter, Cesia, did not have good jobs or much money, so they lived with us. Mrs. Kahane cooked for all of us, and we lived together like a family.

For the *seder*, I arranged for a beautiful table to be set, with *matzoh*, wine, and the ritual foods of the seder plate. Mrs. Kahane was going to prepare the rest. Many people were invited, and I was looking forward to the holiday. The only hitch was the monthly report I had to give to my superior in Chortkow. The war was still raging—it did not end until May—and the factory's alcohol production was considered a top military priority. I had calculated that I could get back in time for the *seder* if, instead of taking the once-a-day commuter train, I hopped a later freight train, which transported coal and cattle. But when I got to the station in Chortkow, I saw there was no carriage for passengers, so I persuaded one of the train crew to let me ride with him.

"Will you stop in Trembowla?" I asked.

That man assured me the train would stop, but unfortunately he was wrong. As we sped past my town, I thought of the table all set for *seder* and the hours of preparation that had gone into making the holiday right this year. I was only twenty-three years old at the time and still did not realize that life is more important than any celebration. I jumped.

I hit the ground hard and broke my leg. At the hospital in Tarnopol where I was taken, they had practically no medical supplies because of the war. There was no plaster or gauze to make a cast, no drugs to ease my pain. All they could do was splint my leg on a board and wrap a towel around it. The doctor told me to keep my leg straight, which, of course, was impossible to do and why plaster casts are used in the first place. I moved around some, and my leg hurt terribly. Thank God, my limb healed, but to this day I feel the ache in my leg before it rains or snows.

I remained in the hospital at Tarnopol for the entire week of Passover. I heard that everyone had a wonderful time at the *seder*; even though I could not be there, I was happy that my efforts had not been in vain.

While I was in the hospital, tragedy struck again. My dear friend, Jan Gorniak, who had saved Arie and me, was shot to death. People in the area said he shot himself, but his wife, Josefa, insisted that he had been murdered. To this day, no one knows exactly what happened to Jan Gorniak. The loss to his family and ours was enormous. Josefa was left a young widow with three small children: Maria, Bronek, and Yola. Today, Yola's eldest son, Darius, lives in the United States with his wife, Barbara, and their son, Salvador, who is employed in my company.

*

In early 1945 while the war was still on, the Russians passed a law stating that anyone who had been born in what was the prewar territory of Poland could now return. This ruling meant that people like me were no longer bound to stay inside Russia. Thus, when the war with Germany finally ended, I decided to leave Russia and head west into Poland. Mr. Pekar, the supervisors in Moscow, and the townspeople I had befriended could not understand why I would decide to leave the rather comfortable life I had built.

Nonetheless, I felt compelled to go. I did not want to stay in the area where my mother and father had been killed. I had always known that the moment I had the opportunity to leave, I would. All along, people had been slipping into Poland illegally, not wishing to live under Russian authority. Although I had often thought about doing likewise, I had decided that I would return to Poland only when leaving Russia became legal. With my decision firmly made, I approached my boss.

"Please, Mr. Pekar," I said, "I would like you to release me from my job because I want to return to Poland. I was born in Poland, and I want to exercise my right to return."

This explanation should have been enough for him. The law was on my side, and he could not keep me in Russia against my will. Of course, he would never have thought of holding me back, but he was surprised and reluctant to lose me.

"You're going to Poland? You're a big man here. What's waiting for you there?"

Then he took out a newspaper.

"Look, read," he said. "They're still killing Jews in that Poland of yours. The war is over, and the local Poles are still beating and killing Jews! They're throwing them from trains and cracking their skulls. That's where you want to go, after everything you've built up here?" He was getting increasingly agitated. "You're going to Poland? You don't know what you're doing!"

Mr. Pekar became so upset that he ripped up the paperwork I had handed him and threw it on the floor. I understood his position. I had been manager of the factory for a little over a year, from the end of April 1944 to May of 1945, and he had grown dependent on my good service. Because he liked me, he was also concerned for my personal welfare. He did not want me going to a country where my life would be endangered. I had a horse and driver, a nice place to live, a prestigious job, and a boss who really liked me. He was giving me fatherly advice.

I decided that I would have to tell him the whole story. From my pocket I pulled out a tattered postcard from my uncle Paul in New York, in America! On the front was a picture of New York harbor and the Statue of Liberty, and on the back my uncle had written, "Leave everything and come to America."

"You see, Comrade Pekar, I'm not going to Poland because I love the Polish people. But I have to go to Poland in order to reach America. My entire family was killed here, and I can't stay. There's nobody left. I have one uncle, and he lives in America. He wants us to come to him."

I handed Pekar the postcard. He turned it over, looking at the photo and reading the words "Leave everything and come to America."

America was then held in great esteem. Mr. Pekar, being an intelligent man, quickly grasped my situation.

"If you're intending to go to America, then I won't object, but you still have to train a replacement to run the factory."

I readily agreed to these terms, and four weeks later Arie and I took a train bound for the west. Before we boarded, Mr. Pekar hugged and kissed me good-bye. He felt a paternal, protective love for me, and I felt deep gratitude toward him. By giving me the job of manager he not only saved me from the battlefront but provided me with the responsible position that enabled me to head west with some assets.

"Good luck," he said to me as the train pulled out of the Trembowla station.

Mr. Pekar was already an elderly man, so by the time I returned to Trembowla years later to look for all those who had helped me, he was no longer alive. I would have enjoyed seeing him again and telling him how I was blessed after our parting. I think he would have been pleased.

A few days before Arie and I departed, we decided to convert all our Russian money into a tangible commodity with real value. We did not trust paper money. Taking Russian rubles over the Polish border could render it worthless. So before leaving, we bought a ton of flour. We assumed there would be a great demand for this basic commodity even in the absence of the shortages we expected.

When we arrived in Poland, we went to the city of Bytom. There, scouting out the local market, we were soon approached by some men who wanted to purchase our flour for fifty zlotys a kilo. While we were discussing the proposition, I overheard at a nearby stall that flour was being sold to a retail customer for a hundred zlotys a kilo. I pulled Arie aside.

"If they were making twenty percent on us, as is usually done wholesale to retail, I wouldn't mind," I told him. "They pay fifty zlotys and sell it for sixty. But they want to pay fifty and sell for a hundred. Do we have pressing matters to handle? No. Then let's sit here in the market and sell it ourselves."

I approached the market attendant and said, "I need a stall to sell some flour."

He took me over to one at the far end of the market where few customers ventured. I pressed some money into his hand and said, "Now, give me a good stall."

As soon as we were set up, a line of customers formed, and within three days we had sold all the flour. Since the transaction was so profitable, we started to buy flour wholesale from others who had just crossed the border from Russia and then retailed it in the market. After three weeks in the outdoor market in Bytom, we were doing very well.

Soon, though, Arie and I grew tired of this process and sold our stall to Arthur Patrontasch from Zolkiew. With the proceeds, we opened a large wholesale business. Why should I sell a kilo, I said to myself, when I could be selling a ton?

From May until December we remained in Bytom, buying flour mainly from the surrounding mills and selling it to market stalls throughout the area. We decided that eventually we would leave Bytom, even though here, too, we were prospering. Although there were no officially organized anti-Semitic outbursts, random killings of Jews were still taking place. The environment just wasn't safe. I had Poles and Germans working for me, and for the most part everyone got along. I must say, thank God, that I personally never encountered any violence, but I did know of serious incidents in which Jews were hurt. In the city of Rzeszow, a pogrom took place after the war in which sixteen Jews were killed. I felt this was reason enough to leave Poland. Who knew what other pogroms would follow? Indeed, a year after we left, in 1946, there was a terrible pogrom in the town of Kielce. In any event, America beckoned, and our goal was to reach its shores.

The young Jewish people in Bytom would gather together in the evening. We organized a Zionist organization, which we called Yichud (meaning unity). It included all political factions—right, left, center of the road—young and old. We used to talk about our experiences during the war and about the future. Most of us went to synagogue on *Shabbat*.

On *Shmini Atzeret* that year in Bytom, Dr. Rabbi Kahane, who had just returned from Russia in the uniform of a high officer of the Polish Army, came to the synagogue and led the *Yizkor* (memorial) service for the dead. Everybody was present. Before the prayers began he said, "We are about to say Yizkor for our fathers, our mothers, our sisters, our brothers, our aunts, our uncles, and for one million of our pure, innocent children who perished at the hands of the Nazi henchmen." All present burst out crying.

Friends and family would also meet with one another and exchange information or just hang around together to have a good time. One day

Sam with his fiancee and her mother in 1945.

Gladys (first row, second from right) with her class in Zolkiew

Top, left: Gladys' father, Ephraim Landau.

*Top, right: Shifra Rauchfleisch,
nee Landau, Gladys' grandmother.*

*Left: Itzhak Rauchfleisch, Gladys'
maternal grandfather.*

I joined a group of people and was introduced by a friend to a girl who had recently arrived from Zolkiew. Her name was Gina (Gladys) Landau, and she was working as a salesgirl for Mr. Patrontasch, a friend from her home town, the man to whom we had sold our market stall.

"Hello, I'm Sam Halpern," I said.

"Oh yes," she answered, "I've heard the name Halpern mentioned many times. It must be your father."

"Hitler killed my father."

"But I have heard people talk about Halpern, " she continued.

"It's me they're talking about. I'm Halpern."

"I did not expect you to be so young," she answered. "I had an image of Halpern as an older man who was doing business with my friends."

The next day a group of us went to the movies, but I had to excuse myself immediately afterward to attend to some business. I returned to the market the next day, though, and asked Gladys out on a date. She agreed. From that day on we saw one another all the time, and three weeks later I surprised her by announcing:

"I'm going to marry you."

She thought I had lost my mind, deciding on marriage after a three week courtship, but I knew she was the one for me, and it did not take her long to agree. We were engaged to be married in September 1945. I was twenty-five and she seventeen.

*

Gladys' story, like my own, reflects the experience of Jews living through the Holocaust, and this book is as much about her life and survival as it is about mine. We share a European history, immigration to America, a wonderful family, and a profound love for the country of Israel.

Gladys was born in Zolkiew, a Galician town of twelve thousand people (including five thousand Jews) about thirty kilometers outside the city of Lvov. It was a typical town with the usual business and cultural activities for both children and adults.

Gladys' father was one of eight children. There were five brothers: Shimon, Wolf, Yosef, Lippa, and her father Ephraim, and three sisters: Rosa, Malka, and Hannah. All of them had families with a total of thirteen children among them. Josef died at the age of thirty before the war after having a daughter, Giga. Gladys is the only survivor of this large, extended family on her father's side.

Gladys' mother came from a family of six children. Her brother, Jacob, and sisters, Esther and Bina, were killed by the Nazis. Her mother and her two younger sisters, Mina and Rachel, and their sister-in-law, Tony, survived the Nazi occupation together with Gladys.

Gladys says that her earliest childhood recollection was being in an oversized crib and hearing loud yelling coming from a radio. Her parents were listening to the speeches given at rallies being broadcast from Germany. The anti-Semitism was blatant. The screaming from the podium and the enthusiasm of the thousands attending was frightening. Just after 1933 Hitler came to power in Germany, and after the war started Zolkiew was occupied.

Before the war, Gladys' father had often spoken of moving to Palestine. As difficult as it was to get the coveted certificate from the British, her father did have the necessary one thousand pounds sterling per family. With this certificate an immigrant entered Palestine as a capitalist settler, not one who would further burden the British Empire. In the end, however, despite her father's ability to take the family out of Poland, he did not move. First, there was the problem of taking more money out of the country, which the Polish government did not allow. The prospect of reaching Palestine with minimal financial resources did not impress her father as a good solution. In addition, the opportunities for making a living in Palestine were still quite limited. Finally, Gladys' mother was reluctant to leave her family. Her grandmother had been left a young widow and had the full responsibility of raising young children. Gladys' mother was the second eldest child, the eldest daughter, and she was very much involved in helping her own mother care for her siblings. Consequently, Gladys' mother felt she could not go to Palestine. She could not simply pick up and leave the family.

Until the occupation, life in Zolkiew was decent; it was interesting. Many Jews were engaged in the fur trade, and most were rather comfortable. The town had its own cultural institutions, including a gymnasium, an advanced high school that few towns could support. Being close to Lvov, with rail train and bus connections making the trip only an hour, afforded the inhabitants of Zolkiew an opportunity to enjoy a rich cultural life. The Lux-Torpeda, an express to Warsaw, stopped in Zolkiew for just one minute, but people could hop aboard and get to Lvov quite quickly. Gladys remembers her parents attending lectures, concerts, and theater performances in Lvov as well as visiting their parents and shopping there.

When Gladys was little, there was no Jewish pre-school in town, and so her mother and her father's cousin, Sara Schwartz, who had two girls, Clara and Manya, started one. At first they rotated houses but eventually rented a space and opened a full fledged school for children between the ages of three and five. Not long ago Gladys visited her cousin in Israel. The cousin pulled out a photograph of the preschool in Zolkiew. In it a group of about thirty children, scrubbed clean and smiling at the camera, were captured in their innocence. Out of this group, only two survived the war: Gladys and her cousin Clara. The two cousins have remained as close as sisters. Clara and her husband, Sol, have two married sons and five grandchildren. Manya was betrayed by a Polish schoolmate who saw her on the street when she emerged from her hiding place. A fire had broken out in the house next door, and she fled the shelter temporarily. At the age of fifteen, she was tortured to death but refused to disclose that the rest of her family was hiding in an underground bunker built by the Becks, a Polish family in town. This family helped eighteen Jews survive.

Like other shtetls in Galicia, Zolkiew had many different kinds of Jews. There were Hasidim, Mitnagdim, secular Zionists, and religious Zionists. The whole gamut of Jewish intellectual and cultural thought was represented.

Gladys' father had a store where he sold porcelain, crystal, enamel cookware, electrical appliances and radios. He was also a wholesaler for electrical supplies at a time when electricity was just making a slow but steady appearance in small towns and villages. As a result, Gladys' house boasted the latest electrical appliances: a radio, toaster, and iron. Her father also owned the only gasoline station in town. Almost exclusively used by the bus company (in which he was a partner), this gas station was also used by the two privately owned cars in Zolkiew. One of these, Gladys remembers, was a small red sports car owned by a Polish officer's wife.

When the war broke out in 1939, people rushed into the town from the west seeking gasoline. For three or four days, a steady stream of refugees arrived desperate for gas. Many were fleeing further east to Romania or Russia. One afternoon, Gladys' father came home and said to her mother:

"I have been offered a car for a certain amount of gasoline. Maybe we, too, should take the offer and run off to Romania."

Her mother answered, "I have a house full of refugees to feed. If we run, who will feed us?"

The family did not take the offer and remained in Zolkiew. A few days later, after a brief bombardment, German tanks rolled into town. It was a Friday, a day Gladys will never forget because the family had just returned from a spa on Wednesday. Gladys had been suffering from a chronic infection of her tonsils, and her parents had finally decided to heed their doctor's recommendation that she have a tonsillectomy. In those days, people were reluctant to undergo surgery since the risk of infection was high, and almost all the antibiotics we use today had yet to be discovered. Also, Gladys was an only child, and her parents were understandably protective. Nevertheless, the sore throats and colds had become such a problem that they finally agreed to the operation, and to strengthen Gladys before the ordeal, the family had taken her to the local spa, Ivonicz, with its therapeutic iodine bath waters. However, the German occupation of the town that Friday ended all medical plans. Curiously, from the day the Germans came into Zolkiew until Gladys was twenty-eight years old and living in New York, ready to give birth to our third son, she never even sneezed, let alone had tonsillitis. Gladys claims the Germans cured her of this illness!

Synagogue in Zolkiew.

The afternoon following the German arrival in Zolkiew was *Shabbat*. All the men in the building came into the Landau apartment and entered one of the back rooms. Gladys did not understand what was happening, but a little while later there was a loud knock on the door. Her mother opened it to two German soldiers.

"We are looking for men," they said.

Her mother answered, "Well, you'll find no men here. Would you care to check for yourselves?"

The soldiers declined this bold invitation and left the building. This incident was the family's first encounter with the German army and the first close call to be experienced. Luckily, it was the last for quite some time.

A few days later news came that the Russians were on the way. Russia and Germany had agreed to partition Poland, and the Third Reich's armies were pulling back. Naturally, the Landaus were relieved. They knew that Germans killed Jews whereas Russians merely confiscated property and sent some wealthy people to Siberia. While they waited for the changeover, Gladys' mother filled and lit the kerosene lamps in the house. The electricity had already been cut off, and all the appliances had become useless. Gladys recalls in vivid detail how a kerosene lamp was glowing on the table when her mother explained what to expect in the coming days.

"You should know there's a whole new world coming," her mother said. "You will only have one dress. One pair of shoes. Everything will be different."

The Russians arrived in the middle of September, and until December, Gladys' father was still able to go to the store and conduct business as usual. The Russian soldiers would come in, always critical of the merchandise. They only wanted the best of everything and claimed they had everything back home. It was not yet widely known what life was really like in the Soviet Union where such items were scarce.

Gladys was about to start sixth grade at this time, but the Russians instituted their own system of education. The gymnasium became a Polish school, and the former boys' school became a Ukrainian school. Gladys had been going to a school run by nuns, which was converted to a Jewish school where the language of instruction was Yiddish. Although her parents knew Yiddish, Polish was the language spoken at home, and Gladys was forced to learn Yiddish quite quickly to keep up with her studies. The Jewish communist teachers made the students come to school on Friday night and Saturday, forcing the pupils to breaking the Sabbath laws. This violation was very difficult for the majority who observed *Shabbat* faithfully, but they had little choice but to comply. The contrast with the schooling under the nuns was extreme. Theirs had always been a school for girls, and one of the courses for instruction was cooking. The nuns would teach the Jewish girls how to keep a kosher kitchen: how to salt the meat, how to separate the dishes, how to keep the foods apart. These Christian nuns had more respect for the laws of Judaism than did the Jews the Russians had installed.

In December the Russians brought a Jewish woman from Kiev and her little daughter to the Landau apartment. The family was told that this woman was the new tenant, and she proceeded to live in the dining room. One morning the NKVD came to the apartment and waited for Gladys' father. They took the keys to his store and proceeded to nationalize the entire household. Everything was inventoried, from dresses to handkerchiefs. They also confiscated an enormous bundle of furs found in an armoire in the back of the apartment. The armoire was chained shut and the contents declared property of the state. The pelts had actually been hidden by a neighbor whose son-in-law, a furrier, had hoped to keep these expensive, high-quality goods out of Russians hands. That night, the neighbor sneaked over to the apartment, opened up the back of the armoire, and took out all the furs, replacing them with an exact number of cheap pelts. Cunning and fast maneuvering were the only way to salvage assets.

In the summer, the woman tenant left, and the head of the NKVD took over the apartment. Gladys and her parents were now forced to move into the dining room.

Because her parents were identified as capitalists, they had been given passport number eleven, which made travel and work impossible. Gladys was still attending school, but the whole household was on edge. People were being taken off to Siberia all the time, and Gladys' parents were quite nervous now that the head of the NKVD lived with them. Any suspicious act on their part might condemn them and result in their being exiled to Siberia.

The family therefore decided to move to Lvov. At first, Gladys' father lived with his father, and Gladys and her mother lived with her grandmother. Then they went to the authorities to apply for new passports, claiming they had been living in a house that had just been bombed and that all their papers were lost. This ploy succeeded. Had it not, had they been discovered, this act would have been considered a capital offense. The family would surely have been sent to Siberia.

With a new passport, Gladys' father was able to get some work, and the three rented a room in a house that belonged to her uncle. Gladys went to school, and the family managed to sustain themselves until June 22, 1941 when the Germans arrived once again. The family braced for the worst, not knowing the extent of the Nazi barbarism. One morning, only a few days after the Germans arrived in Lvov, soldiers came knocking on the door of the apartment in which they were living. A Polish professor who lived there answered.

"Are there Jews here?" the soldiers asked, just as they had asked for the men many months earlier in Zolkiew. But this time there was no clever Jewish woman answering the Nazis. Even now, Gladys does not know whether the professor understood the implications of his answer.

"Yes," he said and pointed to the back room where the Landaus lived.

The Germans came down the hall and ordered the family down the stairs and onto the street. Once outside they were told to take off their shoes. All along the main boulevard of Lvov, Jews were being marched downtown. Lining the streets were large groups of Poles and Ukrainians thoroughly enjoying the spectacle. As the family began to walk, Gladys' mother decided to take a chance. She boldly went over to a German soldier.

"Do you take children?" she asked.

He looked down at her and her child and said, "No, go."

"But the child's father is in the group too," the mother continued.

"Take him and go."

Not waiting for the German to change his mind, the couple and their child quickly walked through the crowd and away from the long procession of Jews marching downtown. As Gladys made her way through the crowd, she recalls that someone spat in her face. This was her introduction to the Holocaust.

Days earlier when the Russian army was retreating, some soldiers had gone into the local Lvov prison where political prisoners were being held. Priests were being detained there and many Jews, among them Gladys' great-uncle, Reitzfield. The Russian authorities jailed anyone they deemed dangerous. Vicious dogs were let loose in the cells and when the attack was over, everyone inside was dead. The Germans had decided to make use of the grisly incident by letting the local population vent its rage on the Jews, orchestrating the fatal pogrom that was to greet the rest of the Jews who were not so fortunate as to leave the procession. When the Jews reached downtown, the German army stood back and watched the local population kill Jews with wooden planks studded with nails. Many people were also shot. Almost everyone was killed.

In the meantime, Gladys and her parents had returned to their Lvov apartment but after only three days decided to go back to Zolkiew. There was no work in Lvov and very little food. In Zolkiew the Landaus had family and old friends.

For a while life in Zolkiew was not so bad. Food could be found and, most importantly, they felt strong being at home, surrounded by people they knew and loved.

Then the Germans began taking some of the men to work. Next the Germans demanded gold from the Jews. Gladys' father collected all the family jewelry, including a little gold ring Gladys wore. He tried to console her by saying they really had no choice. Gladys' mother, though, refused to relinquish her wedding band, which she kept throughout the war. Today, Gladys has that ring. How grateful she is that her mother's insistence enabled her to hold onto this symbol of her parents' loving union.

The Germans soon demanded silver. Then they demanded furs. Not complying with these orders could bring a swift and fatal punishment. Every day there were new demands. Finally, all Jews were ordered to wear a white arm band with a blue star of David.

The first evacuation took place in the spring of 1942. People in category A, those able to work, were allowed to remain. Everyone in categories B and C, those unable to work, would be "resettled" in Belzec. In the summer the Landaus moved to an aunt's house. At that time they first heard about random shootings of Jews on the streets. They began to hear rumors that Jews were not being resettled in Belzec but massacred, shot to death and then burned in large ovens. Such reports seemed outrageous, and no one believed these stories. Then, in November of 1942, the first *Aktion* took place, and the ghetto was created immediately afterward. Jews from all parts of Zolkiew, and from surrounding towns and villages, were crowded into a fenced-in area in the town. Many families had to share the same apartment. There was little food and sanitation, and hope declined rapidly.

Awareness of what was really happening to the Jews was spreading. One source of information was Jews who had escaped from trains on the way to Belzec. There was a sharp curve in Zolkiew where trains had to slow down, giving Jews an opportunity to jump off. Knowing that certain death was awaiting at the end of the line, whoever could, jumped. Many were shot right away, but some managed to roll away undetected. A system was organized within the ghetto to go to the tracks every night and search for bodies. Whoever was still alive and could be saved was brought into the ghetto and tended. The others were buried.

By January 1943, hunger was widespread in the ghetto. Sometimes, local Ukrainians would slip in to sell food to starving Jews for a very high price. One day Gladys' father came to her and said:

"I've arranged for you to go into hiding. There is a Ukrainian farmer who has agreed."

"I'm not going," Gladys said firmly. On that day she did not go.

A few days later her father said, "Get dressed, you're going." His tone of voice indicated he would not be contradicted. Being a respectful and obedient daughter, Gladys knew there was no point in engaging her father in a fight. His tone indicated that there was nothing left to discuss.

In order to get past the ghetto gate, Gladys' father paid off a Ukrainian guard. The two walked through, and there stood a man waiting to take Gladys away. She had already said good-bye to her mother, who promised she would be following soon. Then she hugged and kissed her father and began to walk away with the man. She looked back at her father, standing there waving in a reddish tweed coat with matching hat. This would be the last time she would ever see him. It is the image that always remained with her.

The man took Gladys by train to Lvov. He told her to hold on to him and not say a word. They went to an apartment in a formerly Jewish area. Once inside, the man sat down beside his wife at the gas stove to warm himself while Gladys was told to go to sleep in a cold, dark bedroom in the back. The couple had also taken Gladys' winter coat under whose fur collar her mother had sewn in some

Marian Halicki.

money. Terrified and cold, Gladys wondered why she had allowed herself to leave her parents. Better to die with them, than be alone with people who might kill her, she thought. Somehow, Gladys managed to sleep through the night, and in the morning when she got back her coat, it was clear that they had found the money but had not taken it. This stopover was all part of her father's arrangement for her, and eventually for her mother and other family members, to go into hiding.

The next morning, Gladys went with the man to a big house on a corner on the other side of town. There was a great deal of activity going on inside, and the man told her to sit down and wait. After a while, another man entered. He was, she later learned, only fifty-seven years old, but to Gladys, at fourteen years of age, he seemed ancient. She immediately felt comfortable and safe with him. His name was Marian Halicki, and he reminded her of Wolf, a man with no family of his own who worked in her father's gasoline station, ate meals with her family, and slept in the local synagogue.

Afraid of being caught on a train, Mr. Halicki decided to take her by foot to his house on the outskirts of town. The snow was deep, and the going was rough. Finally, they reached the house and when they got inside, there was another young woman there. Mr. Halicki introduced them, but before anything more could be said, there was a knock on the door. "Go," he said to the woman, and she took Gladys to hide inside a cupboard built into the wall.

It was only his brother who had knocked, but everyone was afraid of everyone else, and there could not be enough caution exercised. After some time, Gladys' aunt arrived. After that another aunt came. Finally, her mother arrived. They were in hiding for a few weeks when they received news that the entire ghetto had been liquidated. Gladys' father had remained behind. Because of the bus company, Gladys' father knew many Poles and Ukrainians with whom he was on excellent terms. He had calculated that when the time came, he would have an opportunity to get both himself and his aged father out of the ghetto and into hiding—if not with his wife and daughter then with any number of other Gentiles he knew. Tragically, he had misjudged the Germans' efficiency and had not had time to make further arrangements. He was killed on March 25, and his father, Itzhak Landau, was killed a week later.

In June when people learned that the liquidation of the Lvov ghetto was going to take place, Gladys' mother asked Mr. Halicki to get out her brother, Yaakov, and his wife. Mr. Halicki agreed. At that point, Mr. Halicki was hiding Gladys, her mother, two aunts, the young woman Gladys met when she arrived, and her mother and brother, and there was no financial incentive for him to take an additional risk. The family had no more money to give him. Rather, he was taking this risk for moral reasons. He wanted to save them.

Mr. Halicki returned from Lvov with only Yaakov's wife, Tony. When asked what happened, he explained that Yaakov had said he still had to go into the ghetto to retrieve something and that Mr. Halicki should return for him in half an hour. When he came back to pick up Yaakov, he saw that he had already been loaded onto a German truck. Uncle Yaakov was taken to Janowska, a labor camp in Lvov, where he perished.

For eighteen months, this group of people lived together in hiding, in Mr. Halicki's workroom. Mr. Halicki was a locksmith, and with the money he had been given, he had fixed up the room so his neighbors could not detect that people were living there. There was one window in the room covered by a curtain. Even so, everyone in hiding walked around crouched as low as possible so they would not be seen. Not once did anyone dare to peek through this curtain to look at the blue sky or the stars at night. Even when alone in the house, they spoke to one another only in whispers.

When people came into the house, family members would creep up the ladder into the attic and stay there until the coast was clear. The only thing that might have given away their presence was Mr. Halicki's little dog. It had grown very attached to them, and when they climbed into the attic, the dog would sit and stare up at the ceiling, yearning for them to come down.

They had nothing to eat. Mr. Halicki had no money, and there was almost nothing left to sell. When they could, they embroidered pretty patterns on a pieces of torn clothing for Mr. Halicki to sell in the market. Sometimes he would find them old sweaters. They would un-ravel them, wash the wool, and knit new sweaters. These, too, he sold to help buy a little food from time to time. With small snippets of left-over wool, they knitted a pair of gloves or a hat, also for sale. Despite all the efforts, they were still starving. During the last three months of the war, there was absolutely no food. Mr. Halicki would pick leaves from a nearby tree, and they would cook them in water to make a pretend soup. There were simply too many of them and virtually no money.

Mr. Halicki was not only committed to saving this group of Jews but was also a member of the A.K., an underground organization that fought the Nazis. He made gun parts in his workshop and transported weapons from one part of the city to another.

And his neighbors were suspicious. One woman in particular kept track of the water he drew from the well, and one day she confronted him.

"Why are you using so much water?" she asked.

"I have to keep clean," he answered. "My wife comes every Sunday, and she wants to see the house in perfect shape."

The wife did come to visit every Sunday after spending the week in town with their daughter. She was too frightened to stay in the same house with hidden Jews and the gun-running operation.

The neighbor across the street, an old man named Balitzki, was also suspicious. "Mr. Halicki," he would say, "why are you always carrying so much water? You must have Jews." To put these suspicions to rest, Mr. Halicki washed the dog in the yard and then took out every stick of furniture and washed it thoroughly. Of course, this activity was all a show. The water was for the Jews, who needed to bathe and drink as much as they could since they were not eating.

When the Russian bombs started falling, the camp in Lvov was liquidated. The Germans burned the Jewish bodies in an area called Piaski not far from Halicki's house, and Gladys and the others could smell the stench of burning bodies. They were terrified. Then the Hungarian soldiers came into the town, retreating with the front. When word got out that they were looking for places to live, everyone was sure they would come to Mr. Halicki's house. They were extremely frightened of this possibility. After all, how long could they go undetected in the attic? Fortunately, the Hungarians never came.

Then, in an ironic twist, the Ukrainian neighbor who had confronted Mr. Halicki about his water usage was afraid that the Russians would take her husband away when they took over the area. She begged Mr. Halicki to hide him. He did, putting the husband in the shed in the garden while the Jews remained in the house.

When the fighting ended not long afterward, Mr. Halicki had the Jews walk out two by two. He was still afraid that his neighbors would discover that he had hidden Jews. July 26, 1944 was their day of liberation.

After a couple of false starts, Gladys and her mother hitchhiked a ride to Zolkiew on a military truck. Frightened by stories of Russian soldiers raping and killing as they crossed the countryside, the two stayed close together and picked up another mother and daughter team traveling in the same direction. On the open wagons to Zolkiew, despite the coverings they had been given by soldiers, they became badly sunburned. What did sunburn matter? What did hunger matter? They were alive. The war was over, and they had survived.

All along the road to Zolkiew they saw dead bodies of both soldiers and civilians killed in battle. Corpses were piled in ditches. It was a terrifying sight. When the four reached the town of Kulikow, between Lvov and Zolkiew, they went into a bakery that was operating all night and asked the baker if they could sleep in the back. They were desperately afraid to sleep in the open because of horror stories they had heard. The baker agreed, and the women slept on a table usually used for baking bread.

Early the next morning, Gladys and her mother caught one last ride and at 5 A.M. arrived in Zolkiew. They were looking for Gentile Poles whom they had known, like the pharmacist her aunt had once worked for, in hopes of learning what happened to the Jewish community. On passing her cousin's house, Gladys said to her mother:

"Let's go see if anyone is there."

"What are you talking about?" her mother answered. "Everyone is gone. No one is alive."

Gladys insisted, and as they approached the two-family house, members of her family began to emerge from the balcony doors on either side. There was the Schwartz family, Meier Berish and his wife Sara (Gladys' father's cousin) and their daughter, Clara. And then there were two young children of Sara's sister, Ucka, who had been killed in the ghetto because Beck, a local Pole who had hidden Jews, was afraid to take her with the children. In the end, after the mother was killed, the children showed up at Beck's doorstep one Sunday afternoon. The boy, Zygo, who was eight years old, said, "Mr. Beck, my Aunt Sara is here. Take my little sister, Zosia. I will take care of myself." Beck grabbed both children, bathed and fed them, and took them to their family in the underground bunker. With these relatives was also the Patrontasch family, close friends, and Lola Elephant. There were the three brothers, Mundik (her father's closest friend) with his wife Sabina and ten-year old daughter Clara, Arthur, Cuba, and their sister Clara. Only Manya was missing, betrayed by her Polish schoolmate and neighbor after the fire.

Gladys and her mother were overcome with emotion because the family had survived. They burst into tears and fell into their arms. Once the sobbing had subsided, they immediately wanted to know the whereabouts of everyone else. The reunion was both painful and joyful. It was wonderful to be with the few members of the family who were there but painful to recognize that the majority had not survived.

They learned that Esther, one of Gladys' aunts, and her husband had been taken from Rotterdam, where they lived, to Westerbork. From there they were taken to Auschwitz where both perished. Her Aunt Bina survived the liquidation of the Zolkiew ghetto and went into hiding, but the people who had taken her money delivered her to the police the following morning. She was shot in the Jewish cemetery in Zolkiew.

Not long afterward, Arthur Patrontasch and Lola Elephant were married. Today they live in Montreal with their two sons and five grandchildren. The little boy, Zygo (Alex), celebrated his Bar-Mitzvah on the ship, the *Exodus*, made famous in Leon Uris' book. Today he lives in Israel with his wife, three daughters and two grandchildren. His sister, Zosia, also lives in Israel with her three daughters.

Years later in 1972, Gladys met another cousin, Lillian, who had managed to survive. The circumstances of this meeting were amazing. Izzi Haliczer, a friend of mine and fellow ex-inmate of Kamionka, moved to New Jersey with his wife, Ronnie, in 1972. During a conversation, the name of their friend, Lillian, originally from the city of Przemysl in Poland, came up, and the fact that Gladys' maiden name was Landau was also mentioned. Ronnie said that her friend Lillian was a Landau too, but she was certain that none of her family survived the war.

Hearing this news, Gladys became agitated. Her father had had a cousin in Przemysl, Dr. David Landau, who was a well known lawyer in Poland and throughout Europe. David's father, Avigdor Landau, was Gladys' grandfather's brother. It was from Avigdor's house in Lvov that Gladys and her parents had been taken to the pogrom in the center of town.

After the war, Gladys and her mother had heard that Dr. Landau's young daughter, Avigdor's granddaughter, had survived. Her mother, anxious to find and care for the girl, had tried to locate her, but the last they had heard was that the child had been brought to the United States and adopted by her mother's family.

Gladys was determined to find out if Lillian was her cousin. Ronnie and Izzi arranged a meeting between the two women. Lillian had pictures of her family, and they confirmed that Lillian and Gladys were cousins. Both of them felt the reunion was a miracle. Lillian was

Together with my wife and our son David, with Sharon and Jeremy in July 1995 at the dedication of the monument in Zolkiew.

married to a wonderful man, Sam Ettinger. Unfortunately, she passed away a number of years ago. She and her husband have two sons, a daughter-in-law and two grandsons.

For a year after liberation, Gladys and her mother eked out a living in Zolkiew sewing dresses and doing other odd jobs. Gladys worked for a time as a secretary in an office because of her knowledge of Russian and Ukrainian. After a year, they repatriated to Poland, together with many other Jews. In August of 1945, Gladys and her mother came to Bytom.

*

During my entire stay in Bytom, I made weekly tax payments to the municipality. Normally, taxes had been due at the end of the year, but at that time the authorities were concerned about people moving away, and they insisted that everyone pay taxes on their workers and

צום הייליקן אנדענק
פון די' 3500 קדושים
אין דשאָוקוועו,געטאָ
ת'נ'צ'ב'ה'

СВЯЩЕННИЙ ПАМЯТІ
3500 ЖЕРТВ
ЖОВКІВСЬКОГО
ГЕТТО
25.03. 1943 РОКУ

*Inset of monument to the 3500
Kedoshim in Zolkiew.*

profits weekly. Then one day, after I was again warned that because I was doing a large volume of business I might be targeted by local anti-Semites, I decided to leave Poland and go to the American zone in West Germany. I took the threat seriously because random killings of Jews were still occurring, and that day I sold everything I could, gathered up my few belongings, bought one-way train tickets to Munich, which was in the American zone, and left Poland for good. My brother Arie, my future wife Gladys, her mother, and my cousin Mina were all with me.

We were stopped at the border where the Poles wanted to send us back. We succeeded in talking them out of it, but not before our valises were stolen. We left Poland with only the clothing on our backs.

To get to Munich, the train had to go through Czechoslovakia, which we entered that night. Although we had tickets for the train, we did not have the necessary transit visas to travel through Czechoslovakia. We were unaware that it was illegal for us, Polish nationals, to cross Czechoslovakia and then enter Germany. In the Czech city of Morawska Ostrava, policemen entered the train to check everyone's documents. When they discovered that we did not have transit visas, they promptly arrested us and the several hundred other passengers on the train who shared our predicament.

We were taken to a large ballroom that was being used as a detention center. Of course, we were frightened—not for our lives, as we had been under the Germans, but for an interminable stay. Some of the detainees told me that they had been waiting for visas for three or four months already. I decided that this approach would not do for us. I had not survived and escaped from a Nazi labor camp to be imprisoned in some little Czech detention center when freedom was within arm's reach.

After two days, I told my traveling companions, "It is morning now, but tonight when it's dark we are leaving. Don't ask questions; just do as I do, and we'll get out of here."

I had thought the plan through carefully. The large room was crowded with people, and only three guards lazily watched over the group. Our chances of escaping undetected seemed quite good. In any event, I realized we had nothing to lose. If we were caught, we would merely be brought back to this room. If we were not caught, we would be that much closer to freedom. When night came, I waited for the guards to fall asleep, and the five of us simply slipped out the door.

We ran until we reached the train station, and since we still did not have the all-important transit visas, I bribed the train conductor with a ring to let us ride the train until Prague. There, we went straight to the offices of the Jewish Agency where we were helped by one of the staff. He took us on foot to another station where we could catch a train to Bratislava. Before boarding, he gave us some important advice. "As Polish Jews," he began, "you are not permitted to enter Germany. The Germans claim that you have your country back, and that it's up to you to make your way. You can, however, enter as Greek Jews since Hitler deported many Greeks into Poland for slave labor. The rationale is that you are going home, and Germany is therefore just a stop on the way. By being Greek Jews, neither the Germans nor the Czechs will bother with you."

This suggestion made sense to all of us, and it did not seem like much of a problem until he added something else.

"All of this means that none of you can speak Polish," he explained. "It means none of you can speak Yiddish since Greek Jews know Ladino and not Yiddish. You can speak Hebrew, however."

With that comment, he bid us farewell and good luck. We left Prague in a train headed for Bratislava. From there it was possible to reach Vienna and then, finally, Munich.

Not long into our journey a couple of police officers came to our seats and asked to see our papers. One officer asked for them in Czech. None of us answered. He then asked for them in Polish. None of us answered. And again he asked for them, this time in Russian.

None of us answered. Finally I said, "Shma Yisrael," and Arie said, "Ma Tovoo Ohalecha Yaacov," lines from prayers, just to show them we were not deaf mutes but in fact Greek Jews who knew Hebrew. The truth is that aside from our prayers, we knew little Hebrew and so could not communicate to one another, but we went on with the pretense using phrases snatched from the prayer book. This plan seemed to work until someone else in the group said, "mayim" (water), which we all understood but could not respond to. The soldiers were baffled. One said to the other, "That they don't understand us, I can see. That we don't understand them, I know. But they don't even understand each other!"

We were nervous, wondering whether they would put the facts together. Luckily, they did not and, fed up with us, they walked away and left us alone until we reached the border. In the meantime, we decided to shred any evidence that could link us with our Polish past. I had to destroy the few pictures I had managed to maintain of my parents and older brother as well as some important letters that, although they meant the world to me, were written in Polish. Gladys, too, had to destroy dear letters from her father. These acts of destruction, severing the last links to our homeland and the place where our parents and so many others were buried, were extremely painful, but the future was more important. If this was the cost of survival, we felt we had little choice but to pay.

We stayed in Bratislava for two days and then walked eight kilometers across the Danube into Austria. From there we traveled to Vienna where we stayed at the Rothschild hospital that was serving as a transit center for Jews arriving from the east. Vienna had been largely undamaged during the war and so was still a beautiful city. We spent a few days walking around, seeing the sights, and even went to an opera one night. Then we made our way to the American zone in Germany.

Like almost all Jews, when we arrived in Germany we entered Fehrenwald, a DP (displaced persons) camp located near Munich in Bavaria. After a few days there, I told the others that I absolutely would not stay.

"The war is over," I said to them. "I am a free man. I cannot go to a soup kitchen every day with a small bowl in hand waiting for others to

Mina Feder, Sam's cousin (Sheindel Diner's daughter) with Gladys on her wedding day.

give me food. I do not want to live ten people to a room anymore."

I did not condemn the many who found refuge and relief in the DP camp, but it was not for me. After all, I had just come from Poland and Russia where I had prospered in business and had already enjoyed some luxuries, the most important being freedom.

We decided to go to the city of Bayreuth near Nuremberg, home of the famous Wagner Festival. We rented two rooms with German families, one for me and Arie, the other for Gladys and her mother. My cousin Mina had, in the meantime, been diagnosed as having tuberculosis and went to a special hospital near Munich.

Gladys and Sam at their wedding.

Our wedding was attended by only 28 guests in June 1946.

The only family members who survived attended our wedding

Soon after arriving on June 30, 1946, Gladys and I married. The wedding was held in our rented rooms, and a rabbi from Bayreuth officiated. Since food was still being rationed, I had to go on bicycle for ten to twelve miles to the surrounding villages to buy provisions on the black market for the wedding. Gladys' mother then prepared what I had managed to buy for the wedding meal. Twenty-four guests, the few family members who survived with us and some friends, were in attendance. Although we were not officially in mourning, our mood of loss remained with us. My parents, may they rest in peace, were no longer alive. Gladys' father, may he rest in peace, was no longer with us. There had been too much loss and suffering to hold a major *simcha*. The wounds were too fresh. We celebrated this enormously important moment in our lives with a small meal and no music.

Arie and I had some money we had brought with us from Bytom, and we decided to open a grocery store. As it turned out, we were barely able to make a living. In addition, I did not especially like the work. I told Arie that we could make more money in textiles. He liked that idea, too, and we decided to make the attempt. There was one major obstacle, however. We needed a government permit issued only if the West German secretary of commerce, the governor of the county, and the mayor of the city approved it. I knew that the government bureaucrats were reluctant to hand out these permits after the war because they wanted to control commodities that were in short supply. People discouraged us by saying the required approvals were impossible to obtain, but I was undaunted. If I failed, then at least I knew I had tried; and if I succeeded, we could go forward with our plans.

On a Wednesday afternoon when I knew the offices of the Department of Commerce were open only half a day, I went to try to see the secretary himself. I waited until everyone had left and then, with a stroke of luck, the receptionist was nice enough to let me in to speak with the man.

"You know we are already closed," he said. "Today we work only half a day."

"I know, sir, but I've been here twice before, and I could not come any other time." I paused and decided he was receptive. I summoned up all my *chutzpah* and continued. "Please listen to me, and if you tell me I have no right to be here, I'll leave."

His expression showed that he was willing to wait.

"I recently came from Poland. There I sold flour wholesale and was doing well. With a different economic system, I would not have to come to you to ask whether I could open up a business. I know business. My father had a business. I could perhaps do well here without help.

"During the war, Nazis first took away our businesses and all our possessions. Then they put us in ghettos, and I was in a camp. Nazis killed my father, mother, brother, all of my friends, destroyed our business and the entire city.

"I want to make a living in my line of work. Some people are lawyers or doctors. Some have a talent for singing or playing the piano. I am a businessman. Why should you want to help me? Because of what I went through, I would hope you would want to. I want to get back on my feet."

He understood and told me to return the following week. When I arrived a week later, he handed me the documents from the federal government. They read:

"I recommend that Sam Halpern receive the necessary permits to own and operate a wholesale textile business in Bayreuth. He is an experienced businessman and deserves this opportunity."

With this letter I went to the governor of the county and then the mayor of Bayreuth and received the required permits. I was in business! Everyone had thought it was an impossible dream on my part even to try and get this permit. People had been known to wait five years for one. I received the papers in a week. Arie and I opened up a retail store, but doing business proved quite difficult. Even though the fabrics were spun and dyed in the region, they were very hard to acquire. When we did manage to get some, selling it was no problem. The shortages were so severe after the war that people would stand in line to buy fabric.

However, we knew that the money was really in selling wholesale, so we became friendly with the managers of factories and began to buy and sell textiles in quantity. The business grew, and before long we were doing quite well for ourselves. We had a truck, I had my own private car, and we employed two chauffeurs, four salespeople, and two bookkeepers. Arie and I worked hard and prospered.

Although I was deeply involved in the business, I never forgot that it had been the Germans who had killed my people. Every day I thought about my mother and father and missed them profoundly, but I was also young and alive and had a beautiful wife with whom I went dancing and to the new movies from Hollywood.

On Purim, there was a ball and more than 100 couples entered the dance contest. Gladys and I entered as well, and we danced waltzes all night long. We received the first prize for being the best dancers, and

Gladys received the second prize for being the most beautiful woman at the ball!

Arie and I were busy all day long with the business. In continuing to work hard to build a new life, I felt I was celebrating our survival despite all the horrors we had experienced. I believed in forging ahead and succeeding. Had I dwelled on the Holocaust all the time, I would have been overcome with anger and grief. This, then, would have been Hitler's ultimate victory.

All my personal friends were Jews, but in business I dealt with Gentile Germans all day long. Not once was there a trace of anti-Semitism. In fact, people were excessively polite, and no one seemed to know anything about the Holocaust.

I focused on my long-term goal. We had come to the American zone in Germany in order to emigrate to America when our turn came. Although living comfortably, we never intended to stay permanently in Germany. We were merely waiting until our visas were granted. And we were waiting to feel ready to make yet another major change in our young lives.

After the war, the United States only let in survivors reluctantly, fearing that they would be a burden on the country. As David Chase, a survivor who now lives in Connecticut, pointed out at the Gathering of Survivors in Washington, D.C., not only did the survivors not become a burden, but they became very productive citizens. Many became scientists, doctors, lawyers, and prosperous businessmen, employing thousands of American citizens. One became a U.S. Senator in California, Senator Tom Lantos, and my good friend, Elie Wiesel, won the Nobel Prize for Peace.

*

A major cause for celebration occurred on Saturday, November 29, 1947, when the United Nations voted on the partition of Palestine into two separate states: one for the Jews and one for the Arabs. Arie, Gladys, and I were sitting by the radio, keeping track of the votes. This country voted in favor, that country voted against. When the decisive vote was cast, when the state was a reality, we began to cry and dance and hug. Then we sang "Hatikva." I almost could not believe it. After almost two thousand years of exile, after the Holocaust, the sovereign state of Israel was reborn. My generation has seen the worst of times for the Jews and the best of times: the Holocaust and the resurrection of the state of Israel. *Am Yisrael Chai*!

The following day, a Sunday, we had an enormous party at our office in the warehouse. Almost all of Bayreuth's five hundred Jews attended. We served all sorts of food, and there was lots to drink. We sang Israeli songs and danced Israeli folk dances. I kept looking at the pictures of Theodor Herzl and Chaim Weizmann that were hanging on the walls of the warehouse office. When non-Jews would ask who these men were, I would simply answer that they were family members. Go tell them that they were two of the great leaders of modern Zionism! It was a great day, one that I will never forget. It felt like the day of liberation, with utter rejoicing and gratitude. This was, after liberation, the happiest day of my life.

Even before the state was created, we had used our office as a center for Zionist get-togethers. About four evenings a week, when all the employees and sales people and customers who came to buy and sell left for the day, the Zionist organization would meet there. This organization was begun by Holocaust survivors in Europe right after the war, and people associated with the right, left, and center of the Zionist movements were all involved.

Often we invited speakers, who would tell us about the activities of the Jewish underground in then British-ruled Palestine. We were asked to contribute funds and always did. We were asked to do whatever we could to help refugees reach the shores of the land of Israel, and often we did. On Sundays, I would donate the truck of my business and even my personal car to transport Jews from Bayreuth and other little towns to Munich, from which they went on to various ports, usually in Italy or the south of France. From there they embarked on ships bound for Cyprus and then, hopefully, to Israel. I would often do the driving myself since my workers wanted Sundays off.

This was before the creation of the state when it was illegal for Jews to enter Israel under British law. As in the book and movie *Exodus*, we helped get passage for people who had pinned all their hopes on reaching the shore and getting past the British blockade.

When Ben-Gurion came to Fehrenwald, I went to hear him speak.

He told us about how the land was being built up by farmers, trades-men, teachers, businessmen, and scientists; how Tel Aviv was a rapid-ly growing city by the sea; how Jews were returning to live in Jerusalem, building new communities outside the Old City walls; how the Hagana was fighting the British army and the Arabs. He recounted how refugees from Europe were being smuggled past the British blockade by Palmach members who swam out to the ships after nightfall and brought the people to shore, one by one, on their backs. I was very impressed with him and with his vision of an independent Jewish state.

While we did not then go ourselves, we seriously thought we would. Arie's mother-in-law and two sisters-in-law were already there, and he shipped over trucks and machinery to Israel. In the end, though, our decision not to go to Israel at that time was influenced by the insistence of my mother's brother, Paul Wolfson, in New York. After losing so many people in our family, he wanted, more than any-thing, for those of us still alive to be together. He kept writing to me: "Please come to America. I know you're a Zionist, but you can always go to Israel from here. You may not be able to come to America from Israel, though, if it doesn't work out for you there."

Our support of the young state of Israel continued after inde-pendence. Two leaders from Bayreuth's Jewish community, Mr. Geller and Mr. Brillant, came to our office one day on what was one of the first major appeals to Jews in the Diaspora.

"Halpern brothers," Mr. Geller said, "we want you to give us three hundred dollars. The state desperately needs weapons."

Now three hundred dollars was a substantial amount of money then. Most people were donating to the organization, but they gave five, ten, or at most twenty dollars. But three hundred dollars?

"Listen," I said, "can I negotiate with you? We'll give you one hundred dollars."

He answered, "No. You two brothers should give three hundred dollars. God helped you. You survived. You have a nice business."

I turned to Arie and said, "He's right." And we gave it to him.

There was a synagogue in Bayreuth that the Nazis used as a warehouse during the war. When the Jews settled again in Bayreuth, we opened it and brought in a *Sefer* Torah. We celebrated a dedication, and from that time on we had a service every Friday night and *Shabbat* morning. During the week, we would convene a *minyan* only when someone had to say *Kaddish*.

Heinrich Heine, the German-Jewish poet, once said: "More than the Jews kept the Sabbath, the Sabbath has kept the Jews." I think this formula is also true of the state of Israel. More than protecting the state with our contributions, the state will protect us with its existence.

Soon after Gladys and I were married, we went to Bad Kissingen for a vacation. It was an elegant resort with therapeutic baths. Actually, Gladys stayed there with her mother for a month, and I visited on the weekends. One weekend I decided to look up Yacob Kirschner, the engineer who had worked for the Otto Heil construction company and had overseen the road works in Kamionka. He was the man who had warned Goldfliess about the *Aktion*. I knew the Otto Heil company was based in Bad Kissingen since their address had been included on their signs. When I walked into Kirschner's house, he became very pale. He seemed to recognize me right away and looked afraid. He must have thought I had come to denounce him since it was not uncommon for Jews and other ex-inmates from the camps to seek out former tormentors to try and bring them to justice.

"So, how are you? I'm glad to see you," he said to me. He hesitated. "You know, I always helped Jews."

"I remember everything about you," I said. "I remember when you beat one of the inmates, but I also remember that you told Goldfliess about the *Aktion* and that we escaped. You liked me because I was a good worker."

"Yes, I remember you were a good worker."

"Don't worry," I said to him. "I will not do anything to you. There are those people who are guilty of crimes, and they deserve to be punished."

The truth is I had sought Kirschner out not to frighten him or even remind him of his dark past but to see if he knew the whereabouts of some friends of mine who had worked for him directly. If they were alive, perhaps he would know. I had fled hours before the *Aktion*, and so I knew nothing about any of these people. It turned out that he knew nothing either. I left Kirschner's house soon after, thinking about Kamionka and the thousands who had been worked to death,

Sam and Gladys on the eve of their departure to the United States.

killed arbitrarily, and finally murdered one fateful Sabbath in July of 1943.

On February 26, 1948, Gladys and I were blessed with our first child, a son. He was one of the first Jewish children born in Bayreuth after the war, and the entire Jewish community attended his *brit mila.* We named him Ephraim, after Gladys' father, and Mordechai, after my father. After all we had lost, the beginning of a new generation in our family, thank God, was a time of tremendous joy.

*

A year after Israel won the War of Independence, I decided to leave Germany. We were not going to bring up our son in that country. Even though our business was prospering and we were living very well, I had had enough of Europe, the continent of my birth and of my family's bitter destruction. I wanted a fresh start in a new place, a new country, without all the ghosts of the past. We decided that Arie would remain in Bayreuth for a while and would then liquidate the business and join us in America.

In December 1947, Arie married Frieda Geller. With the passing of more time, our mood of loss had diminished, and we decided to make a big celebration. We hired a hall, paid for musicians, and hosted 150 guests. On March 5, 1949, Frieda and Arie were blessed with a baby girl, Bella, named after our mother.

In July of 1949, Gladys and I, her mother and our son, Fred, traveled to Bremen where we left the European continent and set sail for America.

Sam and Gladys with their first child, Fred, in 1948.

The New World

After eight days at sea aboard the SS *General Eltinger*, a warship that had been converted for passenger use, we arrived in Boston harbor on July 18, 1949. I was immediately struck by the

At an early gathering of our family. First row, left to right: Arie Halpern, his late first wife Frieda Halpern, my son Jack, Sam Halpern, my wife Gladys, Cousin Mildred, Cousin Harry Halpern. Second row, left to right: Gladys' mother Mrs. Sara Landau, Cousin Clara, Cousin Sol, Cousin Joe, Cousin Anna, Cousin Shimon, Aunt Betty, Uncle Paul Wolfson.

Sam's uncle, Paul Wolfson, who encouraged Sam to join him in the United States, with his wife Betty at Fred Halpern's Bar Mitzvah.

automobile traffic (there were so many more cars than in Europe), and by the hustle and bustle of the people. Everyone seemed to be rushing about on serious business. Of course, Boston's pace would eventually seem slow compared to New York City's.

From the harbor we made our way to the railroad station and caught a train to New York. After five hours of traveling through a few of the states of our new country, staring out the window at the lovely landscape of New England and New York, we finally reached Pennsylvania Station in the heart of Manhattan.

When we emerged from the train station, we were overwhelmed. Rising like a needle from the earth, the Empire State Building shone right before our eyes, and a little beyond was the elegant, intriguing Chrysler Building, sights I had only heard about or read of in the newspaper and only dreamed of seeing. Yellow taxi cabs were weaving in and out of the heavy traffic, and everywhere there were people

*Cousin Eugene Wolfson
with his wife Toby.*

Cousin Marilyn with her late husband.

on the go. Nothing in Europe had prepared us for the reality of New York City, its sheer size and wealth. Everything, from the buildings to the cars to the hats women wore, was big. Big and glorious. I could sense immediately that wonderful opportunities awaited us on these shores. We were full of excitement and charged with hope. We had made it. We were in America.

I was also anxious to see my uncle, Paul Wolfson, whom I had not seen for eighteen years, since I was a boy of ten. He had always liked me very much, and I had looked up to him. In 1929 his future wife, Gitel, an American, had come to visit relatives in Trembowla. There she met Paul, and they fell in love. He followed her back to America, but before leaving, he had said to me: "When you grow up, I'll bring you to America." Unfortunately, Gitel died some time later, but Uncle Paul remarried Betty, a wonderful woman whom I was looking forward to meeting. Indeed, it was Paul's dog-eared postcard begging me to drop everything and join him in the States that I had carried with me at all times.

We were standing in such a large crowd of people that I wondered how I would ever find my uncle—would he recognize me? After all, I had been just a child when he last saw me. However, as I scanned the crowd, looking for his familiar face, I spotted it immediately. I went up to him and said, "Uncle Paul, it's me, Shmerele." He fell upon me and held me tightly and cried and introduced me to his daughter, my twelve-year-old cousin Marilyn.

The family lived in the Bronx, and we all took a taxi to their pleasant apartment. There we met Aunt Betty and their son, Eugene. Aunt Betty had prepared a beautiful dinner for us, which we thoroughly enjoyed after a week on the ocean. Fred, unaccustomed to the food on the ship, had barely eaten a thing the entire journey, and my mother-in-law and I had been seasick the whole time and could not keep much down. Only Gladys, pregnant with our second son, and feeling wonderful, had been able to enjoy the ship's fare.

After the meal, we were given a bedroom in which to sleep. It was only in the morning, after I noticed my uncle sleeping in a chair and my aunt curled up on a small couch in the living room, that I realized they had given us their bedroom. Because Gladys and I had seen a lovely dining room and living room, we had assumed that we had been given an extra bedroom. But no, Uncle Paul and Aunt Betty had given up their own bedroom.

It was so generous of them, and I was genuinely moved, but I could not allow them to sleep that way one more night. When Uncle Paul woke up, I told him of my decision.

"Today, not tomorrow, we must find a furnished room. Whatever it costs."

At first he protested, wanting so much for us to stay with him. I was one of the only three family members who had survived the Holocaust. The second was Arie, and the third was our cousin Mina Diener, who now lives in Kitchener, Ontario with her husband, her two children, Sidney and Shirley, their spouses and seven grandchildren. Throughout the war, Mina worked as a governess for a German SS officer. She had used a Gentile friend's report card to create a false identity for herself. But while she was able to work in the SS officer's home during the day, she had not been able to go to the housing authorities with her false documents and was forced into sleeping outside under a stairwell at night. She was liberated in Lvov, four months after Arie and I, and then found us in Trembowla. She came with us to Bytom and Bayreuth. There she met her husband, and they then moved to Canada. It was Mina's mother, little brother, and sister who had been betrayed by Anna Bartetsky for five kilos of sugar. Uncle Paul, all too aware of the great loss our family had suffered, wanted to stay close to me. In addition, it meant so much to him that I had been in Kamionka with his brother, my Uncle Dudio. Dudio was killed in the final *Aktion* after being released from camp and returning to Trembowla. I had been the last one in the family to see him alive.

"We'll live nearby," I said. "I'll see you all the time. But I cannot have you sleeping in a chair one more night, and my wife, her mother, my baby, and I, too, need a bed. Believe me, this is what's necessary; this is for the best."

By late afternoon, we had found a furnished room on Mosholu Parkway in the Bronx. It was a tree-lined block not far from a park, which would be good for Fred. The tenants of the apartment were going away and gladly rented us the room. We started to unpack, and a little while later I went out into the street to look at the stores. Even though I had been involved in business in Russia, Poland, and Germany, I knew right away that business in my new country was different.

I was twenty-nine years old. I had arrived in a completely new country with some money. I didn't know more than a handful of English words, and I was totally unfamiliar with Anglo-American culture. I had no connections. As I walked around the Mosholu Parkway neighborhood, I decided that since I did not have enough capital to start my own business and that since there was so much to learn right away, the right way to proceed would be to work for someone else. I would make a living and could learn the ropes.

I went to a store to buy a crib for my son and then asked the young man who brought it and assembled it what his weekly salary was. When he told me he earned fifty dollars, I became discouraged. This man, a college graduate, earned in one week what I had just spent on a crib for my baby. Of course, I had bought the top of the line, but even if I had bought a cheaper one, there would still have not been much left over with that salary. I quickly calculated how much money was needed to live in New York and discovered how low wages were relative to the cost of living. I began to wonder why I had ever left Europe where I had been doing so well.

I said to Gladys, "Why did I do this to myself? I am twenty-nine years old and I know no English. A college graduate is delivering cribs and cannot even afford to buy for his own child the very bed he is delivering to other people's homes. If he, a native-born, English-speaking, college graduate, can barely get by, how will I?"

Her answer was simple and direct but contained the most important words for me to hear, words that have stayed with me ever since. Gladys said, "You always found a way to make a living in Europe. Everyone here makes a living. You, too, will find a way. I know it."

Her moral support and faith in my abilities made all the difference at that critical moment in my life.

Not long after this conversation, I was offered employment in the garment business doing piece work. After living as I had in Europe, as a successful, independent businessman, I knew myself well enough to know I would be very unhappy in that situation. After all, I did not even know how to thread a needle. I wanted to work with the public where I would be forced to speak English. In the factory, everyone spoke Yiddish, and I would never learn the new language. I declined the offer and started to look for work on my own.

We used to shop in a Daitch dairy store in our neighborhood, and this gave me the idea to approach Mr. Paul Daitch, the owner of a chain of dairy stores and supermarkets.

"I don't know much English," I said to him, "but I know how to work very hard, and I'd appreciate your giving me an opportunity."

Mr. Daitch was a middle-aged man, and he liked my directness. He also knew that I had recently arrived from Europe. Considering what all of us who survived had just been through, he knew we needed a chance to start over. He spoke to me in Yiddish and said that he still remembered when he himself came to the United States. He was only too happy to provide me with an opportunity.

"Fine," he said, "you have a job as a stockman at the Daitch store on Tremont Avenue You will fill the shelves with merchandise and keep them in good order."

I thanked him and started work the following day for thirty-five dollars a week, which was less than what I had been offered at the factory. Gladys, her mother, Fred and I moved to our first apartment on Webster Avenue in the Bronx. On December 16, 1949, on the second night of Chanukah, our second son, Chaim David Itzhak, was born. He was named after my second eldest brother, Chaim, after my Uncle Dudio, and after three great-grandfathers who bore the name Itzhak.

For a year and a half I worked at the Daitch supermarket, earning small raises along the way and learning English from the products I carefully shelved. I would read English words all day long. Even if I was not sure of their meaning, I would say them softly to myself so that they would become familiar to me. I worked until six o'clock in the evening, and then I went home to see my family. After supper, I walked to nearby Fordham University to attend night courses in English. I knew that if I were to succeed in this new country, I would need to learn the language as fast as possible.

One afternoon, Daitch's supermarket was very crowded. One of the regular cashiers had not shown up for work, and a long line began to form at the one open register. Customers were becoming restless. They were beginning to complain. I was putting away cereal boxes on a shelf near the front, and I watched the tension mount as the line of customers continued to grow. Finally, I couldn't stand the situation anymore. I walked behind the second cash register and called out, "Open." A dozen or so people shifted to my register, and without skipping a beat I began to ring up items, take money, and pack groceries. I already knew all the product prices from stocking the shelves, and I knew how to work fast. Most important though, I knew that in business pleasing the customer is essential. I was so absorbed in my work that I didn't notice when Mr. Daitch walked into the supermarket. He did a double-take when he saw his stockman working the cash register and stopped to watch me for a while. When the crowd was gone, he approached me.

"What happened?" he asked in a friendly tone of voice.

"Well," I said, "I was putting away the cereal when I saw the line getting longer and longer. Since I know the customers have to be served, I decided to take the place of the absent checkout man and help out." I was hoping he wouldn't be angry with me. Who knew how someone would react? After all, I wasn't trained to work the register.

"I like your spirit," Mr. Daitch said. "And I think from now on you'll work the checkout. That'll mean a raise."

"Thank you, Mr. Daitch," I said.

"I think you have a bright future at Daitch, Sam. I can see that you'd make a wonderful store manager."

"Thank you, Mr. Daitch," I repeated, knowing he meant the compliment.

However, I hadn't told him everything. As well as things were going at the supermarket, I knew that I could not stay there, that it would never fulfill my ambitions. I was born to be an independent businessman, to reap the financial rewards of starting new ventures and taking risks.

I began to look around for an appropriate business and thought I found the right one. I did not do anything, though, until November 1950 when Arie arrived in New York from Germany. He brought with him his wife Frieda and daughter Bella. On January 26, 1951, Shelley was born, named after Frieda's father, Shalom. And on September 29, 1961, another daughter, Nanette, was born to them.

Before leaving Europe, Arie had sold our textile business, and between the profits from that sale and the little he and I had in savings, we felt we could invest in our own business. Almost immediately after Arie arrived, therefore, I went and had a talk with Mr. Daitch.

"I want to thank you again, Mr. Daitch, for giving me a chance to do good work, for giving me time to learn English, and for helping me start my life over again in this wonderful country. But the time has come for me to leave the store. My brother is here, and we're going to open up our own business."

Mr. Daitch was shocked. He never expected an immigrant off the boat a year and a half to go into business for himself. He expressed regrets at losing me but wished me luck.

Since I had become familiar with the supermarket from working in one for a year and a half, I decided that the grocery business was a safe area in which we could invest, so Arie and I bought an existing supermarket on Broadway and 141st Street. At the time, in 1950, the population of this section of Harlem, lower Washington Heights, was heavily German, mainly German-Jews, who lived in large, elegant buildings on Riverside Drive. Even though we knew little English, we could communicate with our clientele, and in no time the business was doing much better than it had been under the previous owner.

The previous owner was just waiting for us to fail so he could take over the store once again. We purchased the store with a cash down payment and a three-year mortgage held by the seller for the remaining sum. He was sure that two brothers fresh from Europe, who barely spoke English and who did not know the ways of America, would not succeed. If we defaulted on the mortgage, as he expected, he would not only have the cash down payment but could repossess his supermarket.

The Halpern brothers were not so easily defeated, however. Together, Arie and I worked very hard, much harder than I had at Daitch's or in Europe. We renovated the supermarket, putting in new shelving, lights, and display racks. I had learned a thing or two about supermarkets working for Mr. Daitch, and I knew that a better looking store would attract more customers. We were also courteous and friendly and kept the store very clean. The area residents really appreciated this service as well as our scrupulous honesty and competitive pricing. They showed approval through frequent patronage.

Within six months, not only were we not bankrupt, but business had improved fifty percent. Our expenses remained the same, but our revenue had gone up considerably. We continued to work very hard, and within a year and a half we paid off our three-year mortgage! Then, owning the store and its merchandise free and clear, we decided to invest in another store. We scouted around and selected on a store on Broadway and 123rd Street. It also did well, and after a while we opened another store on Broadway and 148th Street. Finally, we opened a fourth store in the Bronx.

Arie and I ran from store to store all day long, but for some reason our income from the four stores was less than what we had been making from two. We were not sure exactly what had gone wrong. Perhaps our store managers had not been handling things well.

In any event, we knew we had to sell two of them. And something else began to influence our thinking at the time.

In all the years that we had been in America, our homes were

strictly kosher, and we prayed every day, but the nature of the supermarket business was such that we needed to keep our stores open on
Saturday, which was the busiest shopping day of the week. Having to
work on Saturday, on *Shabbat*, began to bother us terribly. We knew
we had to find a way to make a living without working on *Shabbat*.

One day Arie said, "I am willing to give up five years of my life
not to work on *Shabbat*."

It was such a radical statement. Five years of his life! I did not
want him to lose one day of his life, much less five! Of course, I understood this statement expressed the depth of his longing and since I
shared it, I decided we had to make an aggressive effort to find other
business options. But first, I told him he could no longer work on
Shabbat. Then we began exploring other business opportunities.

Before this difficult issue was resolved, however, my family had to
solve another problem. Our son, Fred, was ready to start school. We
had moved from the Bronx in 1952 and were living in a spacious, airy
apartment on Riverside Drive and 140th Street, not far from our first
supermarket, so we decided to send Fred, who was six years old, to the
Breuer yeshiva, the community of the late Rabbi Samson Raphael
Hirsh from Germany on Bennett Avenue in upper Washington
Heights. The only problem was that Mr. Joseph Breuer, head of the
school, told my wife children were only accepted from households
that strictly observed the Sabbath. He suggested that Gladys send Fred
to the local public schools where administrators did not care about
such matters. Mr. Breuer insisted that he would not make an exception
to this policy.

When Gladys came home, I could see from the expression on her
face that she was upset. When I asked her what had happened, she
recounted what the head of the school had said.

I replied, "Let me go and talk to the rabbi, I come from a family of
many rabbis and I know how to talk to them."

The next day, despite being extremely busy in the stores, I went
uptown to see the head of the Breuer yeshiva. My child's education
was more important to me than anything else. I found the rabbi and introduced myself:

"Rabbi, I pray every day, and my house is kosher. My father and
grandfather were Chortkover Hasidim. I've only been working on

Shabbat in this country because it is the nature of this business, but more than anything, I want to stop. It may take me a little while longer to figure out how to make this work, but in the meantime my son has to go to school. He cannot wait. I don't want to send him to a public school now and then a yeshiva later. I want him to start with a real Jewish education from the beginning. I promise you I'll soon be able to observe *Shabbat*. Please make an exception."

He did. Somehow I convinced him of my sincerity, and he agreed to let Fred come learn at his yeshiva. A year and a half later my son David and niece Bella also began attending the yeshiva. Both boys continued to study there until we moved to Elizabeth, New Jersey.

Five years after our arrival, Gladys and I became naturalized citizens of the United States of America. The ceremony took place at Ebbets Field, the famous baseball stadium that was home to the Brooklyn Dodgers. As far as I know, the naturalization ceremony was the largest of its kind up until that time. More than five thousand new American citizens were sworn in that day. Gladys, my mother-in-law, and I were very proud. Fred automatically became a citizen of this country on that day, too, although he received his papers in a separate ceremony in 1956.

Our third son, Jack, was born on March 30, 1957. We named him Jacob, after Gladys' uncle, and Naftali, after my eldest brother. The same year, Arie and I started a construction company in New Jersey. This business allowed us not to work on *Shabbat*. I would spend every day on the job site, observing the mechanics and details of the trade. I spoke with contractors and learned from job supers. I watched how construction workers put parts together and learned the prices of materials and labor; I learned to identify reliable suppliers and the necessity for coordination among all parties.

In the evenings, I rushed back into Manhattan to supervise the supermarkets. In the meantime, Arie worked at the supermarkets all day long, waiting to see, as was I, if construction was the alternative business for which we had been hoping.

After we sold some of the houses, we saw with certainty that the building industry was a viable option and decided to sell two of our stores. When I told my lawyer that I eventually hoped to sell the other two stores and move into the building business full time, he thought I was making a mistake.

"What's the matter with you? You are a couple of newcomers, and you already have four supermarkets. Everyone envies you."

This observation was true. We had college graduates working for us who could not understand how two men just "off the boat" were doing so well.

"I know," I said, "but I must find a way not to work on *Shabbat*, and we will never accomplish this goal if we stay tied to supermarkets. With construction, I can make *Shabbat* a true day of rest. It's final. I've made my decision."

The first two of the four supermarkets were soon sold. The liquidation had begun.

At the beginning of the first major construction project, I realized that one job could overlap another, and so capital from incoming sales of one could finance the start of a second. Arie and I then bought land in Edison Township and built thirty-six single family homes. We built two model homes and then advertised. People came to look, they liked what they saw, and then they bought what was yet to be built. As the homes were selling, we took in a partner and purchased yet another parcel of land in Woodbridge and developed 104 houses on it too.

We were expanding during the Truman era, and the Veteran's Administration was offering veterans home mortgages with no down payments. Tracts of land in New Jersey were wide open for development, and the idea of suburban living was spreading like wildfire in the American imagination. Conditions were favorable for this kind of development. However, I believe there are opportunities just as good today. There is always something for a businessman to do. Business never goes out of style. Sometimes it is slower. Sometimes it is better. But if you know what you are doing and pay attention to the world around you, success is possible. And sometimes you do even better.

I am often asked how I could have jumped into the construction industry, a technically complicated field, without any prior knowledge or background. It's a good question, and I think I have a good answer. First, there is the issue of crossing frontiers and defining them by the act of doing. No one knew that a human being could fly across the ocean until Charles Lindberg showed how it could be done. I learned

Left to right, Senator Frank Lautenberg, Rabbi Pinchas Teitz, and the author.

about construction and development by doing. One house after another, one architect after another, one subcontractor after another, one business deal after another. Before too long I was familiar with the technical language, the idiosyncrasies of the trade, and the financial details.

The second part of my answer is that business is business whether one is selling diamonds, salt or houses. Everything I know about business I learned from my father in his store where I absorbed his approach to people. The quantities may have changed, but the act is essentially the same. I drew on everything I had noticed in my father's store, in the marketplace of Chorostkow, in the Russian distillery, the factory, the Polish grain and flour wholesale market and the German textile business. The same principles apply. Only the goods are different. The supermarket business is very difficult, harder than construction in many ways, a fact I learned soon after arriving to this country without connections and few language skills. What I did have was a willingness to work hard, energy to invest in the learning process, and determination to succeed.

Tired of commuting back and forth between Manhattan and the building sites in New Jersey, I decided to move the entire family to an apartment on Elmora Avenue in Elizabeth, New Jersey in 1958. We chose Elizabeth because of Rabbi Pinchas Teitz's school, the Jewish Educational Center of Elizabeth. In fact, our first apartment was right across the street from the yeshiva. My sons had been going to the Breuer yeshiva, and I was determined not to make a break in their Jewish education. I had heard only wonderful things about the beautiful school in Elizabeth, so Gladys and I decided that this city would be our next stop.

In 1959 we sold the last supermarket. Nine years in that business had taught us a great deal about commerce in America and enabled us to support our families. The stores provided enough capital to jumpstart us in real estate development. That same year, we bought land in Bloomfield, New Jersey and developed seventy-four rental garden apartments for the first time. The following year, we began projects in Scotch Plains, Woodbridge, and Parsippany, all central Jersey locations. Eventually, we also built houses and garden apartments in Rockland County, New York.

In 1960 when the business began to take off and I realized I could not be everywhere at once, we instituted a policy that proved to be wonderfully successful. We began to give our project managers a percentage of the profits in addition to a good salary. We felt that they would have more interest in pushing the job along and making sure everything worked well if they were partners in the process.

Most developers paid their managers a good salary, but they did not give away shares. I wanted more, however. Of course, I wanted to ensure that the project made money, but I also wanted the manager to know first hand that if the project made money, both of us would prosper. This policy has worked wonderfully for us. In this way, I was confident that my management was on top of things, and I was free to take care of other critical aspects of a growing business: I could meet with bankers, be available to negotiate for land, and make appointments with engineers and architects. Essential to understanding this profit sharing structure is the realization that for the project manager, who is the person on the job site every day, the person who knows every detail and transaction, his ten percent is as important to him as our ninety percent is to us. Today, many other people are using this system to boost efficiency and loyalty in business. We started it back in the 1960s.

Aside from the business angle, what has been most satisfying for me about this profit sharing is the way people have learned to give charity. Some people who became our "partners" in this way went on to become wealthy, and for this outcome I am only too happy. When the profits were divided and everyone was assured a sizable gain, I would say time and again: "Now that you have made; it's time to give. The job made money; let's all give a certain percentage to charity." And people did, for they saw us behaving this way all the time, and they knew I was right to ask. Teaching people that giving charity is the right thing to do has meant a great deal to me.

We encouraged our associates to become involved in various organizations and schools: the United Jewish Appeal, hospitals in New Jersey and New York City, the Jewish National Fund, Israel Bonds, American War Veterans, the Jewish Educational Center, and the Red Cross. As with the ways of business, making charity a part of life was something I learned from my father and grandfather. Although they were not rich, they were comfortable, and they always gave more than they could. In proportion to his means, my father gave more charity than I do. When he gave, he was left with much less.

In 1961 after three years in an apartment, I finally built a house for my family in Elizabeth, and I was pleased with all I had managed to do in the twelve years I had been in the United States. In this house we were blessed with our youngest son, Murray, who was born on February 20, 1966. He was named after Gladys' great-uncle, Moshe Landau, and her Uncle Yosef.

Before this wonderful joy, though, tragedy struck our family. Frieda, Arie's wife, died of cancer. A few years later, Arie married Eva Krenkel, a close family friend from Chorostkow. Eva had two sons from a previous marriage to Baruch Stein who had passed away a year before Frieda's death. Together they created a loving, close-

My mother-in-law, Sara Landau.

knit home for all their children.

Twelve years later, in 1973, we sold our house and built a larger one in Hillside. Our motivation for moving was my mother-in-law, Sara. Gladys wanted her to come live with us in our Elizabeth home, as she had before we moved to New Jersey. Although at the time Sara was still spry and able to climb stairs with ease, we envisioned the day when reaching her bedroom on the second floor might not be so easy for her. Anticipating this situation, we decided to build a new house where her bedroom would be on the ground floor. No matter how much room we had, no matter how many times we asked her to live with us, she always answered gently, "Yes, I'm glad you have a room for me in case I need it, but as long as I can be in my own home, that's where I prefer to be."

My mother-in-law was a wonderful, independent woman who came from a prestigious line of rabbis, most notably Noda BiYehuda, the chief rabbi of Prague. A generous and kind spirit, she joyfully helped Gladys raise our sons. During the many years when I was immersed in our growing business, I could not help much with the children or the home. Thank God, Grandma could.

Since my mother-in-law, may her memory be blessed, remained in her own apartment, Gladys visited her every day if she was not already at our house helping with the children. Each *Shabbat* we walked over to visit Grandma, and in the end she never did use the room we built especially for her. She lived on her own until 1985 when she passed away suddenly at the age of eighty.

Several years after we moved from Washington Heights to Elizabeth, New Jersey, Rabbi Teitz appointed me to serve on the board of the Jewish Educational Center. I gladly accepted. Over the years, the school continued to grow, and a school building for boys was added. Then a girls' high school, called the Bruria school, was built. Most recently, in 1991, another addition to the main building was completed. It houses a large gymnasium and other facilities. This building was named after our dear friend, Harry Wilf, who remained involved in Jewish education, especially with the JEC's growing needs, even through his final illness. In memory of our parents, Arie and I built and dedicated a study hall, the Halpern *Beit Medrash*, in this addition. Arie not only contributed financially to this project but also spent many hours on the site. On a daily basis he supervised the construction and negotiations with contractors to help save the school money. I served this wonderful institution of Jewish education for three years as president, contributing as best I could in numerous ways. Since then, I continue to serve as a member of the Board. Today, there are over nine hundred students in the religious day school that many say is one of the best in the country.

Everything centers around Rabbi Teitz, a truly remarkable man. Originally from Riga, he was not only a gentle personality and great American rabbi but was one of the first rabbis to build a yeshiva in a smaller American community. Before the JEC was built, yeshivas were found only in large cities. Rabbi Teitz had the foresight to recognize that Jews were beginning to move from cities to suburbs and that wherever young Jews lived, there was a need for Jewish education. The school he founded and built became a model for other schools in smaller American communities. With this act, Rabbi Teitz was instrumental in reviving Judaism. As an outstanding orator and charismatic teacher, he was most effective in developing a love for Judaism in the young generation.

When I first came to America, I saw mainly old men praying in daily services. The young had little interest in Judaism or Jewish learning. They were too involved in their work. This situation has changed, thanks to people like Rabbi Teitz. Today when I go to synagogues in our area and elsewhere around the country, I see many younger people interested in learning Torah, involved in prayer and doing *mitzvot* (good deeds). When our youngest son, Murray, was born in 1966, Rabbi Teitz was his *sandak*. We respected the rabbi so much that we wanted him to be even closer to our family, and we were honored that he accepted this important role.

When Rabbi Teitz came to this country from Riga, he married Rabbi Preil's daughter, Bessie. Rabbi Preil, Senior, was the chief rabbi of Elizabeth, and Rabbi Teitz eventually succeeded him. Later, he established the school, which opened with about twelve children. However, the rabbi's efforts did not stop there.

Rabbi Teitz began weekly radio broadcasts dealing with Talmud, the *Daf HaShavua* (page of the week). Thousands, including myself, learned a great deal from the rabbi's lectures and enjoyed them tremendously. The rabbi would explain the Talmud in Yiddish, and now his son, Rabbi Eliezer Teitz, also a great scholar who studied at the Ponevish Yeshiva in Bnai Brak, lectures on the radio in English.

Not only young people were affected by the rabbi's teaching. Often students wound up teaching their parents about Judaism, many of whom, for one reason or another, had missed out on a Jewish education, and so the older generation was brought back into the fold.

At a time when not many people were paying attention to the millions of Jews trapped inside of Russia, Rabbi Teitz made more than

In front of the Moscow Yeshiva, founded by Rabbi Adin Steinzaltz.
Left to right, Sam Halpern, Councilman Noach Dear, the current
Rosh HaYeshiva, Harry Wilf, and Lenny Wilf.

twenty trips to establish contact with the Jewish community in the former Soviet Union. On these trips he brought religious articles, such as kosher wine, *matzot, etrogim,* and *lulavim.* He also shipped cases of these items to Russia and was unafraid of defying the Soviet authorities in order to supply what he knew the Jews there needed. In addition, he had special Russian-language prayer books printed.

Inspired by the rabbi's example, Gladys, my son Jack, and I traveled to Russia in 1979, and we too "smuggled" in prayer books and other religious articles. One *Shabbat* in a synagogue in Leningrad, I was handing out the prayer books I had brought, and suddenly a man came up to me.

"You just gave that man a book," he said. "He's not going to pray with it. He'll sell it on the black market."

"Good," I answered. "He will then have money to make *Shabbat,* and the other man will pray with the book. This is excellent; nothing wrong at all!"

Rabbi Teitz is also an ardent supporter of the state of Israel, having met with Ben-Gurion many years ago and become good friends with Menachem Begin.

Working for Jewish education is not a new activity for the Halpern family. My father and grandfather were actively involved in supporting schools and yeshivas, and so it was only natural for Arie and me to continue this tradition. The JEC is not the only yeshiva I support with time, energy and funds.

Avraham Ofer, the former minister of the state of Israel, my childhood friend from Chorostkow, whose brother, Dov, so impressed the entire shtetl by walking to Israel, worked very hard on behalf of Mivasseret Zion, a yeshiva for Chortkover Hasidim on the way to Jerusalem. He was a real Laborite, and everyone thought he would never support a religious institution. I know how wrong this assumption was, though, because he worked hard to raise money for the yeshiva. Because of Mr. Ofer's continuous efforts, I too became involved with this yeshiva. After all, we were Chortkover Hasidim ourselves, and we remembered Rabbi Meshulam Rath from Chorostkow. Avraham and I knew that too many of our people were lost in the Holocaust; we recognized as vital support of Jews devoted to studying Torah. I help this particular yeshiva and continue, to the best of my abilities, to support a number of others both in the United States and Israel.

I strongly believe in the need for solid institutions of Jewish education, from the earliest years when a student learns the *aleph bet* with drops of honey, to the college and universities, and on through a wide spectrum of yeshivas.

After the war when I looked around at those of us who had survived, I saw only adults, no children. Hitler had killed the children first, so often right in front of their parents' eyes. No matter where I was—in Russia, Poland, or Germany—I did not see any Jewish children, and I became concerned. I knew that if there were no children, there would be no future for our nation. All those who had filled the benches of the *heders* and yeshivas; all the Jewish youth who were members of B'nai Akiva, Hanoar Hatzioni, Betar, Mizrachi, Ha-Shomer Hatzair; all the children who accompanied their parents to the synagogue on *Shabbat*; all those who helped their families sell at the stalls on market days; all those who played soccer and tag and filled the fields with laughter and excitement, all of them were gone!

Not until I came to the United States were my fears stilled of never again seeing a Jewish school full of children. Here, for the first time, I again witnessed normal Jewish life. My cousin, Eugene, was in Yeshiva High School, my other cousin, Marilyn, was in a Talmud Torah school. When I went with them to pray at Rabbi Faderbush's synagogue in the Bronx, I saw scores of little children running up and down the aisles and watching as the holy Torah was taken out of the ark for public reading.

Who knows how many future Rambams, Rashis, Vilna Gaons, Einsteins, Freuds, Herzls, Wiesels there were among more than a million children who were brutally killed by Hitler's hordes, whose potential was never realized? We are the remnants of that great Jewish civilization which existed in Poland and throughout Europe, and educating our children is where it all begins. Jewish education is the secret source of our strength through the ages; it is the foundation upon which our meaning and faith is laid. *ViTalmud Torah keNeged koolam*: And the study of Torah above all else.

Because of this belief, I am also involved in Yeshiva University,

*In Yad Vashem: Sam Halpern, Michael Gorniak,
Josefa Gorniak, and Gladys Halpern.*

which I consider to be a jewel of Jewish education. Touro College, where I am a member of the board and one of the trustees, is also a remarkable achievement. Dr. Bernard Lander, founding president of the college, has accomplished a great deal in the twenty years of the school's existence. In addition to the New York and Jerusalem campuses and the law school on Long Island, there is a Touro College in Moscow with over five hundred students. Another building is currently being built on a Brooklyn campus in New York. Students at these institutions study both secular and religious subjects and receive degrees in either or both. Today there are more than eight thousand students involved with Touro worldwide, an astonishing achievement.

I firmly believe that the commitment of Jews to education has helped us survive when the odds were clearly against us. In our communities, not only a small, select group of leaders have been literate and knew how to think through complicated problems, as is often the case in other nations. Our tradition, as the People of the Book, was to teach every child to read and write and study the Bible. Most boys were taught the *Mishna* and some even the *Talmud.* Our people have

As I steadily work for Israel Bonds, UJA, and other causes, I meet with Israeli leaders both in the United States and Israel, during my frequent visits there. I am glad to work with members of the ruling parties as well as leaders of the opposition parties. Above: With the late Prime Minister Menachem Begin.

Below: Together with my wife, at a meeting with Prime Minister Itzhak Shamir.

I am greeted by the head of the opposition party, Benjamin Netanyahu.

*At the Ben Gurion home in Tel Aviv, I introduced Foreign Minister
Shimon Peres to UJA leaders.*

had to think their way out of problems, and this has not only worked for us but has, I believe, made us a special nation in this complex world.

                                        *

Not long after we moved out of our apartment and into a new home, one of the chairmen of the UJA approached me and asked if I could donate $180 to the organization. I said I would but asked him to come to my house so that we could discuss the matter further. Of course, I was more than interested in giving as much financial support to the new state of Israel as I could. Had we had a country of our own ten years before the war, the Holocaust might not have happened; certainly, the Nazi plague would have had less tragic consequences. When the world kept silent and closed its gates, we would have had a place to go, a place of our own. Today, Israel welcomes Jews from all over the world. The Russians Jews have a place to come; the Ethiopians have realized their dream of returning to Zion. Jews from Europe, North and South America, Africa, and Asia keep immigrating to Israel, hoping for a better life for themselves and their children.

The man from the UJA agreed to come to my home, and in the meantime I organized a parlor meeting to which we invited a number of friends, builders among them, and Gladys provided everyone with coffee and cake. When the UJA representative came, he was surprised not only by the reception waiting for him but by my announcement that instead of pledging $180, I was interested in donating a larger sum. This commitment began a series of substantial pledges. In that one evening, a significant amount of money was raised for the UJA.

My involvement with the UJA and its board began that day, and to this day I work closely with the Federation, helping to raise funds in my community and participating in worldwide missions to Europe and Israel. This was not the first time I was involved with a major Jewish organization, however.

In 1951 Ben-Gurion had come to the United States to sell Israel Bonds. I went to hear him speak on the Grand Concourse in the Bronx. The hall was so crowded I could not get in, but I stood outside and listened to his speech through a loudspeaker. I heard Ben-Gurion

Vice President Dan Quayle addressed the Israel Bond Drive dinner.
Left to right: Ambassador Meir Rosen, Elie Wiesel, Vice President Dan Quayle,
Sam Halpern, and Mayor Ed Koch.

proclaim that whoever purchased a hundred dollar bond would be entitled to go to Madison Square Garden for a Chanukah performance. Arie and I eagerly bought a bond each. Through this act we knew we were investing in Israel's future, giving the new country the capital it needed to build an infrastructure, fund research and development projects, and feed and house the needy. This investment made us partners in Israel and gave us the most satisfaction, as it continues to do.

Today, I am the general chairman of Israel Bonds in my community as well as a member of the national cabinet. Thank God, my family and Arie's are now able to purchase a considerable number of bonds. With each purchase, we feel the sense of partnership grow stronger. I am not only delighted to buy bonds, but I also take great pleasure in selling them. In fact, because people who purchase bonds become the best salesmen, I strongly believe that buyers should also become sellers.

In 1989 I was greatly moved to receive the fifth International Elie Wiesel Holocaust Remembrance Award, which is presented annually by Israel Bonds to an individual for "outstanding and exemplary leadership on behalf of Israel and the Jewish people." At that presentation dinner, Elie Wiesel spoke of the need to publish survivors' memoirs. "We need these testimonies," he said, "especially in this crucial decade, the last decade of the century." He predicted that in the next century the world would tell the Jews to "stop talking, it's enough!" People would refuse to hear any more about the genocide of the 1940s and Jewish suffering at the hands of the Germans and their collaborators in many European countries. I agree wholeheartedly with him, and in this spirit I am telling my story.

In the spring of 1994, I led a mission of a few hundred people for Israel Bonds to Poland and Israel to participate in the March of the Living. This biannual journey to Auschwitz and Birkenau, made by several organizations and youth groups, is followed by five days in Israel. The trip traces the road of the forced three-kilometer march of death between Auschwitz and Birkenau where millions of Jews died in the crematoria. More than six thousand children and adults marched. Everyone wore blue jackets imprinted with the "March of the Living" in white. This march is not only a gesture of solidarity with the victims of the camps but also an effort to ensure that the Holocaust remains part of our living history.

Among many interesting people involved in the March of the Living was a man from Vienna who told me that in 1939, after the *Anschluss* (Germany's annexation of Austria), he was sitting in the classroom of his Jewish school one afternoon. Outside, a band of Nazi youth began to chant anti-Semitic slogans and screamed "Heil Hitler" over and over. The students were frightened, but their teacher, in an attempt to mollify their fears, thoughtfully said: "Dear students, I do not know what tomorrow will bring, but I can tell you that long after the Germans and Austrians have finished screaming 'Heil Hitler,' we Jews will still be saying, '*Shma Yisrael.*'"

After the Israelis' swift and brilliant victory in the Six Day War in

June, 1967, raising funds for Israel became much easier. Jews all over the world felt proud and stood taller. The danger to Israel's existence had also become clearer, and the combination of national pride and a continued threat spurred world Jewry to greater participation. Again, after the terrible Yom Kippur War in 1973 when Israel was caught by surprise on this holiest of days, American Jews responded with generous support.

From early childhood, I collected money for *Keren Kayemet Li-Yisrael*. The famous blue boxes were visible signs of developments in Israel. Land reclamation, road building, tree planting, desert agriculture, and water management were accomplished with these funds. In addition to our annual contribution, some years ago, after the start of the Palestinian *intifada*, the Jewish National Fund forests became arsonists' targets, so Arie and I bought one of the urgently needed state-of-the-art fire trucks to help Israeli fire fighters work more effectively. I know Moshe Rivlin, the world leader of *Keren Kayemet*, very well, along with Dr. Samuel Cohen, executive vice president of JNF America. The work of this fund has been invaluable to the development of the land of Israel.

In May of 1988, I was honored by Mizrachi at an international dinner attended by a thousand people. I have long worked on behalf of this organization, especially for the benefits of the *Hesder* yeshivas, the schools where students divide their time between religious studies and army service.

Although I am a devoted Zionist and continue to contribute to many Israel-related organizations, I also believe, as I learned in my parents' home, that charity and kindness must apply to those very close to home. Therefore, in addition to my involvement with national organization, I also work with institutions in my local community such as the Jewish Family Service in Elizabeth, which helps poor Jewish families get apartments and furnishings, pay school tuition, find jobs, put food on the table and clothing on their backs; and the YMHA, which provides recreational, sports, cultural and educational activities for all age groups in the community.

I am also honorary vice-president and one of the original founders of the Jewish Home for the Aged in Franklin Township, near New Brunswick. Harry Wilf, *z"l*, Senator Norman Tanzman, Herb

Goldstein, and I helped raise the funds for this facility and supervised its construction ourselves. It was the first Jewish facility for the elderly in central New Jersey and filled an important need.

In terms of hospitals, I donate regularly to Elizabeth General, Perth Amboy General, St. Elizabeth's, Kennedy Hospital in Edison, New York University Hospital, Columbia-Presbyterian, St. Peters in New Brunswick, and others.

Even though I come from Chortkover Hasidim, I am not a member of the Lubavitch movement. I am, though, a strong supporter of Lubavitch and help the Rabbinical College of America in Morristown, New Jersey. I have seen evidence with my own eyes of the wonderful work the Lubavitchers do. Once when I was on a trip to Hong Kong, I found that the local Habad house had a *minyan* in the Hilton Hotel for travelers. I was staying at the nearby Mandarin Hotel and could walk to the *minyan* on *Shabbat*. Habad had provided a space for people from all over the world, from the United States, Canada, South Africa, and Israel, to come together to pray, sing and enjoy a delicious *kiddush*. Coincidentally, the rabbi who ran the Hong Kong Habad house was a graduate of the Morristown Rabbinical College, a man whom I knew from home.

Another time, Gladys and I arrived in San Diego not long before *Shabbat*. As we drove around looking for a supermarket where we could buy some kosher food to take back to the hotel room, I spotted a group of men with long beards in black hats and black suits and white shirts. Right away I knew they were observant Jews. I stopped the car to ask what they were doing there.

"Oh, around the corner there is a Habad house," one replied.

"A Habad house?"

Well, Gladys and I went over, and we saw that a great deal of food was being prepared. When I asked for whom they were cooking so much, they explained that there were Jewish students at a nearby university and that many of them came for meals. Some of the young women were dressed quite immodestly, and they would be given some clothing. Some of the students could not afford to eat very well during the week, and they would fill up over *Shabbat*. Some were even given ten or fifteen dollars pocket money for the coming week. About fifteen to twenty students showed up weekly. So I support such efforts, know-

On one of our UJA trips to Europe, Baron Rothschild, who headed the French Jewish Federation, introduced me to the gathering.

ing that the Lubavitchers are only trying to provide a forum for Judaism in areas where few others go.

I had the privilege of meeting the great Lubavitcher rebbe, Rabbi Menachem Mendel Shneerson, *z"l*, a number of times. I always received my blessing and a dollar, and once I even sat quite close to him when a group of us, representing various Zionist organizations, were invited to stay for a gathering, a *farbrengen*, at the 770 Eastern Parkway headquarters. He spoke to us about Israel, its past, present, and future. The passing of this towering personality is a great loss to the world Jewish community.

My wife Gladys who shares my interests, is a full partner in our work for American and Jewish causes. In addition to the organizations that I have already mentioned, she works for Hadassah, Amit, and the Women's Auxiliary for the Home for the Aged, and she has her own interests and organizations to which she donates time and financial support. Throughout the years when a number of leaders of world Jewry came to speak at meetings at our house, Gladys was always a gracious and delightful hostess. No doubt the aura that she created helped inspire the generous donations of the guests.

After years of working and contributing to organizations that dispersed funds to different projects in the state of Israel, Arie and I started to think of how to get more intimately involved with the country. The obvious answer was to develop projects there, on the ground. I knew the old saying: "Give a man a fish, and he will eat that night; teach him how to fish, and he will eat for the rest of his life."

One day in 1970, an opportunity presented itself. Mr. Pinchas Sapir, then finance minister of Israel, approached a group of people and asked if we would be interested in investing money in Israel. Among those present were many friends of mine: the Wilf brothers, Harry, *z"l*, and Joseph; the Schwartz brothers, Steve and Henry; the Dunitz brothers; and Arie and I.

"Charity is very nice," he said, "and important, but Israel needs investment. If people did business there, the young country would grow much faster."

"We agree with you," I said. "And we are interested in investing directly in Israel."

He was delighted.

"The best thing for Israel," he said, "would be to have new factories built. And if that factory could produce a product that would be marketed and sold to America and Europe, then many jobs would be created and a lot of revenue would also be generated for other sectors of business and the government."

Again we agreed that this strategy was excellent, but it was not exactly what we had in mind.

"Running a factory is a full-time job," I said from experience. "We would have to be there all the time, which we cannot do. We live in America, and our business is here."

"So what do you propose?" he asked us.

"My partners and I would be interested in a good location," I answered immediately. "We want to build a five-star hotel in Tel Aviv."

Sapir told us that if we were serious about building such a hotel, we should come to Israel soon to meet with Rabinovich, the mayor of Tel Aviv, to discuss the availability of land and other important aspects of the project.

Not long after this meeting, representatives from our group flew to

Israel to meet with Rabinovich. We told him that we were extremely confident in Israel's future, and we pointed out that Tel Aviv had only two five-star hotels, the Hilton and the Dan. We were sure that with each year more and more tourists would come to Israel and want to spend time in this beautiful city by the sea. Once, only small planes crossed the oceans and continents, but we had entered the jet age, and suddenly four hundred people per plane were landing, and there was a clear shortage of hotel rooms. We proposed building a sixteen-story, 345-room ultramodern hotel with banquet halls, restaurants, and bars that would appeal to sophisticated travelers.

This project excited Rabinovich very much, and he showed us plans for Kikar Atarim—a large, wonderful plaza of shops and cafes on the beach, and for the *tayelet*, a pedestrian promenade modeled after the French Riviera, which would snake along the beach all the way from Tel Aviv to Yaffo. Although my friends and I liked the plans and were excited at the prospect of being part of this seaside development, I must admit that we were also skeptical about its realization. How delighted I am today to be able to state that the promenade and plaza exceed the proposed plans in beauty and utility. The mayors of Tel Aviv, and in particular Mayor "Chich" Lahat, helped make this grand scheme a marvelous reality.

After showing us plans for the future development, Rabinovich personally took us around to look at various sites that might meet our needs. He showed us the sites where the Sheraton now stands, the Plaza, and the Ramada Continental. We said we liked the locations very much and closed the deal.

The Ramada Continental on Yarkon Street officially opened its doors in the spring of 1974. It is a lovely hotel right on the beach, and all around it hotels and a large plaza have grown. A sleepy shoreline has become the busy hub of this metropolis.

We were all as pleased as could be, and for nine years we were content. Then we began to think that the time had come to build another hotel. We knew that this time we wanted to build in Jerusalem. We scouted around and eventually found a piece of land on Wolfson Street near the Givat Ram campus of Hebrew University. As I was negotiating for this property right before I was about to close the deal, a broker called me.

"Sam," he said. "I understand you want to build another hotel here in Israel, this time in Jerusalem. I can tell you, if you want another hotel, the Jerusalem Hilton is for sale. And it will probably cost you considerably less than it would to build from scratch."

I had to stop and think about this proposal. The Hilton is a beautiful hotel, and the price was certainly attractive. I decided to meet with the hotel's representative. Afterward, I returned to our hotel in Tel Aviv and called Harry Wilf, my friend and partner.

"Harry," I said, "the Hilton is available, and the figures come out much better to buy than building new. It's a beautiful, prestigious hotel, fully equipped, custom made, and fully cliented. It's something to consider seriously."

Harry was quiet for a moment, and then he answered me thoughtfully, as he always did.

"Sam," he said, "people already invested in the Hilton. It has already been built. The *mitzvah* is not to own a hotel in Jerusalem but to build Jerusalem. *Bonei Yerushalayim* the prayers say. Those who build speed up redemption, not those who purchase already built properties."

"Harry, you convinced me," I said, knowing he spoke a deep, spiritual truth. Without hesitation, I shared his conviction and pressed forward with our new hotel.

The Ramada Renaissance opened with great fanfare in 1983. A five-star facility, it has become Jerusalem's most modern and largest hotel. Former Mayor Teddy Kollek came to me after the opening and said, "Sam, this hotel is a flower of Jerusalem." He was very impressed and said, "It's good for Jerusalem. It's good for tourism. It's good for the country."

A few years later, a developer started erecting a hotel on the plot next to ours. Unfortunately, soon after the shell was constructed, the finances went awry, and the bank took over the project. My partners and I decided to buy it from them and continue development. On the land in between the two hotels we built one of the largest ballrooms in Jerusalem. It has the capacity to hold more than sixteen hundred people theater style and a thousand people for dinner. Not long after this addition was completed, the name of the hotel was changed to the Jerusalem Renaissance.

In the continued spirit of building Jerusalem, my partners and I decided to contribute to a much-needed synagogue in the large new community of Gilo. We believed strongly in the development of new Jerusalem neighborhoods and felt we should do our part to make them complete.

Our next project was a joint venture with Ashtrum, a very fine Israeli construction company. Together we built a 200,000 square-foot office building in Tel Aviv right near the Ayalon Highway. Around 1990, we again joined with Ashtrum to build a hotel called the Riviera Club in Eilat. We do not operate it but lease it to David Luis. We have also built an industrial park in Jerusalem.

We use Israeli labor almost exclusively to staff our projects. With the exception of Italians who are brought in for marble work and sometimes cabinetry, we rely for the most part on local labor and recognize that doing so is an invaluable part of contributing to the growth of Israel. More than a thousand people are working, thank God, in our various properties in Israel.

*

I travel to Israel three or four times a year, and each time I land, just like the first time I came in 1966, I think of my older brother, Avrum Chaim, the ardent Zionist, and I cannot stop myself from weeping. "He should be here," I cry when the doors of the airplane open and my feet touch the tarmac. "He would love this place so much," I say through my tears as handsome Israeli soldiers watch over the disembarking passengers. "He should be living here, making the country grow, making it work," I think to myself as I survey the terminal at Ben-Gurion International Airport in Lod.

On that first two-week trip in 1966, I was overwhelmed with what had been accomplished in the country in so short a time. I visited with friends, Avraham Ofer among them, whom I had not seen since 1933 when we were young boys. Gladys and I traveled up and down the country, seeing as much as we could fit into our time table. I was awed by all I saw: the Mediterranean and the Dead Sea, the Galil and the desert, Tel Aviv and Haifa, Tzfat and BeerSheva. And then, of course, there was Jerusalem. In 1966 there was still a wire separating the

*The Chief Rabbi of Israel, Rabbi Yisroel Meir Lau, stepped in to congratulate
me when we celebrated the 10th anniversary of the Renaissance Hotel in
Jerusalem.*

divided city. It even ran through the gardens of the King David Hotel
where I was staying. Where the hotel pool is today was then Jordan. I
was able to see the Old City walls and had to imagine what it might be
like to see and touch the *Kotel* (Western Wall of the Second Temple).

One of the places that especially left an impression on me, for
practical and historical reasons, was Zichron Yaacov, Baron Edmund
de Rothschild's investment in the holy city during the late nineteenth
century. Rothschild had believed in returning to the land and had invested heavily in the first European-style farms in Palestine. After a
few unsuccessful starts, grapevines were eventually planted, and the
vineyards of Rishon LeZion and Zichron Yaacov along with the nearby gardens are a beautiful success.

I was impressed with this enterprise not only because it is a working, profitable business, producing kosher wines for world Jewry, but

Avrum Wolf Gelbart, Sam's great uncle, his children, grandchildren, and other members of his family, which today number over one hundred.

Avrohom Ofer, a member of the Israeli cabinet, on Sam's right, was invited to address a dinner gathering for Israel Bonds.

because it stands in stark contrast with another resettlement effort begun at the same time. This was the vision of Baron Morris de Hirsh, who also recognized that Europe's Jews needed to rebuild their lives somewhere else. However, Baron de Hirsh did not believe that national redemption was tied to the ancient homeland. When Herzl visited him to ask for funds for his early Zionist enterprise, de Hirsh rebuffed him. He thought of the New World and bought thousands of acres of land on which he began two farming communities for Jews, one in Argentina and one in Vineland, New Jersey. De Hirsh paid all the expenses for families to establish themselves in both settlements, and for a generation or so things seemed to be going well. However, for all of de Hirsh's good intentions, his plan could not provide for future generations of Jews. Today, little remains of either of these great efforts, these alternative communities. In Israel, though, the vineyards and other communities, like Benyamina, Rosh Pina, Petach Tikva, Zichron Yaacov, and Rishon LeZion into which Baron de Rothschild funneled money, have flourished.

As I walked around the grounds of Rishon LeZion, I wished that others had shared Rothschild's vision and invested financially in the land of our ancestors a hundred years ago. Moses Montefiore, from London, did, constructing Yemin Moshe, one of the first communities outside Jerusalem's Old City walls. He visited the country seven times, which was no simple task in those days. I wonder why we as Jews at the beginning of modern Zionism, and even earlier with the Hovevei Zion movement in the nineteenth century, missed numerous opportunities to purchase land in Israel. Many of the problems the nation encountered under British rule and certainly with the Arabs might have been avoided had we acted earlier. When Herzl was negotiating with the Turkish Sultan for more land for Jewish immigration, the Sultan was willing to sell the country to him for a few million dollars. Wonderful as this prospect was, Herzl was unable to raise the money. Of all the wealthy European Jews, Baron Edmond de Rothschild was one of the very few who was willing to invest in the idea of national redemption.

We cannot allow ourselves to miss any more opportunities. The fact that Israel has been able to absorb half a million immigrants from the former Soviet Union within a five-year period proves the country's ability to absorb Jews and thereby save lives. How many untold thousands, perhaps even millions, might be alive today had Jews acted in the first few decades of this century? Even today, the majority of Jews in America never visit Israel, never take advantage of their opportunity to be a part of one of the most dramatic national resurrections in world history.

On one of our following trips, I met again with Avraham Ofer, my childhood friend, who by this time had become a minister in the government. We had lunch at the Knesset restaurant.

"Look, Sam," he said to me, "if somebody in Chorostkow had told us that one day we would have a state of Israel, that I would be a minister in the Israeli Cabinet, that you would be doing business in the sovereign state of Israel, and that we would be having lunch in the Knesset cafeteria, would we have believed him?"

"No," I answered. "I think we would have had a very hard time believing this."

We laughed out loud and thoroughly enjoyed ourselves. Until this day, even after Ofer's tragic death, our families, our children remain good friends. This relationship with the Ofer family, which goes back a hundred years, is very important to my family. We cherish it.

Unlike on my first trip, all of Jerusalem was now in Jewish hands. I was anxious to visit the *Kotel* and see the Temple Mount. Gladys and I slowly walked through the stone streets of the Old City, and as we approached the *Kotel*, we began to cry. I wished that my father were alive to see what my fortunate eyes beheld. How he would have rejoiced! He would have danced and sung and praised the Almighty!

I touched the large, cool stones and wept. For thousands of years Jews prayed three times a day to be restored to this city, to the Holy City of Jerusalem, and here I was, a survivor of the Nazi camps, embracing what had been elusive to so many for generations. Again, I felt that my generation had seen the worst and the best of times for Jews: the Holocaust, the annihilation of a third of the entire nation, and the emergence of an independent state of Israel, the redemption of our people, Jerusalem in Jewish hands.

*

In the early 1970s, I received a request from the German government to come to the German consulate in New York to testify against
Paul Rebel, who had been the *hauptsturmführer* at Kamionka. He had
just been arrested as a Nazi war criminal. The German authorities had
searched the Kamionka records for survivors, found my name, and
contacted me. There were so few survivors of Kamionka still alive
that they wanted me to testify as soon as possible.

When I entered the consulate on the appointed afternoon, I was introduced to three men. One of them identified himself as my lawyer.

"Feel free to tell me whatever you want, whatever you know. I'm
here to represent you as best I can, Mr. Halpern."

He introduced one of the other men as Rebel's lawyer, and the
third man was the judge, there to listen to both sides.

They proceeded to ask me many questions. I told them everything I
remembered about my own experience in Kamionka and what I had
seen happen to others. I knew I was a good witness, not only because I
had been young at the time yet old enough to absorb and retain a lot of
information but because my working in the *hauptsturmführer*'s house
had given me more intimate knowledge of this man than other inmates
could have had.

After hearing everything I had to say, I was asked whether I had
ever witnessed Rebel kill anyone. I thought about the question for a
few minutes before answering.

"No," I said, "I never saw him kill anyone with his own hands, his
own gun, or his stick. But I heard and saw him order people killed on
many occasions. Once, when someone had run away from the camp,
he had four people randomly selected and shot in the head in front of
the entire camp. And many other times, for the slightest mistake, he
would order the Ukrainian chief of police to shoot or beat someone to
death. All the men in the infirmary whose legs had become
gangrenous were killed on Rebel's orders. The soldiers just came into
the infirmary, took out seventeen men, and shot them, one bullet a
piece."

When I was finished testifying, my lawyer took me into an adjoin-
ing room.

"Mr. Halpern," he said, "with all you know about this man's deeds,
why can't you tell us you saw him shoot people himself?"

"Because I didn't," I insisted. "And I refuse to lie. I would not be able to sleep again if I lied about something so important. I must tell you, though, that when Rebel gave an order, it was just as important, if not more important, than doing the actual shooting. The man who shoots can try to hide behind the excuse that he was just following orders. But the man who gives the order has nothing to hide behind. Because of Rebel's orders, hundreds of people are dead."

The lawyer said he understood my position and that my testimony was completed. I had decided not to tell them how Rebel had said to me "Katzman is here" the day before the *Aktion* in Kamionka. I did not want them to interpret this phrase favorably, for as I said earlier, I had no idea why Rebel said this to me on that fateful Friday. The man was a murderer, killing people all around me with his orders. He deserved to be severely punished.

A few months later I saw in a Yiddish paper that Rebel had been sentenced to life imprisonment. It was the maximum that could be imposed, since Germany does not have the death penalty. Not long afterward, I read that Rebel had died in prison.

The Mayor of Jerusalem, Ehud Olmert, hurried to congratulate us when, by chance, he heard that our son Murray was being married at the Renaissance Hotel in Jerusalem.

Gladys and I were soon fortunate to attend the wedding of our son David. He was the first of our four sons to marry. The wedding took place in the New York Hilton on July 11, 1972. Our daughter-in-law, Sharon, is a wonderful "daughter." Their first son, Jeremy, our first grandchild, was born on August 19, 1976. Today he is in college, and we are very proud of the young man he has become. His sister, Mindy, the first girl in our family, was born on April 21, 1979. She, too, has grown into a lovely young lady whom we love dearly.

Fred, our eldest son, married Cheryl on June 12, 1977. Their wedding also took place in the New York Hilton. With this marriage, Gladys and I gained another special daughter in our lives. Their first daughter, Yonina, was born on July 27, 1979 and is now a lovely and accomplished young lady. Her sister, Meira Zahava, was born on May 21, 1982. We love her dearly. And Alexander arrived on August 15, 1985. He is nine years old going on twenty!

Jack, as of this writing, is still not married, and we hope to hear good news soon.

On August 24, 1993, our youngest son, Murray, married a lovely woman from Israel. Batsheva and Murray's wedding took place in the Jerusalem Renaissance, which made it even more of an emotional and beautiful occasion for us. We are only too happy to have gained another daughter through this union.

Gladys and I are so very proud of all our children and grandchildren. God has blessed us with them.

*

I had not been back to Poland since I left in 1945 and thought I might never return. I changed my mind, though, after Gladys and I went touring through Spain in 1975. We had just been to Israel for the wedding of our niece, Shelley, and on the way home we decided to stop in Spain. I had never been there, and I am always interested in seeing new places.

In Spain we hired an excellent tour guide who took us to see synagogues and other historic sites in Toledo, Seville, and Cordova, which were a moving testament to the large Jewish community that had once flourished in that country. Walking the streets of the cities

At my grandson Jeremy's Bar Mitzvah:
First row, left to right: Fred Halpern, Cheryl Halpern, my grandson Jeremy Hal-
pern, Sam, Sharon Halpern, David Halpern, Murray Halpern, Jack Halpern.
Second row, left to right: Gladys Halpern, my granddaughter Maiera Halpern,
my granddaughter Yanina Halpern, my grandson Alexander Halpern, my
granddaughter Mindy Halpern, David's daughter.

where many Jews had lived, paying our respects in old stone
cemeteries where generations of Jews were buried, standing inside the
Iberian synagogues, remarking on the grace and distinctiveness of the
Sephardic sanctuary, all gave me a different perspective on the vanquished communities of Poland. Seeing evidence of the destruction of
the Spanish communities five hundred years earlier enabled me to see
the horrendous end of Polish Jewry historically, something I was
never been able to do before. My memories of Poland had always
been highly charged and emotional, but the distance of historical

perspective allowed me to consider setting foot on that soil once again. I finally asked myself, "Why shouldn't I go see the graves of my mother and father, my brothers and grandparents?"

A few month later, Gladys and I traveled to Poland for ten days after a thirty-year absence. In those years, not many Jews went to Poland to see, to remember, to find out what remained. We traveled to Belzec where my father had been killed, where thousands and thousands were murdered and burned and buried in the surrounding forests. Right after the war in 1946, the Poles erected a memorial there, a block of granite with the inscription: "Here in Belzec, 600,000 Jews and 1,500 Poles who helped Jews died horrible deaths." A few yards behind this marker is another memorial, a statue of one skeletal figure supporting another. The Polish inscription reads: "In memory of the victims of Hitler's terror murdered from January 1942 through early 1943." Behind that a row of concrete blocks, possibly a reminder of the gas chambers, stands among birch trees. And six urns filled with ashes remind the visitor of 600,000 souls who brutally perished there.

The camp and memorial were hard to find. There were no signposts in the village to direct a visitor to the site. We had asked people the way there, but many were not sure what we were talking about. I was surprised by the fact that there wasn't a single Jewish emblem, not a Hebrew word or star of David, to remind visitors of the Jewish victims who had been slaughtered in this place. But I stood before the granite block whose etched words spoke of thousands who died there and said *Kaddish* for my beloved father. The weight of his loss, the father I so loved, filled my entire being.

Our next stop was Chelm, about a hundred kilometers from Belzec, the site of the POW camp where my brother Avrum Chaim had been held prisoner as a Russian soldier and executed by the German for being a Jew some time in the fall of 1942. By the monument, which memorializes all the soldiers who were held prisoner there—Russian, French, Italian, some American, but mostly Jews—I said *Kaddish* for my beloved brother, my role model.

Then we traveled to Trembowla, which today is in the Ukraine, to the site outside the town of Plebanowka where my mother was killed. Nothing marked the murder site. All I could do was say *Kaddish* near the mass grave and weep. Later on, along with a friend, Ulo Kimmel, who then lived in Tarnopol, we had a memorial built there. When we visited the location where the Kamionka labor camp had once stood, the site was also barely distinguishable from the surrounding countryside. The ditch, though, into which thousands of Jewish bodies had been dumped and then burned and buried, was honored by the local farmers. We were told by one of them that there was an unspoken agreement not to use that large piece of land for farming. They recognized it as a gravesite and respected it as such. Amid fields and fields of crops, the site of this large ditch of death lies fallow.

When I traveled to Chorostkow, I was in for a shock. Nothing remained. All the houses had been razed. All evidence of the five-hundred-year-old Jewish presence there had been utterly effaced. Local residents had torn down everything, whether in search of hidden treasure or building materials or deliberately to erase any memory that Jews had once lived peaceably among them. Whatever the reason, it was extremely painful for me to travel through the area and see that absolutely nothing of our Jewish history remained. The entire Jewish center of town reminded me of an ancient archaeological site one might see in Israel, just piles of stones and rubble. There wasn't a breath of life, only an air of long neglect.

Even the Jewish cemetery had been destroyed. Although I learned about its destruction during the war, I was still unnerved to see residential houses sitting on top of graves. In one of the letters I received from my father when I was in Kamionka, he had said that he was working in the Jewish cemetery chopping tombstones to be used in repairing the highway. He was a firm believer in the resurrection of the dead and thought it was important to know the names of the individuals buried there, so he carefully wrote down the names and put them in a glass bottle that he buried not far from the site. He instructed me how to locate this bottle, but by the time I got there, thirty years later, the place had been entirely built over and the bottle was impossible to find. Today, there are plans to build a major commercial project on the ruins of Jewish Chorostkow, and even the rubble that had been the only testament to the lives once lived there will be buried under a new chapter of history. Recently, though, a memorial was built on a farm nearby commemorating the Jewish inhabitants of Chorostkow.

Gladys and I then traveled to Zolkiew, most of which was still standing. Gladys' childhood home and her father's store were still there. Where there had once been three mass Jewish graves, however, there was nothing. The graves had been dug up by local vandals looking for gold in the dead peoples' teeth or for any other item of value they could find. The Soviet government had reacted to this desecration by excavating and leveling the entire place so that nothing remained at all.

Gladys is in touch with Siegmund Leiner, a Jew who still lives in Zolkiew, and together they are working on erecting a memorial at the site of the mass graves. Even the old Jewish cemetery in town vanished. A marketplace had been built on the site, with tombstones used as paving. Out of a Jewish community of five thousand people before the war, only four families remained there afterward. The trip was very painful for both of us. With the rush of memories, the sense of loss was great.

Since that initial trip, we have returned to Poland every two or three years. First of all, I want to go to Belzec, Trembowla and Chelm to say *Kaddish* for my parents and brother. Second, I want to continue to help the Gorniaks who saved my life. I helped build them a house and continue to assist them in numerous ways since the economic situation in Poland is very difficult and these people deserve a better life. I had located the Gorniaks soon after the war and began helping them after I arrived in America. Once back on Polish soil, though, I had an opportunity to see them in person, and visiting them has become an important part of every trip I make there.

In Paris, in October 1992, I led the Jewish Federation's *Am L'Am* (People to People) mission to Poland. We met with a representative of the Polish government and visited the sites of our ancestors. When asked why I continue returning to Poland, I say that it was my home where Jews had lived for a thousand years. It was home to rabbis and scholars, writers, artists, doctors, lawyers, poets, and statesmen. From their ranks came the people who had the wisdom to understand the need of establishing an independent Jewish state. In traveling back to Poland on the missions I lead, everyone has the opportunity to learn about this rich past so we can know what was lost and how much we have to ensure that the great, tragic destruction that occurred there will never be repeated.

In 1989, Israel Bonds bestowed on me the Elie Wiesel Holocaust Remembrance Award. Left to right: Ambassador Meir Rosen, Muyles Lernman, Sam Halpern, Elie Wiesel, Sigmund Struchlitz, Gladys Halpern, George Klein, and Ben Mead.

Of course, I am very involved in Yad Vashem and as a member of the American Society for Yad Vashem, I was involved in helping build the Valley of Destroyed Jewish Communities. This memorial was completed in the early 1990s. A big meeting to discuss and raise funds for the Valley was held in my house. Eli Zbrowski came and told me about this idea. I thought it was essential and pledged to support it with time and resources.

Built mostly by survivors, though some non-survivors participated as well, the Valley of Destroyed Jewish Communities cost over twelve million dollars and took years of fund raising, travel, and work to create, but when finally completed, it was—as it continues to be—an extremely moving monument to all that we lost in the Holocaust.

Shaped like the map of Europe, it is the first memorial to commemorate every vanquished city and town. It is not dedicated to people per se but to their communities. The Valley is a powerful addition to Yad Vashem, one of the most important monuments in Jerusalem.

Whenever a world leader comes to Israel, he or she is taken to Yad Vashem and guided through it to make sure that the impact of the Holocaust is communicated. Soldiers, after induction into the Israeli army, are also brought to Yad Vashem to remind them what they are defending. A visit to this crucial institution is made even more powerful by the Children's Pavilion, built by my good friend Abe Spiegel from Los Angeles in memory of his son who was killed in Auschwitz.

In 1992 I was very glad to be recognized by the American and International Societies for Yad Vashem as a recipient of the "Remembrance Award." This award was presented at an international dinner, and as I surveyed the crowd of faces, I felt moved and relieved that so many were helping insure that the world would remember what Hitler had done to us.

While I was working on behalf of Yad Vashem, I was also beginning to feel that something had to be done here in America. Only about twenty percent of American Jews ever visit Israel, so the vast majority never have the opportunity to see Yad Vashem. The story of the Holocaust is so important that millions of Americans, Jew and

One year later I congratulated Dr. Henry Kissinger when he also received the Elie Wiesel Holocaust Remembrance Award.

*At a Yad Vashem reception. Left to right: Joseph Wilf, Sam Halpern,
Senator Frank Lautenberg, and David Chase.*

Secretary George Schultz graced us with his presence at one of our functions.

non-Jew alike, need to be taught this piece of history, and I decided to become involved in bringing the story to light here. The impetus to tell about the horrors does not stem from fear, as if another Holocaust can occur here at any moment. Rather, the need to share the suffering, to give other people and nations the opportunity to learn from this horrible chapter in human history, motivated survivors living in the United States to organize an American Holocaust museum.

We met at a hotel where Elie Wiesel, already named general chairman of the project, told us about the proposed United States Holocaust Memorial Museum to be built in Washington, D.C. He said that President Carter had proposed building a monument to the victims of the Holocaust, but Wiesel had told the president that the world already had many monuments and that what was needed was a museum that would educate the public about the fatal consequences of anti-Semitism and racism. Wiesel told us that President Carter agreed and had already allotted a wonderful location for the recommended museum, right on the Washington Mall. In my opinion, we had been given the best location in the world. When standing in front of the building, visitors can see the Capitol, the White House, and the Lincoln Memorial.

"Look people," Wiesel said to those of us gathered to discuss the museum, "we have to raise money."

He told us that the U.S. government had given us the land, but the expense for everything else had to be raised privately. Citizens would have to pay for the architect, Jim Fried, of the internationally famous firm of Pei, Cobb and Fried; and for construction of the museum, designing exhibits, collecting artifacts, installing the computer network for a research library, and funding the staff necessary to get the museum running.

Like all federal museums on the Washington Mall, once the institution was open to the public, there would be no entrance fee. The U.S. government assumes all operating expenses.

I was one of the first people to make a commitment. I donated a sizable amount, which led the way to numerous pledges. After this meeting, we all set to work raising funds from our communities and others, from Jews in all walks of life, through mailings, newsletters and any means available. Miles Lerman, a dear friend and campaign

The President of the United States, George Bush, appointed Sam Halpern
"a Member of the United States Holocaust Memorial Council."
Left to right: Arie Halpern, Mrs. Bush, President George Bush, Sam Halpern.

manager, must be given credit for doing much of the fund raising. He is now, deservedly, chairman of the museum. Thanks to his efforts and those of hundreds of people who helped raise funds and coordinate the project, we succeeded, as anyone can see who visits Washington and goes to this extraordinary museum. Harvey Meyerhoff, chairman of the museum while it was under construction, was instrumental in making the educational institution a reality. In addition, Jeshajahu Weinberg, director of the museum—the man who organized Beth Ha-Tfuzot in Ramat Aviv—was asked to program this enormous under-taking and did so with great energy, efficiency, and aplomb. For my efforts and involvement, President Bush appointed me to the museum's council.

From Jerusalem to Washington, D.C. to my own hometown of Hillside, New Jersey, I am involved in telling the story of the Holocaust for those who are not here to tell it for themselves. I helped organize a Resource Center for Instructors at Kean College in New Jersey, which is dedicated to educating teachers about the Holocaust.

Once, at the 25th anniversary party for our friends, Murray and Lucy Pantirer, in Elizabeth, New Jersey, I met Oskar Schindler. I had heard about him from good friends, Murray and Abraham Zuckerman, whose lives he saved. I saw that Schindler was wearing a very old suit, so I walked over to him and offered some money.

Secretary Jack Kemp at the swearing-in ceremony at the United States Holocaust Memorial Museum.

"Buy yourself a new suit," I said.

"Why are you giving me money?" he asked. "I did not help you."

"You didn't help me, but you helped over a thousand Jews, many of my friends," I answered. "Like the Talmud says, and as is engraved on your ring, 'Whoever saves one life, it is as if he has saved the entire world.' You are a very fine man."

Who knows if Schindler ever bought himself a new suit. He was terrible at holding onto money, but I knew I had to help someone, even in this small way, who had saved the lives of so many Jews.

Of course, there are those in the Jewish community who don't share my opinion of Oskar Schindler. When the Holocaust Museum's council was debating whether to give Schindler a posthumous award for efforts on behalf of the Jewish people, there were people on the council who felt he did not deserve such an honor. In particular, one person had the following to say:

"First, Oskar Schindler was a Nazi. Second, he was a womanizer. Third, he was an alcoholic. And fourth, he was a businessman."

I could not believe what I was hearing, so I stood up.

"Mr. Chairman, I'd like to speak," I said politely. "I agree that Schindler was all of the above. But if he had not been a Nazi, he would not have been in the position to save anyone. If he were not a drunk, he would not have wanted to do what he did. The man who saved me also drank. It takes a little extremity of personality to risk one's life for another. That he was a womanizer, well, this may not be the nicest thing in the world, but it certainly is not the worst. Some of our most prominent personalities, past and present, have had some weakness in this regard. Womanizing is his wife's problem, not mine.

"And being a businessman is not such a terrible thing. After all, I myself am one. However, and I can testify personally to this—yes, Schindler was a businessman, and he made a lot of money using free Jewish labor. But he also spent everything he made off the Jews to save Jews. After the war he was broke. When I saw him several years later, he didn't even have enough money to buy a decent suit. He had nothing."

I had many friends on the council who agreed with me, and in the end the body voted to extend the posthumous award.

When Steven Spielberg's movie *Schindler's List* was released, the initial screening was in Washington, D.C. Everyone was there, including Spielberg, President Bill Clinton and Hillary Clinton. Gladys and I, along with a number of others involved with the Holocaust Museum, were also invited. When the president entered, he shook hands with many people. He was congenial and friendly. As it turned out, I was sitting about five seats away from him in the same row. When the movie was over, the president looked very distraught, and Hillary was crying so hard her entire face was red. Of course, I don't like to see people so upset, but when I saw this reaction, I realized that Spielberg had done his duty by his people. He had succeeded in giving others a glimpse of the unimaginable suffering endured by those who survived and, more importantly, by those who did not.

The motivation behind my ongoing support of various American and Jewish institutions, of educational and social services, and those directly contributing to the growth of a strong Israel, is a belief that I survived in order to be able to tell the story for those who did not, to make sure that this tragedy will never happen again to my people or any people. I do not think that it is merely "nice" that people give charity; it is an obligation to future generations and to generations past. Because of this conviction, I not only make financial contributions, for writing checks isn't the hardest thing to do when you have funds, but I give a great deal of my time. I sometimes sacrifice important business meetings to attend various functions. When I am asked to go to Israel with a group, I work the trip into my busy schedule.

At the beginning of August 1993, I received a phone call from the White House requesting my presence at a meeting with President Clinton to discuss how to help get the economy started again. Thirty-two citizens from New Jersey were invited, including doctors, lawyers, bankers, and developers. The meeting was scheduled to take place on the day of our departure for Murray's wedding in Jerusalem. I was deeply honored. For me, a survivor of the Holocaust, to be invited by the president of the United States to the White House for a discussion on the nation's economy, was quite extraordinary. I changed our travel plans so I could attend this important meeting.

Just as my father and other Chorostkowers arranged a soup kitchen for needy Jews after the German invasion, and just as there were always guests at my parents' Sabbath meals, so I learned about the all-

My family joined me at my 75th birthday celebration in July, 1995.
Seated: daughters-in-law Sharon and Cheryl. Standing, back row, left to right:
Maeira, Yonina (Fred and Cheryl's daughters), David, Jack, Jeremy (David and
Sharon's son), Murray. Standing behind Sam is Fred, BatSheva (Murray's wife),
Mindy David and Sharon's daughter) and Alexander (Fred and Cheryl's son).

important *mitzvah* of giving charity, which is an integral part of what
it means to be a Jew. A hand that gives is higher than the hand that
takes, and there is great pleasure in giving. I also believe that the more
you give, the more God gives to you. Of course, I do not mean that a
system of giving should be embraced in order to be rewarded. However, the more you help the world, the better place it becomes, the better the spiritual quality for everyone. The concept of *tikkun olam*,
repairing the world, is based on everyone's contributing to right im-
balances and bring the world closer to its original harmony.

*

I was liberated in early spring, two weeks before Passover. Many years ago when my children were still small, I took them to see the movie *The Ten Commandments* at Radio City Music Hall. When they saw how hard Jewish slaves were working in the brick pits, they became very upset. I said to them, "My dear children, your father worked much harder in the slave labor camp. People were beaten every day; there was very little food. You can see that in Egypt, hard as it was, they apparently had more food than we had, and they were not murdered systematically as we were."

And at the Seder, I am always compelled to talk about how I was a slave and that I was liberated not only from the Egyptians thirty-three hundred years ago but also from Hitler's camps and ghettos only a few decades past.

Every year, in the Hulon cemetery on the outskirts of Tel Aviv, the survivors of Chorstkow, Trembowla, and about six other nearby shtetls hold a commemorative ceremony. About 120 people come to mourn at a monument we built in the cemetery. We say *Kaddish* together and afterward go to our hotel in Tel Aviv, the Ramada Continental, for a reception. There we talk about the people lost and life in our towns Before the war. We tell stories about our families and friends before the war.

*

I asked Gladys to report briefly on our 1995 trip to our home towns and the camps.

Our first stop was Zolkiew, where after 52 years we dedicated a memorial to the 3,500 Jews who perished and were buried there on March 25, 1943, among them my father and members of our extended family.

When we visited Zolkiew ten years ago, we found the cemetery had been desecrated and only large ditches remained where the graves had been. Some of the bones had been buried in a far corner of the Christian cemetery. Mr. Leiner, one of the four Jews left in Zolkiew, said he would erect a monument there.

When we returned four years ago, we found the spot was under

Monument to Chorostkow in Holon Cemetery. The Chorostkow Synagogue is seen on the monument.

water and overgrown with tall weeds. Horrified, we stressed our obligation to memorialize the place where the killings occurred. There was no one else to do this.

We asked Mr. Leiner to deal with the town authorities, and assured him that we, the Kramers and the Patrontasches would finance the memorial. In the summer of 1995, we took our son David, his wife Sharon, and our grandson Jeremy, to see the results.

My cousin Clara, her husband, family, and friends, with their children, came from Israel, Canada, and the United States to join us in a commemorative service, where we recited *Kaddish* in memory of our *Kedoshim*.

We showed our children my former home, my father's store, the attic where I had hidden for eighteen months, and other personal landmarks. Although the interior was destroyed, the main synagogue still stands, a historical monument to the Jewish life which had flourished in Zolkiew for hundreds of years.

Our family then went to Tarnopol, Chorostkow, Trembowla, and Kamionka. In Kamionka, we arranged with the mayor for a monument which is to be erected in memory of the 5,000 inmates who were killed when the Germans liquidated the camp in 1941.

We traveled to Belzec where Sam's father was martyred in 1942, and Chelm where Sam's brother Avrum Chaim perished at the hands of the Nazis. From Chelm we went to Majdenek and from there to Warsaw, where our sad journey ended.

It was an emotional, sad, and difficult trip, but after ten years of effort, we felt a sense of accomplishment. We don't know how long these monuments will last, but we do know that we fulfilled our obligation.

March 22, 1994 was the fiftieth anniversary of my liberation. About fifty people gathered at my house to celebrate. Most of them were also liberated on that day, and the rest within the next few months. Even though this year the anniversary fell only days before Passover, with all the cleaning and preparations the holiday demands, Gladys managed to create a wonderful evening. This commemorative reception also came one day after the Academy Awards ceremony in which the film *Schindler's List* won Best Picture and its director, Steven Spielberg, won the award for Best Director.

I recounted to my company Spielberg's words on accepting his award. Speaking to the camera, he told hundreds of millions of viewers all over the world that today there were only 350,000 survivors of Hitler's camps still alive. He beseeched the audience to seek out the survivors and listen to them, to hear their stories while there was still time.

Yes, I thought the movie was important. Yes, I personally knew Schindler and have good friends who were *Schindler Juden*, whose lives he saved. But hearing one of America's most famous directors telling the world to listen to the stories of the survivors, of people like

At a conference in Washington, DC in November 1995,
Sam Halpern is greeted by President Clinton.

me and my fifty guests, was a validation of everything for which we had survived.

As we raised our glasses to toast *l'chaim* (to life), I turned to my friends and said, "We are gathered here to celebrate our liberation from Hitler fifty years ago. We are able to celebrate, and we should celebrate. At the same time, we cannot forget those who did not live to see the day of liberation.

"Nor should we forget those who were liberated but are no longer with us." And I took out a list of the twenty-six friends from Chorostkow who survived but have since died; I read their names aloud.

When I finished and the weight of the loss enveloped us, we all stood for a moment of silence. This heaviness, the memory of our darkest days, was broken by the joyful singing of "*Hatikva*" and repeated in the last verse: "to be a free nation on our land, the Land of Israel and Jerusalem!"

I felt overwhelmed by the press of time—the war, the liberation, the postwar years in Europe, and then the rebuilding of our lives in this great country. The United States of America has not only been a faithful friend to Israel but has given so much to mankind the world over.

I thought of more than a hundred offspring of my grandmother's brother, whom I met after arriving here. My great-uncle had emigrated from Poland in 1910, and because this one man was spared the Holocaust, a hundred Jews were born. The proportions of loss and of blessings are enormous. The United States provided a sanctuary for our people, and it has allowed us to grow and prosper. More importantly, America gave me, my wife and children, and my brother the opportunity to start again. Sometimes I think that no one appreciates this country as much as survivors. We whose existence is the sign of Hitler's defeat can never underestimate this country's democracy, its passion for human rights, its commitment to world peace.